The boy in 7 billion

A TRUE STORY OF LOVE, COURAGE AND HOPE

Mirror Books

Published by Mirror Books,
an imprint of Trinity Mirror plc,
1 Canada Square,
London E14 5AP, England

www.mirrorbooks.co.uk

ISBN 978-1-907324-62-8

First hardback edition

Some names and personal details have been changed to avoid identification

Printed and bound in Great Britain
by CPI Group (UK) Ltd, Croydon, CR0 4YY

Every effort has been made to fulfil requirements with regard to
reproducing copyright material. The author and publisher will be
glad to rectify any omissions at the earliest opportunity.

Front cover image: Becky Williams
Sleeve images: Richard Payne, iStockphoto

THIS BOOK IS DEDICATED

to the beautiful children who gained their
angel wings far too soon. Those who walked
the path before us, inspired us and showed us
what true bravery looked like. And to their
families, who continued to shine throughout
the most harrowing of times.

*They are the inspiration for my
continuation to fight for what is right.*

The boy in 7 billion

Contents

Chapter 1

STANDING IN THE DIMLY LIT BEDROOM IN THE HOSPICE LOOKING over the body of my sleeping eldest son, I couldn't hold back the words, or emotion, any longer. As tears rolled down my face, my thoughts came tumbling out loud even though it was the early hours of the morning and I was the only one awake.

'This isn't fair, this isn't right. You're only 14 years old, you haven't even had the chance to live yet.'

I immediately felt a pang of guilt as I realised that I'd woken Deryn up. He looked up at me through half open eyes and took my hand.

'It doesn't matter how old we are when we die, it's about what we did while we were here,' he whispered. 'We all have to die at some point, whether it's 14 or 94, it doesn't matter. Please don't be upset, you will be okay.

'Life will go on.'

Deryn had arrived in this world at 4.43pm on the first day of December 1999 with a full head of black hair, weighing in at 8lb 1oz. After the usual checks, he was declared fit and healthy. I was overjoyed but exhausted. I wasn't quite sure if I was old enough to take responsibility for another human being but I had no doubt of the overwhelming love I felt for Deryn when I first laid eyes on him.

Motherhood came quite naturally to me. I had turned 20 just a couple of months before Deryn was born and had been married for two years to my husband Dan, who was a soldier. We were based in London, near the West End.

Deryn was a dream baby, sleeping through from nine weeks and barely crying at all. He made it very easy for me to be a good first-time mum, which I appreciated as, sadly, his father didn't want to be involved with him at all.

Motherhood was a joy but it wasn't without its issues. I started to suffer from panic attacks just after the birth and would stare at Deryn for hours to make sure that he was still breathing, worrying myself sick that something was going to happen to him.

When Deryn was five weeks old, I noticed that he wasn't breathing normally. As he lay in my arms, I could see that he was struggling and taking only very small, shallow breaths. Within a few seconds, his lips had turned blue.

I was terrified. I immediately thought that he was going to die and although inside, I was falling to pieces, auto-pilot kicked in and I managed to get Deryn to hospital.

He was diagnosed with bronchitis, put on a nebuliser and kept in hospital for four days. It was traumatic to find myself sitting with my five-week old baby lying helpless with a mask taped to his face. I was filled with turmoil and anxiety and felt incredibly alone as my husband had stayed at work. When I later called him to update him about Deryn's condition, he was out clubbing with his friends. Feeling let down, isolated and scared, I cried as Deryn held my finger with his tiny hand.

Life soon returned to normal after that worrying episode, though, and Deryn continued to develop at a rapid pace. The health visitors would often comment on how advanced he was for his age. Needless to say, I was incredibly proud of him.

However, my marriage was starting to disintegrate and when Deryn was 15 months old, after much soul-searching and agony, I finally made the decision to leave his father. It was an amicable parting – we both realised that we had married far too young.

CHAPTER 1

We knew nothing about one another. With a heavy heart, I felt it would be better for Deryn to have just me rather than a father who ignored him.

That said, I was far from the perfect mother myself. Still young and immature, it wasn't long before my newfound freedom went to my head and I went off the rails. I started to go out regularly with my single, childless friends, leaving Deryn for weeks at a time with my mum and dad in Norfolk.

After two months of non-stop partying and socialising, my irresponsibility forced my mum into action. One day, she took me aside and made me an offer that pushed me to take a long, hard look at myself.

'Would you like me and your dad to look after Deryn for you?' she asked. 'He can live here and you can get on with your life.'

I suddenly realised that Deryn was my life and that my unacceptable behaviour would have to stop. My baby son was far more important than going out and drinking myself into a stupor. Quite simply, I had to grow up.

From that moment on, I stepped up to the full responsibility of being a single parent. It certainly wasn't easy; money was short and I became anxious about living on my own with a small child to support. I did my best and Deryn never went without because I was lucky enough to have the support of my parents.

We gradually saw less and less of Deryn's father until all contact ceased. He had started seeing someone else and she became more of a priority to him than his son. He made it very clear that he wanted nothing further to do with Deryn and hasn't seen him since he was three years old.

When Deryn was 22 months old, I met Simon.

I was chatting online to a friend one evening when she told me that she was talking to a 21-year-old ex-RAF rugby player on a dating site.

'He's far too young for you', I joked.

She introduced us and Simon and I chatted well into the early hours. We had regular conversations over the next few months and finally met face to face at Slough station. Our relationship developed quickly and in time, I introduced him to Deryn.

From the second they met, it was clear they were going to get on. Deryn presented Simon with a lovely gift of a full potty as he stood with a beaming grin on his face and the relaxed way Simon reacted told me everything I needed to know about him. He was a good guy, the kind of guy that I wanted Deryn to look up to.

Simon was thrown into the deep end of fatherhood and fully immersed himself in the role of step-dad to a toddler within a few days of us moving in together, back near my parents in Norfolk, always treating him as if he were his own child.

He had always loved children and they in turn loved him. Kids would gravitate towards him and he relished it. Meanwhile, Deryn had a man to look up to, a father figure who cherished him as much as I did. Deryn thrived on the attention and it wasn't long before he chose to call Simon 'Daddy,' a moment which made my heart swell.

It was when we took Deryn swimming for the first time as a family. Deryn was sitting in a little yellow rubber inflatable and I was pushing him around the rapids when we noticed that Simon had disappeared out of sight. I wasn't worried but Deryn had noticed and wanted him to come back.

The next thing I heard was Deryn shouting at the top of his voice: 'Daddy Simon, Daddy Simon!'

Simon swam back with tears in his eyes and Deryn flung his arms around his neck, hugging him hard.

❖

When Deryn turned three we started to notice that he was

CHAPTER 1

different from other children his age. He began to make funny faces over and over again. It seemed to come out of nowhere and these funny faces would change from one month to the next – sometimes he would open his mouth as wide as he could; at other times he would open his eyes as far as possible. None of the other children at his nursery were displaying the same traits and I became concerned as this didn't seem like normal behaviour.

At the age of five, the vocal tics started. He would go 'hmm hmm hmm' all the time, which drove me mad. At first, I thought he was just being difficult, but having been such an easy, undemanding baby, this didn't ring true.

I decided to start doing some research on Deryn's little idiosyncrasies. The more I researched, the more I found myself drawn to information about Tourette's Syndrome. Surely there was no way he could have Tourette's? All I knew about the condition was that it caused people to shout, swear and say inappropriate things.

However, the late nights I spent at the dining table doing my research led me to the extraordinary discovery that only 10% to 12% of Tourette's sufferers have coprolalia, a very fancy word for excessive and uncontrollable use of obscene words, socially inappropriate and derogatory remarks.

Simon and I became increasingly concerned so I decided to take Deryn to see our doctor. His blood pressure, weight, height and reflexes were checked and Deryn was given a clean bill of health. Despite sharing my views with the doctor, he felt there was nothing wrong with him and I was told it was quite common for children his age to have tics. I later discovered that a diagnosis of Tourette's Syndrome is only made if a child has had motor and vocal tics for more than three years. It was a case of waiting to see if Deryn would grow out of them.

He never did. As time went on, the tics became more

pronounced and more debilitating, which was excruciating to watch. Sometimes they would cause him to walk into a wall. On one occasion, when Deryn was about six, we were walking through town and his tic of the month was to look repeatedly over his left shoulder. He looked back just as he walked straight into a solid glass door.

Humour became our default setting. He had one tic that we christened the T Rex, which involved him obsessively bending his arms at the elbows in a jerking motion. This one had us all in hysterics and even Deryn had a laugh about it.

When Dylan came along in 2004, Deryn was almost five and had just started primary school. A gregarious and friendly boy, he loved school and being with his friends and he absolutely loved having a baby brother. There was no jealousy or sibling rivalry and he often asked to hold Dylan.

As Dylan got older and more fun to be with, Deryn paid him even more attention and I loved watching them laughing and giggling as they tumbled around together in the garden.

My journey into motherhood second time around was very different to the first. Dylan was similar to Deryn in his good behavior but having someone supportive and loving by my side to help me was wonderful. I hadn't realised until Dylan was born just how much I had taken on by myself when I had Deryn. I felt more at ease and less anxious and started to really enjoy being a mum to two cheeky, adorable boys.

In autumn 2007 Deryn started junior school and he was lucky enough to end up in the class of Mrs Blackman, a wonderful teacher who had a nephew with Tourette's. Because she had looked after him regularly, she recognised the signs in Deryn almost immediately.

One day after school, she took me to one side for a chat. She was very careful about how she worded her feelings as she didn't want to upset me. In fact, I was utterly relieved that at last, someone else was noticing the same signs that I had and she was quietly reassured when I told her that I thought the same.

Instead of getting frustrated with Deryn, Mrs Blackman adapted the way she taught him. She was very inventive, allowing him to lie on the floor and do his work there if he wanted to because he couldn't sit still at a desk. She'd give him 20 minutes' time out here and there and, as a result, the work she elicited from him was outstanding. I will forever be thankful to her for the way she helped Deryn through those early school years.

The doctors, however, were harder to convince and once again told me there was nothing wrong. But, despite hearing the same platitudes from a number of paediatricians, we refused to accept their view. Call it mother's intuition but I just knew something wasn't right.

When Deryn was eight, we were sent to a specialist mental healthcare centre in Norwich. At the end of a two-hour consultation with a specialist, Deryn was diagnosed with Tourette's Syndrome and autism.

Tourette's we expected – but autism?

A few years earlier, I would have been panicking at such a frightening diagnosis but I had grown up a lot. Whatever this meant for Deryn, we would deal with it as a family unit. With my unofficial researcher hat on once more, as soon as I got home I started reading into autism.

I couldn't deny that all the factors added up. Deryn was quite the introvert, he didn't play with any imagination and he didn't care about hurting your feelings. In fact, if you wanted the truth about anything, you asked Deryn. He was happiest in his own company and he completely lacked any empathy, struggling immensely to see things from outside his point of view.

However, his symptoms were manageable and the most

important thing for us as parents was to try to understand him more. We had to come to terms with the fact that he wasn't likely to be loving or caring. Rather than try and change this, though, we accepted Deryn for the way he was. And fortunately, everyone around him did the same. Despite his problems, he was so likeable and engaging that his friends loved him unconditionally.

It wasn't all plain sailing – far from it. Deryn would sometimes drive Simon and me mad with his repetitive and obsessive compulsive behaviour. Food had to be cooked and presented in a particular way, clothes had to feel a certain way and certain rituals had to be completed before the day could continue. It was draining.

These rituals and patterns of behaviour would change regularly, which made it almost impossible to keep up with his needs but at least we had a reason for his behaviour.

I can't deny that there were times when he was incredibly hard to deal with. He would often melt down in temper tantrums and sometimes even became physically violent. No matter how hard I tried, often I couldn't calm him down and on two occasions it turned physical between the two of us. I hated having to restrain him but I knew that I could safely do it and it was the only thing that made him stop.

I had been a bouncer for five years, working on doors at nightclubs. There wasn't a lot I hadn't seen and I knew exactly how to deal with violence, but to be on the receiving end of it from my 10-year-old son was very distressing.

It was awful to watch him smash up his room. I stood frozen to the spot, talking myself into restraining him but fearful because I didn't want to hurt him. It took every ounce of strength I possessed to take him to the floor. Once Deryn stopped thrashing about, he would become limp in my arms and we would sit on

CHAPTER 1

his bedroom floor in tears.

Thankfully, the good times far outweighed the bad and Deryn was always at his happiest outside, riding his bike or playing with his friends in the fields surrounding our little house. During the warmer months, I would rarely see him as he was never short of things to do or people to do them with. Deryn had a love of all things physical; he played rugby, trained in jujitsu and loved nothing more than riding around on his BMX, just like any other boisterous young lad.

Chapter 2

I<small>T WAS THE SUMMER HOLIDAYS, SEVEN MONTHS AFTER HIS</small> 10<small>TH</small> birthday and Deryn had been feeling under the weather. He complained that his food tasted odd and, despite training with an adult rugby club twice a week, he had lost his appetite.

Tourette's Syndrome and autism could cause him to be picky with food but alarm bells rang in my head when he was physically sick one morning. He told me he could feel something large in his stomach and when he lay on his side, it felt as though something inside was 'falling' so I took him to the doctor.

The GP examined Deryn and noticed that his tonsils were extremely large. She was concerned that his spleen was also enlarged – it was the size of a small cat – and diagnosed glandular fever.

'It's nothing to worry about but I suggest you take him for a blood test at the hospital,' she advised. 'Leave it until after the weekend if you like, there's no rush.'

I had no intention of leaving it until after the weekend; I wanted answers as soon as possible. I couldn't help feeling sad for Deryn. I'd heard about glandular fever and I knew that it was something that could hang around for a few years.

The following morning, I got up and headed off to my first job as a self-employed businesswoman. I had set up a mobile valeting business and managed to secure a contract with a local golf club. The morning went well and by midday I was in the car with Deryn, Simon and Dylan, heading for our nearest hospital, 20 miles away.

When we got there Deryn took ticket number 58 and I could see that he was starting to panic. He had never had a blood test before and was worrying about how much it was going to hurt. I tried to reassure him, although I was also feeling sick inside. I also hated blood tests but I couldn't let Deryn see how scared I was. Before we knew it, number 58 flashed up on the illuminated board.

Deryn quipped that the chairs in the treatment room looked like the kind murderers were strapped into before being given a lethal injection. The phlebotomist laughed and assured him that this wouldn't be happening. I offered him my hand to squeeze. Once his bloods had been taken, she pressed a cotton wool ball against the puncture wound and taped it to Deryn's arm.

'That wasn't nearly as bad as I expected,' Deryn told me as we left the room. 'I don't know why I was so worried.'

We decided that there was no harm in heading to the A&E department to try and get a second opinion on Deryn's spleen, which concerned me more than anything.

A doctor there confirmed that it was the largest he had ever seen. Like our GP, he was also surprised that Deryn didn't have a sore throat and concurred with the diagnosis of glandular fever. My mind was put at ease. There was no need to worry myself stupid and drum up thoughts of horrible diseases.

On our way home, Deryn finally felt hungry. Pulling into a nearby fast food restaurant, he ordered enough to feed a small army but after managing just one chip, he announced that he simply couldn't eat anymore. I felt my patience running out – it wasn't Deryn's fault but if this was what glandular fever would be like, I wasn't looking forward to it.

Just as we were about to leave, my mobile rang but cut out before I could answer it. The voicemail said: 'This is a message for Mrs Blackwell. It's the doctor's surgery in Watton, could you please ring us straight back?'

I assumed Deryn's blood tests were back so I dialled the number and was put straight through to our doctor.

'The hospital has Deryn's results and they have found something in his blood,' she said. 'They need you to go back to the hospital straight away, they are waiting for you at the Children's Assessment Unit.'

I felt sick. I walked back into the restaurant where Simon and the boys were waiting and explained that we needed to go back to hospital straight away. Despite my outward calmness, Simon could see that I was fretting and tried to reassure me that I shouldn't worry too much at this stage. But I had a feeling of dread, my stomach was in knots and I wanted to run away.

Once there, a nurse ushered us into a large room with an examination bed and a few chairs. The boys were climbing all over the bed, laughing and pretending to examine each other. The nurse explained they might need to run more blood tests or give Deryn some fluids intravenously so the best thing to do was to insert a cannula – a thin tube – into a main vein.

Poor Deryn was not pleased but the nurse told him that once the numbing cream started to work, he wouldn't feel a thing.

Four doctors entered the room. Why do we need to see so many of them, I wondered? My heart started to race and I felt a rising sense of panic and nausea. It was like being on a roller coaster, making the slow and steady climb to what you know will be a fast-falling journey into the unknown. The trepidation was unbearable.

We sat down opposite them and the one in the middle announced: 'There is no easy way to say this so I'm just going to come out and say it… Deryn has leukaemia.'

I was dropping at a million miles an hour, falling into a dark abyss. My heart felt like it had come straight out of my mouth. I couldn't breathe. For a split second, the entire world stood still.

I glanced at Simon, who was silent and looked completely terrified, before turning my gaze to Deryn, who returned it, puzzled and innocent. I heard myself start to sob.

'Mum, what's leukaemia?' he asked.

My first instinct was to protect him but I also knew that I couldn't lie so I told him the little I knew, which was that it is cancer of the blood. Deryn started to cry quietly, followed by his little brother.

One of the doctors chastised me, warning me not to scare Deryn with the details of his illness. Anger replaced my fear momentarily and I retorted that there would be no lying to my son.

'If he is going to fight this and beat this, he needs to know exactly what he's dealing with,' I said.

The doctors admitted they didn't know what kind of leukaemia Deryn had. I wasn't even aware that there was more than one type and it suddenly dawned on me that this was going to be a very steep learning curve.

An ambulance was booked straight away to take Deryn to Addenbrooke's Hospital in Cambridgeshire, 60 miles away, where he could receive specialist care. The four doctors left the room.

We hugged, we cried... then, all of a sudden, something else kicked in: autopilot. Phone calls were made to relatives, we ran through the logistics of getting Deryn's things to Addenbrooke's and arranged who would go in the ambulance and who would take care of Dylan. There was no time to fall apart.

There was also no time to waste. The nurses urgently needed to cannulate Deryn so that he could start having fluids but he was so dehydrated that after numerous attempts and many blown veins, they gave up. He looked fearful as he sat on the bed being prodded and poked.

Only a few hours earlier, he had been worried about having a simple blood test and now needles were going to loom large in his life and there was nothing I could do about it.

We decided that I would go in the ambulance with Deryn and Simon would take Dylan home, drop him at my mum's, pick up some clothes for us both and head over to Addenbrooke's. Simon was told that he mustn't try to chase the ambulance (apparently some parents can't help themselves.)

We filled in some paperwork and there was a lot of medical talk that I didn't understand. It felt like an out-of-body experience, with me spectating from above on what was happening.

Deryn had never been in an ambulance before and, despite the gravity of the situation, he thought it was pretty cool. A lovely paramedic sat with us as Deryn struggled to contain his excitement at the sirens and blue lights that were speeding us along, setting off speed cameras en route. Bizarrely, the atmosphere was upbeat rather than doom and gloom.

The paramedics wheeled Deryn into A&E and navigated us around the building until we reached C2, the Children's Oncology Ward. A nurse came to greet us with a big beaming smile.

'Welcome to C2,' she said, and I was overwhelmed by a comforting sense of calm, serenity and peace.

We walked down a long corridor with walls covered in colourful drawings and vibrant artwork. There was nothing sad or gloomy about the place. I spotted a little girl who was completely bald, hitching a lift as her mum pushed her chemo pump stand along. She was attached to a big bag of fluid administered by a long white tube.

It felt surreal, like I was in a TV advert for Cancer Research, but this was real life for all these people and it was going to be real life for us too.

We were shown into a room with three beds separated by blue curtains and directed to the empty bed in the far corner. By now it was 8.30pm so most of the children on the ward were getting ready for bed. The room was dimly lit, which added to the sense of calm. The paramedics said their goodbyes and wished us all the best before heading off.

A doctor came to talk us through the procedures it would take to discover what kind of leukaemia Deryn had. Our son would be going into theatre first thing the next day to have a Hickman line inserted into his chest.

I was frightened by the prospect of a general anaesthetic. Deryn had had one once before when he was five to have some teeth removed and I'd been terrified he wouldn't wake up. He did, of course, but the thought of them inserting a long line into the main artery in his neck and right down next to his heart pained me.

As we walked to the treatment room at the end of the ward, I took in our new surroundings. We saw poorly child after poorly child, some with no hair, others with tubes, wires and lines coming out of their little bodies. Other parents smiled at me. We didn't know each other but we all had something in common. I knew we wouldn't be alone on this journey and it was a small comfort that we would have support to help us find our way.

The treatment room was white, bright and very clinical. The doctor asked Deryn to get up on the bed and the phlebotomist arrived to do his blood tests. She was from Transylvania, which Deryn thought hilarious because she sounded like Dracula.

To distract him while she inserted the cannula, she asked if he would like to read 'Where's Wally?'. Unfortunately, it wasn't difficult enough to keep him occupied for long.

CHAPTER 2

'Found him', Deryn shouted triumphantly to the dismay of the lovely woman who was prodding around the back of his hand, preoccupied by her own version of 'Where's the vein?' She managed to find one but as the cannula went in, blood came gushing out of the back of his hand. Deryn's platelets – the cells within the blood that cause blood to clot – were dangerously low and blood was pumping everywhere.

Eventually, she managed to syringe a large sample of blood from Deryn as jokes flew around the room about how she was clearly stealing his blood for herself. She was a great sport, joining in the fun and giving her best impression of Count Dracula from *Sesame Street*.

The phlebotomist wrapped a crepe bandage around Deryn's hand to hold the cannula in place, which would administer many infusions through the night until he could be taken into surgery the following morning. Our son rewarded himself with a pot of silly putty from the box of treats in the room.

'Beats a rubbish sticker from the dentist', he laughed.

Simon arrived at the hospital and as soon as I set eyes on him striding purposefully down the corridor, I felt like a heavy weight was lifting from me. Being able to share this surreal, bizarre experience with the only other person who loved Deryn as much as I did was an enormous relief.

Finally, we got our 10-year-old into his PJs and left him sitting on his bed playing with his putty while we wandered down to the parents' room. This was a haven, a place to store and cook food or chill out if you needed time away. We did a lot of hugging and I gave him an update.

Simon and I agreed then that we would always be totally honest with Deryn about everything, good or bad. We wanted him to be armed with all the facts, even if they were not great facts and not easy to hear. I had always been straight with Deryn about why his biological dad and I were no longer together, and throughout the trials and tribulations with autism and Tourette's, I had never hidden the truth from him. He was now facing his biggest challenge yet and honesty seemed like the obvious way to handle it.

❖

Simon and Deryn had a man-to-man chat.

'You like playing your PlayStation games don't you, Deryn?' he began. 'You like shooting zombies and bad guys, don't you? Well, this is just like that. The zombies are trying to get in through the door and you can stop them with your weapons. You're going to be armed with a lot of special drugs that will help you kill the zombies and stop them getting in through that door. Are you going to let them eat you or are you going to fight them with everything you have?'

'Everything I have,' he replied solemnly.

By the time I got back to the room, Simon and Deryn were chatting with another dad on the ward, whose little lad was in the same room as Deryn. Matthew was only two and had machines and pumps attached to him. But there was one thing that struck Deryn more than any of those lines and tubes. Matthew didn't care about any of them. He was sitting up on his bed, playing with the controls to the hospital bed, raising and lowering it over and over again, much to his dad's frustration as he tried to get Matthew to sleep.

Little Matthew was having none of it. Giggling, waving his arms around and generally having a great time, he was totally oblivious to anything other than having a bit of fun at his dad's expense. Deryn looked across at us.

'I'm not going to moan about any of this, I'm not going to get angry or sad. Because if Matthew can deal with this, then so can I,' he said quietly.

CHAPTER 2

❖

We were all exhausted and needed to sleep. I spent that first night in a pull-down bed next to Deryn's. It took me back to when he was just five weeks old when he and I were alone in the hospital. At least this time I had the support of a wonderful husband and no matter what happened, we would be able to get through it together.

I hadn't slept in the same room as Deryn for many years and sharing a room was alien to us both. Pumps were beeping throughout the night, bags of saline needed to be changed, other poorly children on the ward were crying or being sick and, on top of it all, every hour nurses were coming in to carry out observations.

Deryn was attached to a pump on wheels and it soon became clear that manoeuvring this contraption about was going to take some getting used to. Each time he got up to use the toilet, Deryn would bash his robot into every piece of furniture in his path. Not much sleep was had by either of us that night.

The following morning, Simon arrived armed with bread, milk, cereal and some ready-made meals to keep us going. Not that food interested me much; eating was the furthest thing from my mind. All I could think of was making sure that Deryn was okay. He was due to go into surgery first thing and the doctor in charge asked one of us to go with her to learn what they had found and the treatment protocol they intended to use.

I sat down in her office, which was lined with shelf after shelf of books on anatomy and blood diseases, and she explained to me in great detail just how dangerously ill Deryn was. He had been diagnosed with acute lymphoblastic leukaemia.

❖

Understanding the way our blood works is crucial to understanding Deryn's illness. It is made up of a number of factors but key to Deryn's story and the ones that would immediately indicate Deryn's general health are white blood cells (WBC), haemoglobin (HB), platelets (Plts) and neutrophils (Neuts).

White blood cells fight infections and diseases. When we are ill, our body produces more of them depending on how severe the attack is. They are also responsible for eating up the dead haemoglobin. Platelets are sticky and help the blood to clot and neutrophils are one of five different kinds of white blood cells.

Normal levels for each of the four components are:

WBC: between 5 and 12

HB: between 11.5 and 14.5

Plts: between 150 and 400

Neuts: between 2 and 6

Most children with leukaemia have a white blood count of around 50 to 100, significantly higher than normal. The white blood cells are immature and start to eat away at the HB that isn't yet dead, causing anaemia in blood cancer patients. The white cells don't work correctly so they don't fight infection and far too many are produced. This explained why Deryn's spleen was so large, because the spleen is part of the immune system and produces white cells when a person is ill.

I was told that Deryn's white cell count was 286 – the second highest they had ever seen – and his spleen was literally bursting with leukaemic white cells.

The doctors treating Deryn couldn't understand how he had even managed to walk into the ward. Rather bluntly, one told me that he shouldn't still be with us. I was horrified that he was in such grave and immediate danger but the fact that he had walked in unaided gave me great hope for the success of the treatment. For the first time ever, I was proud of him for not doing what he was supposed to do!

CHAPTER 2

His illness was more common in boys and the doctor said he would require three and a half years of treatment.

THREE AND A HALF YEARS!

Chapter 3

ONCE I MANAGED TO GET MY HEAD AROUND THE FACT THAT THIS was to be our life for the next few years, I headed straight for Deryn's room.

I was able to fill Deryn and Simon in on what the doctor had told me. I found myself using terminology that I didn't fully understand but armed with as much information as I could deal with, I felt empowered. Cancer no longer looked quite as scary and I felt at ease knowing that Deryn's doctors were very capable of looking after him.

Deryn didn't look terrified, just a little disappointed that he was going to be spending a lot more time in hospital. We had no idea what was in store for us or what the long-term treatment plans would be. There was no other way forward than just taking it one day at a time.

The doctor returned to examine Deryn and explained that, before he could have a Hickman line inserted to get vital drugs into his body, he needed some pre-operation examinations to ensure he was well enough for the procedure.

Deryn looked mortified when a young female doctor came into the cubicle with four student nurses. She asked if it was okay to have the students there while she carried out his examination and although Deryn clearly wasn't overly comfortable with a gaggle of females looking at his bits, he didn't object.

Deryn squirmed with embarrassment as the nurses pressed him for answers to extremely intimate questions. Although it was all part of the treatment, it wasn't easy for Simon and me to watch this.

The doctor said she needed to examine Deryn's testicles because often leukaemia can lurk in this area. It's the reason why boys have three and a half years of treatment whereas girls have a year less.

She asked him to pull down his pants and Deryn's face instantly turned a vibrant shade of red. I felt so sorry for him that he was having to show his genitals not only to a young female doctor but also to four student nurses.

The doctor examined Deryn, moving things around to get a better look at his testicles. All the while, Deryn just laid there, wide-eyed with a look that begged for the ground to open up and swallow him.

Thankfully, he has always had an amazing sense of humour and Deryn soon became accustomed to answering the most unusual and personal questions on a daily basis. He decided the best way to deal with the embarrassing parts were through laughter and it was a bleak, black humour that was to carry us through.

Deryn had always been fascinated by medical procedures and had long dreamed of becoming a surgeon, but he would laugh it off and talk about the difficulties of being a medic with Tourette's Syndrome.

'One tic and I could cut something off by accident,' he chuckled.

Meanwhile, Deryn's spleen – quite the talking point among medics because it was so large – needed to be measured so the doctor used a black pen to draw its outline on Deryn's skin. Instead of being tucked away neatly underneath his left ribcage, it came out so far that the black line extended all the way from the bottom of his right ribs down to his right hip bone. Each day, a doctor would come in and draw another outline to assess how much it was shrinking.

The go-ahead was given for his operation and the moment I

had been dreading came when the porters arrived to wheel him off to theatre. I had an irrational fear that he might not wake up after the general anaesthetic but I couldn't show Deryn how frightened I was. I didn't want to scare him and it took every ounce of self control to keep a brave face.

My stomach was in knots of fear as we approached the operating theatre. I couldn't quite take in that my eldest boy was about to have his chest cut open and a line permanently inserted into his jugular vein and his heart.

As for Deryn, he had absolutely no fear of the operation. He was wheeled through the corridors on his hospital bed, laughing and joking all the way about how he felt like a VIP. This feeling grew as we made our way through the main hospital and everyone turned to look at him. People were curious about the bright and chatty boy passing through and the attention made Deryn feel extra special.

I was incredibly proud of my son and how he was adapting to all these sudden changes. Just inside the theatre was a lovely nurse beaming a big, welcoming smile. Immediately, I felt relaxed and knew that my son was in good hands.

The anaesthetist fired off a list of questions.

'Have you any loose teeth? When did you last eat or drink anything? Are you allergic to anything?'

Deryn spotted some syringes containing various liquids on a table and wanted to know exactly what each and every one of them did. The anaesthetist was more than happy to comply, answering everything in great detail. One by one, the syringes were emptied into Deryn's cannula and he was asked to start counting back from 10. Instead, he started to narrate exactly how he was feeling.

'I sound like a robot. Oh, now everything has gone fuzzy. There's a buzzing in my ears. I can't see properly…'

Then he yawned the biggest yawn.

'Can I have lasagne please?'

Then he was gone.

I kissed Deryn's forehead before being ushered out of the room by a nurse. The last time I felt this kind of trepidation was the first time I dropped Deryn off at nursery. I had hated leaving him there and walked away with tears in my eyes.

Leaving him now was so much worse.

The recovery nurse gave me a pager so they could bleep me when Deryn emerged from the operation. Meanwhile, Simon and Dylan were waiting patiently on the oncology ward. Dylan was only five and we were mindful that this journey was going to take its toll on him too.

The children's oncology ward was set up brilliantly for Dylan's age group and while Deryn was in surgery, his little brother had great fun playing with a toy garage while Simon and I tried to make some plans.

Our lives had turned overnight into one big logistical exercise. Who would stay with Deryn and who would go home? How could we make sure that Dylan still carried on normal life at school while caring for Deryn over an hour away in Cambridgeshire? How would we make it all run as smoothly as possible?

I barely had a chance to sit down and grab something to eat before my pager went off. Although I'd been waiting for it, the loud, high-pitched beeps still came as a shock. I started navigating my way back alone but when I turned a corner, suddenly I had no idea where I was. I started getting into a panic with all sorts of thoughts tumbling around in my mind.

What if I get there and Deryn hasn't made it? What if I get there and because I'm late, he dies without me by his side?

For many years I'd battled with panic attacks and anxiety but there was no time for such nonsense now. I was going to have to learn to deal with my issues very quickly. My son needed me.

I gave myself a stern talking to and asked someone the way. Thankfully, I wasn't too far off course and was again greeted by the nurse with the big smile.

'Deryn is over here,' she gestured. A wave of relief swept over me as I was directed to a bay with a curtain around it. I pulled this back – and there sat Deryn, bolt upright in bed, eating an egg sandwich!

He was still slightly under the influence of the anaesthetic, his pupils were dilated and he was slurring his words. Then I noticed his chest, which was bright red and sporting a huge transparent dressing holding down the Hickman line – a long, white tube that came out of the left side of his chest. It wasn't as bad as I'd expected.

A nurse asked Deryn whether or not he had been to the toilet yet. They needed to know that everything was working as it should be before letting him go. This led to his first experience with a bedpan, much to his dismay, but he just got on with it without any fuss.

The porters arrived and before long, he was being wheeled back to the ward as he carried on munching away at his second egg sandwich.

I was struck by the fact that something quite profound had happened to my eldest son. He was showing a level of acceptance that none of us was able to achieve anywhere near as easily as he was. Nothing seemed to faze him anymore.

In those very early days, he taught us a lot.

To put the younger children at ease, the nurses on the ward referred to Hickman lines as 'wigglies'. They had 'wiggly' parties to banish their horrible connotations – they were carrying toxic drugs into young and otherwise perfect little bodies, after all. Deryn felt he was a little too old for this term so he dubbed his line 'George'.

Now that George was in and working, the team could start chemotherapy. Back on the ward, Deryn was eager to show off his new implant to Simon and Dylan, who peered curiously at the white tubes protruding out of his chest.

It was an odd experience watching the line being tested for the first time. A nurse arrived with a sterile tray adorned with needles, bungs (the ends of the line had interchangeable sterile bungs to prevent germs from getting inside the line) saline, swabs and many little vials waiting to be filled with Deryn's blood for testing.

He was happy now that the cannulas could stop and there would be no more blown veins or sharp scratches. Having an implant instead of intrusive and painful needles was a good swap in Deryn's eyes, and in mine too. I hated seeing him in pain and although the sight of his line would take some getting used to and learning about its maintenance was daunting, I was relieved to have George around.

I'll never forget the first chemo drug, Doxorubicin, which arrived in a big bag shrouded in a silver cover to protect it as it was extremely light sensitive.

Nicknamed 'red death', it produced ghastly side effects – the doctors advised us not to Google anything about it, their prime concern being that we would frighten ourselves with depressing statistics and figures that didn't relate to Deryn. After spending hours doing exactly the opposite of what they'd advised, I discovered that perhaps they had a point; I had successfully managed to terrify myself.

We watched with bated breath as the nurse set up the Doxorubicin ready to administer. I hated the idea of what it was going to do to Deryn. Hair loss was the most common side effect, as the drug, like many chemo drugs, attacks and kills all growing cells. Hair follicles and soft skin inside the mouth can be seriously affected, causing severe ulceration as far as the nose and throat. Heart damage was another potential complication.

Deryn's immune system would be hugely affected as the bone marrow cells are killed off by chemo drugs and he would have to be very careful about who he mixed with as he would be highly susceptible to germs and viruses and could become ill very quickly. Even a common cold could be fatal.

For my own sanity I decided to concentrate on the fact that Deryn's body was already fighting with all its might despite his leukaemic count.

Once chemo started to work, we were warned, we would see some serious, life-threatening issues.

Deryn's proposed journey was mapped out for us: a three-day course of chemo would kill the cancer cells but it was up to the body to process them out of Deryn's system through his liver and kidneys. These organs were expected to fail once his body started to rid itself of the dead leukaemia cells.

Deryn would need to have a finger prick every 15 minutes to test his liver function and general health – so, unfortunately, the needles would not completely stop with the presence of George – and his urine would be tested every time he went to the loo.

In short, he would be watched like a hawk and at the first sign of liver or kidney failure, Deryn would be moved straight into the Paediatric Intensive Care Unit (PICU), where a bed had been booked for him.

In fact, every single bodily function would be weighed, measured and tested. Using a bedpan or paper vase was going to become second nature.

While changing nappies and wiping babies' bums is standard

practice for a mum, I wasn't sure it would ever feel natural to be standing outside the sluice, where all the waste was measured before disposal, chatting to other parents with a bedpan full of poo in one hand and a paper vase full of toxic wee in the other.

Horrendous though all this was, I felt strangely reassured that the team was so vigilant and prepared for every eventuality. I felt safe and no longer frightened knowing that Deryn was in capable hands.

While we knew that at any moment, Deryn could be carted off to PICU, we still decided to allow him visitors and the many relatives and friends jollying us along helped the time to pass and did us all the world of good.

Unfortunately, Dylan and Simon couldn't stay over at hospital with Deryn and me so each evening, they would go home and return early the next morning. Simon's family travelled from the Midlands and stayed at our house to drive in each morning with Simon and Dylan.

Simon's sister Gemma also came to visit and brought some healing crystals with her. Deryn had always been a lover of the spiritual and supernatural side of life and he was thrilled to have them dotted about his room. Gemma also bought Deryn a beautiful quartz necklace which Deryn put on immediately. After that day, it rarely came off.

The three chemo days passed quickly and we were soon met with puzzled faces from the medical team. Deryn seemed absolutely fine. Nothing had changed, he wasn't any worse or any better.

But picking up on the confusion felt by his team, we started to get anxious about the unknown. Were the drugs working, I wondered? And if so, why hadn't any of the terrible things they said would happen, actually happened?

One of Deryn's consultants told us they had run numerous

CHAPTER 3

tests on Deryn's liver and kidneys and they were still functioning perfectly well. Even his spleen had returned to an almost acceptable size.

Deryn's leukaemia count was now also incredibly low, a result they had hoped to see but certainly not expected without organ failure.

We were all stumped. How had Deryn successfully managed to process a phenomenally high amount of leukaemic cells while remaining totally and utterly unaffected by it all?

He'd managed to basically 'wee out' his cancer. It wasn't something any of them had ever seen before and it puzzled the senior doctors on his case.

'I think that Deryn is going to rewrite the medical books,' his bemused but extremely happy consultant told me with a beaming smile.

Chapter 4

DERYN WENT INTO HOSPITAL AS A CHILD BUT AFTER A FEW DAYS AND nights on the oncology ward, he was no longer a little boy. His cancer battle had turned him into a young man. Deryn was remarkably fit at the time of diagnosis and one of his doctors believed that the reason this 10 year old was able to withstand such harsh treatment with absolutely none of the usual after-effects was purely because of his outstanding general health.

Other than Tourette's and autism, Deryn had never been physically unwell as a child. He'd had few colds but he certainly didn't suffer like some children with recurrent tonsillitis or chest infections.

I was feeling a lot more positive about the months ahead.

I hated hearing small children crying on the ward. It seemed so much more terrible for them because they weren't able to fully understand what was going on. They would often look at their parents with bewilderment as their mum and dad held them down so that drugs could be administered. I couldn't begin to imagine how painful it must be for those parents and felt tremendously fortunate that my child was old enough to understand why certain painful processes were a necessary evil.

One evening, a little boy across the room from us was crying and clearly having a terrible time. He had a tumour in his stomach which was clearly visible through his distended belly and he was in a lot of pain. As he wept, Deryn turned to me.

'I really feel sorry for him, he must be in a lot of pain,' he said sadly. 'It must be awful for him.'

Simon and I looked at each with astonishment. Deryn had never said anything like this before or given a glimpse that he cared about anyone else. Empathy was a quality that, thanks to Tourette's, Deryn had not one ounce of so we were astounded.

I started watching him like a hawk and spotted that his facial tics had also stopped. Suddenly, he could play on his PlayStation without any sign of them.

To see Deryn behaving normally was just awesome. I hadn't seen him without a tic since he was three years old and virtually overnight, they had disappeared. We had no idea how long this might last but it was an exciting development.

❖

Deryn had been in hospital for four or five days when Simon received a phone call from his boss. Simon had kept them well informed about what was happening with Deryn's treatment and had only missed a couple of days off work.

He was summoned to a meeting at the company's Norwich office and told he would no longer have a job. In an incredible about-turn, Simon's boss, who had been really supportive and understanding about what we were going through, accused him of using Deryn's illness to get time off work. Simon told them where to stick their job and drove back to hospital absolutely livid. He told me it made him realise where his priorities lay.

This meant we soon built up a new routine, with Simon coming in every day with Dylan to sit with me in Deryn's room, chatting, playing games and generally looking after Deryn's needs. The hospital ward rapidly became a home from home for us. There were a couple of bathrooms, a shower room and a utility room with a washing machine and tumble dryer for parents to use. This was to come in very handy.

Many of the drugs caused sickness and problems with the

young patients' bladders and bowels. Steroids caused such a large amount of water retention that the doctors would often prescribe a diuretic drug to counteract the water build-up. This worked incredibly quickly, often far too quickly for Deryn to react in time. He had quite a few accidents in the early days although I wasn't the only one stripping my child's bed three, four or more times a day.

There was a deep sense of camaraderie on the ward. Other parents would fold your washing and put it to one side if you weren't there to collect it or pop it into the tumble dryer. We all helped each other.

Deryn also started to experience sickness from the chemotherapy drugs by around day four after each infusion and his already diminished appetite was shrinking further. Nevertheless, there would be times when he had a craving for something, often at 3am. Seizing the opportunity to get some food inside him, I'd get dressed, walk down to the concourse and search in vain for the one thing Deryn was craving... hash browns.

Luckily, there was a lovely chef in the kitchen who was willing to cook hash browns just for Deryn, whatever time of the day or night. But by the time I got them back to the ward, Deryn was either asleep or not in the mood anymore – it's one of the nastier tricks chemotherapy plays on your taste buds, making foods that were once your favourite treats taste metallic and inedible.

The oncology ward also had another secret weapon in the shape of a classically trained chef called Mick. Mick was on call all day long and his job was to feed the children exactly what they asked for. Nothing was too much trouble for him, he knew that most of what he cooked wouldn't get eaten but this didn't deter him from making everything as appetising and attractive as possible. He truly loved doing the best he could for the children.

On Mick's door was a white board and a pen. When your

child showed an interest in a particular food, you would walk down to Mick's kitchen and write your child's name and their order on the whiteboard. A short while later, as if by magic, the food would appear.

The highlight of the culinary week, though, was Saturday night when the Burger King on the concourse would give the children on the oncology ward free food. Whatever they wanted, no questions asked. Needless to say, all of the kids loved being in Addenbrooke's on a Saturday night!

The day-to-day routine consisted of nurses coming in and administering various drugs and Deryn's urine and faeces having to be weighed and measured. The many trips to the sluice became rather monotonous so Simon decided to liven it up by writing one-liners on the big paper vases.

'Deryn thinks that nurse xxxx is hot!'

'(Deryn's phone number) Call me when I'm 18!'

Simon drew the radioactive sign on every bottle and every bed pan in Deryn's cubicle, adding the words 'Radioactive Apple Juice'. He amused himself for hours by thinking up ways to get a giggle out of the nursing staff.

One morning, we had a visit from a woman from CLIC Sargent, a charity supporting children and their families through cancer. One of the ways they help is to offer advice and counselling on various issues to the parents of newly diagnosed children.

The lovely lady arrived holding various forms for us to fill in and explained that she would apply for funding from different charities to help with our stay in hospital until we could get a Disability Living Allowance for Deryn. We were going to need as much help as we could get and, thankfully, there was someone ready to assist us. Life as an oncology family meant learning something new every day. Sometimes it was overwhelming but there was nothing we could do apart from get on with it.

CHAPTER 4

A quote sent to me at the time by a family member pretty much summed it up: 'You never know how strong you are until being strong is the only choice you have.'

Chapter 5

OUR TIME TO LEAVE THE HOSPITAL WAS LOOMING AND ALTHOUGH IT had only been 11 days, we were going to miss the staff, the parents, the children and the safety blanket that had been wrapped around us.

Deryn's form of cancer, acute lymphoblastic leukaemia (ALL), meant he was treated as an outpatient whereas acute myeloid leukaemia (AML) required a more intensive six-month inpatient regime. For these children, C2 really did become their home.

One such child was Tiegan, a wonderful, cheeky, smiley 9-month-old little girl who had been diagnosed with AML only weeks before. She would often scoot around the ward at lightning speed in a baby walker while her poor mum Emma tried to keep up.

A little bundle of energy who was always cheerful with a ready grin, she was universally adored by everyone who met her and inspired Deryn. Meanwhile, I gained a lot of strength from Emma.

Cancer shakes your world to the core and I found I totally lost faith in my own abilities as a caregiver to my son. Calpol and hugs were no longer going to suffice if Deryn spiked a temperature. There were protocols to follow, charts to fill in and journeys to be made as a matter of urgency if Deryn started feeling unwell.

In hospital, the burden of responsibility was shouldered by others. If anything went wrong, the nurses were there to step in. Now suddenly, we were left to manage things ourselves and that was a frightening prospect.

One of Deryn's doctors went through a flow chart and gave us a copy detailing the calendar of upcoming treatments. The chart was overwhelming, with lots of dates, arrows, dots and dashes. But once the doctor explained what the symbols meant, it made sense.

Deryn's outpatient care was transferred to the Norfolk and Norwich University Hospital, 18 miles away from home, as opposed to 50 miles away. Another blessing.

On the day we left hospital, I felt very emotional. Armed with what felt like a million and one different drugs and a list of instructions as long as my arm, we said our goodbyes to the legions of nurses and doctors who had been our rocks.

Deryn walked out of the hospital looking not dissimilar to his healthy self. Only the Hickman line in his chest and his thinning hair marked him out as a cancer patient.

With mixed emotions, we packed his stuff into the car boot. Deryn, meanwhile, was thrilled to feel fresh air on his face again. The warm, balmy breeze made him smile and he sat with the window open most of the way home.

We were on our own now. Going home to normal, everyday life after such a life-changing few days was surreal and a little daunting. Reassuringly, though, a large support network of people was there for us whenever we needed them, day or night.

We made a pact that cancer would not swallow us or define us. Deryn certainly wasn't going to wear cancer like a badge. He wanted to show everyone that they didn't need to feel sorry for him. He'd already met children who were far sicker than he was and he kept the promise that he'd made that very first night.

He could beat this and be positive about it, too.

❖

Deryn arrived back home in the middle of the summer holidays. There was a playing field opposite our house and at some point, he was going to have to face his friends who played out there most days and evenings.

CHAPTER 5

I was intrigued and concerned to see how people would react to Deryn and indeed, how they would react towards us, too. Our lives were very different now but the lives of those around us hadn't changed at all.

We pulled up outside our little mid-terrace house and some of the lads that Deryn had grown up with spotted him and waved as they continued to play football. Breaking the news to his circle of 10-year-old friends was a huge responsibility that I didn't take lightly.

I'd experienced a little of the turmoil that would accompany it a few days earlier. During my stint at home I'd been chatting to Deryn on FaceTime in hospital when one of his friends knocked on the door.

'Is Deryn coming out?' Olly asked when I opened the door.

I had to think on my feet. I didn't want to shock or upset him but I also had to be honest.

'He's not here, buddy, he's in hospital', I replied, before realising that I couldn't just leave it at that.

'Come in, mate, I'm on FaceTime to him at the moment, do you want to talk to him?'

As we walked through the house, I told Olly that Deryn had been diagnosed with cancer and that he wasn't very well but that he was doing okay and still looked the same and felt the same inside.

My iPad was sitting on the kitchen table and as we got closer, I could see Deryn waiting patiently for me.

'I've got someone who wants to talk to you, Deryn,' I told him.

'Alright, Deryn?' Olly asked cautiously.

He didn't know what to say but Deryn managed to put his friend at ease within seconds by being his usual chirpy, cheeky self. They talked for a few minutes before Olly virtually ran out of the house, shouting goodbye as he left.

It had gone far better than I'd expected and I felt relieved that at least one friend now knew the score. About an hour later, I got a message from Olly's mum.

'Olly has just come home telling me the most ridiculous story,' she said. 'He said that Deryn has cancer. I'm sorry, I can't believe that he would make up such rubbish. I've told him off for making up stories.'

I explained that her son hadn't made anything up and was telling the truth.

To their huge credit, Deryn's friends never acted any differently towards him. They were wonderful and supported him as best they could. All Deryn needed from them was normality and that's what he got.

So many of our friends were amazing, offering ongoing, unwavering support and reassurance. Whatever we needed, we had only to ask.

However, we also experienced some strange reactions and inexplicably ignorant behaviour which was very hurtful.

I hadn't been back home with Deryn for very long before I saw a female friend who I'd known since my schooldays. As we got closer, I smiled at her, expecting to engage in conversation as we usually did when we saw each other. Instead, she walked straight past me without even making eye contact.

I was confused and bewildered but didn't say anything as I hate confrontation. Sadly, it wasn't an isolated incident. The same thing happened with other people I considered friends and while some would give me a half-hearted smile and keep on walking, others pretended not to see me.

Clearly, they didn't know how to deal with Deryn's diagnosis or how to make conversation with me but it would have been easier to hear them tell me: 'I just don't know what to say to you', rather than blatantly ignore me.

CHAPTER 5

For the rest of the summer we went to ground and didn't see anyone other than my closest friend Penny, her son Joss and his older sister Marcie. Deryn didn't feel well enough to play with his mates from the estate and it was heartbreaking to sit and watch my vivacious, outgoing son become a hermit who was too ill and scared to mix with his friends.

With George nestled in his chest, Deryn was heavily restricted. There was no more swimming or contact sports of any kind. No more long soaks in the bath. Even showering was difficult.

Our energetic, fun-loving Deryn was struggling with the sedentary lifestyle that cancer was inflicting on him. He started experiencing temperature spikes – when the body temperature exceeds 38°C – which led to a litany of three-day observational stays in the Norfolk and Norwich University Hospital.

I would run around checking Deryn's temperature every two hours with an electronic thermometer. I was paranoid about caring as well for him at home as he would have been cared for in hospital. The burden of being responsible for a seriously ill child weighed heavily on my mind.

I felt powerless and yet powerful at the same time knowing that his wellbeing depended on me being thorough in everything I did. I made sure every room in the house was clean and tidy so that Deryn didn't pick up any nasty bugs. Dirt became my arch nemesis – that and people who sneezed.

Deryn had a strict drug regime and to help me get organised, I bought him a dosette box, in which each day of the week had four separate compartments. After Deryn went to bed, I stood in the kitchen and counted out a week's worth of pills. If I made a silly mistake or didn't pay attention to what I was doing, it would be Deryn who would pay the ultimate price.

Chapter 6

AT HOME, IN QUIET MOMENTS, THE THOUGHT THAT WE MIGHT LOSE Deryn regularly reduced me to tears. In hospital, I didn't get a chance to think about what was happening. There, everything moved so fast, there wasn't time for contemplation.

Standing on my own in the silence of the kitchen gave me more peace and quiet than I really wanted and I quietly sobbed. Simon came in and saw that I was upset.

'He'll be all right, you know,' he told me, squeezing my shoulders tenderly.

I really wanted to believe him but how could any of us know that for sure? The doctors could only give us a balance of probability on Deryn's chances of surviving acute lymphoblastic leukaemia. His success depended on a few crucial factors, which became a pros and cons list in my head.

Age was in his favour, but only just. Once a patient is over 10 years old, their chances of surviving for longer than five years start to decrease. Deryn was 10, a tick in the box for his survival.

Gender plays a role too, with females tending to perform better while undergoing ALL treatment than males. This made it one all.

Deryn's white cell count at diagnosis had a lot to do with his chances of reaching remission. The higher the count, the harder it would be to keep it in remission. His white blood cell count had been horrendously high – the second highest the doctors had ever seen. It was now 2-1 to cancer and I felt myself edging towards a downward spiral of hopelessness.

The final factor to be taken into account was the type of white blood cell that leukaemia had affected. Deryn had T-cell ALL, one of the hardest types to treat.

So the odds were stacked against Deryn – how on earth could Simon tell me that it was going to be all right?

I was beside myself with worry but I knew something in my mindset had to change, for my own sake as well as Deryn's. I had always been a glass half-empty kind of person and wanted more than anything to feel more optimistic and adopt Simon's positive mental attitude. Simon felt strongly that we had to pull together as a family. We couldn't let this get to us so much that our family or marriage fell apart.

Despite his assurances to me, Simon was also going through hell and experiencing the same feelings of concern as me. Simon was Deryn's dad and it cut him deeply to watch his little boy going through so much. It affected him in a way that he often couldn't convey or talk about because he was the one who was supposed to be strong. Sadly, it's still a taboo for a man to have feelings or break down when his child is diagnosed with cancer.

I was asked many times how I was feeling, while Simon barely got asked at all. People assumed he didn't have anything to say about it. He seemed to be an afterthought to the medical staff and I could see that it hurt him. It hurt me, too.

The first morning back at home, Deryn was due to take some medication quite early so we set an alarm. He was not pleased to be woken up at the crack of dawn. Naturally, we got a different reaction to the one the nurses received. Deryn felt he was able to vent on us in a way that he wouldn't dream of doing to anyone else.

We had been through some frightening times, caring for him and giving him everything he needed so it was very upsetting when he snapped at us or was rude or uncooperative. But you hurt those closest to you and I instantly forgave him because if he couldn't take his frustrations out on us, who else would be there for him?

Deryn still had no appetite and wasn't interested in eating as he was starting to suffer the dark side effects of chemotherapy. Simon and I decided that if Deryn didn't want to eat, we weren't going to force him. He wasn't underweight and we figured that missing a few meals wouldn't hurt him as long as he ate when he felt like it.

I desperately wanted to hide away from the world and pretend none of this was happening. Going out of the house meant that people would talk to me about Deryn and with each and every conversation, the reality of cancer hit home.

We decided to have a duvet day together. Snuggled up on the sofa watching films and eating some junk food would surely help Deryn feel better. He loved junk food and because the doctors had told us to feed him whatever he wanted, processed or not, we filled our cupboards with everything Deryn liked. The aim was to get as much into him as possible – doctor's orders.

After a few days at home, and a few more duvet days, we had to go to the Norfolk and Norwich University Hospital for a check-up and to meet the paediatric oncology team. He had the usual blood pressure test done and his height and weight were recorded before we were introduced to his new oncologist.

Dr JP produced flow charts outlining Deryn's upcoming treatment. There would be a lot of different drugs, all given at varying times, and some would be very aggressive. Many of the drugs Deryn was taking were to counteract the side effects of the chemotherapy, protect his stomach, prevent nausea and help his blood recover.

The oncologist examined Deryn. Once she'd turned him

crimson with the testicle check and toilet habit conversation, she explained that everything seemed to be fine physically. Deryn just needed to give some blood so that they could run more tests.

The subject of going back to school also came up as the medical team felt it was in his interests.

The idea of going back to school appealed to Deryn. The staff would need to be onboard and confident at having Deryn in their care as well as tolerant about how often he was able to attend. If he became too unwell or neutropenic – exhibiting a very low level of neutrophils – he simply wouldn't be able to go in.

It hadn't even occurred to me that Deryn would be fit and well enough to go back to school so quickly and I was in two minds about it.

As I mulled over the idea with mixed emotions, Dr JP announced that the blood test results were exactly what she'd expected to see given that Deryn had just finished some pretty intensive chemotherapy and was slowly recovering.

This was amazing news and just what I needed to hear. Before any blood test, there was a certain amount of trepidation and the hour it took for the results to come back was always an anxious wait. I wanted to know that he was okay but a larger, more scared, part of me didn't want to know the results in case they weren't good.

Finally, it felt like we had something to celebrate. Deryn was due to go back to school and rejoin his friends after the summer holidays. More than anything, I wanted him back to being a normal kid again.

❖

Amid the uncertainty of the previous few weeks, I had an experience I can only describe as amazing one day while waiting for everyone to get ready. As I stood alone in the kitchen, a blinding light cascaded through the window, enveloping me with a blissful warmth. It shone so brightly that I could barely see. It was beautiful.

I closed my eyes and immediately had an overwhelming sense of inner knowledge that I'd never felt before. I could still feel the warmth on my chest from the sun but the feeling also penetrated deep inside, filling up my whole body.

It's impossible to describe the feeling of wellbeing that came over me. I was filled with confidence that Deryn would come through this and get well again. I'd oscillated between periods of denial and moments where I was able to deal with everything but on this day, I felt something monumental happening deep inside my soul. It reassured me that Deryn would not die and the tears flowed as I tried to make sense of this profound experience.

Was it all in my mind? Was I going mad? Whatever it was, I suddenly felt that I had every reason to be positive and uplifted about the future. Despite my pessimistic outlook, I had an extraordinary innate sense that everything was going to be okay. I no longer felt scared or at a loss to cope. I felt strong, in control, as if I could take on the world if I needed to. It was a remarkable boost at a time when I really needed something to give me a little faith.

I was reminded of a small stained glass ornament that my mum had in pride of place on her windowsill when I was growing up, which was inscribed: 'God grant me the serenity to accept the things I cannot change, the courage to change the things I can and the wisdom to know the difference.'

Instead of dreading the next hospital rendezvous, Deryn was quite excited about undergoing another general anaesthetic for a lumbar puncture. He did not enjoy the fasting before the procedure, however, as the steroids were kicking in and – to my delight – he wanted to eat everything.

The downside to the steroids was that they caused such severe water retention that Deryn started to look unrecognisable. His face was bloated to twice its normal size and when he laughed, he couldn't see properly because his over-inflated cheeks covered his eyes. To his credit, he didn't let it get to him, even playing up to his new nickname, 'Moonface'.

The day of the lumbar puncture dawned and we arrived at Addenbrooke's. Following some tests, we were called to meet Deryn's haematologist, Dr Mike. I immediately liked this softly spoken and kindly Scottish doctor, as did Deryn.

He asked how he had been getting on before examining Deryn, who was at ease with a male doctor checking him over. We'd been told the timing of the procedure would depend on how many young children were also in for the same thing. Less able to cope with fasting, the younger kids tended to throw hunger tantrums so were pushed to the top of the list.

Deryn was patient to a point – until Mick the chef turned up with some toasted tea cakes for a child who had already had a lumbar puncture, two hours into our wait, and he was beside himself.

'I'm starving mum,' he grumbled.

It was hard watching him go hungry when only a couple of weeks earlier, he couldn't eat anything at all. To make matters worse, the little boy who had ordered the tea cakes decided he wasn't hungry anymore and left them sitting there as Deryn salivated.

On the days when Deryn had to fast for a medical procedure, I decided I would also forgo food. I didn't think it was fair to eat in front of him – it was a small thing I could do to help make him feel less isolated – so I was also starving and I asked a nurse to remove the temptation from both of us.

Eventually, Deryn was installed in a small ward to await his turn in theatre and when he was finally wheeled in, there was a steel table laden with medical instruments that looked like a macabre torture chamber. I was shocked at the size of the enormous needle while Deryn could only gasp: 'Wow, how cool!'

Watching him being put under general anaesthetic wasn't as traumatic this time. It was amusing to note his 'going under the influence' routine did not differ from before. He remarked on the fuzziness, loss of hearing and robotic sounds he was making before letting out a big yawn, asking for a plate of lasagne and seconds later, crashing out for the count.

'Would you like to give him a kiss, mum?' the nurse asked.

I gave him a gentle peck on the forehead and waited outside theatre.

The lumbar puncture procedure was fairly straightforward. The close proximity of the procedure to the spine means the patient has to stay perfectly still to prevent any damage to the spinal cord. Once Deryn was asleep in the foetal position so that his spine was fully extended, a needle and catheter would be inserted with the catheter left in place in between the vertebrae in the spinal cord. A sample of spinal fluid would be taken for testing and a chemotherapy drug would be injected into the spinal cord to kill any cancerous cells that might be present in the spinal fluid and brain.

Deryn was also due to have a bone marrow aspiration, where a sample of the bone marrow fluid and cells is taken from inside the bones.

Deryn's bed was wheeled back towards me 20 minutes later. He was fast asleep on his side with an oxygen mask over his mouth. The nurse explained that it might take a little while before he woke up and he would have to remain lying down for at least another hour to ensure the chemotherapy drug could make its way towards the brain. If he sat up too soon, gravity would make it harder for the drug to travel. Deryn woke up full of beans and impatient to get on with things.

It never ceased to amaze me how well Deryn coped with whatever horrible procedure came his way. He put up no resistance, remained cheerful and upbeat and was a complete inspiration to me and the staff around him.

'How long do I have to stay lying down?' he demanded. 'I'm starving!'

Before the nurse could answer, Mick arrived with Deryn's lasagne.

The nurse told Deryn that he could sit up shortly and while I could see Deryn was desperate to argue with her, he decided against it. Learning to compromise was proving to be a valuable part of his journey.

I fed him the lasagne as he lay on his side and we were able to leave after making an appointment for another lumbar puncture a month later. He had a sore back and a headache and was desperate to get home.

On our way out, we were stopped by the nurse specialist, Hannah, who was liaising with Deryn's school about his return. Hannah wanted his classmates to have all the information about what he was going through before he arrived back in the classroom, to prepare them as much as possible. We agreed that she would visit the school on the first day of term and he would return on the second day.

Not for the first time, I felt incredibly proud of Deryn. At 10 years old, he was showing a spirit and tenacity that someone three times his age would have had to dig deep for. He seemed to have some unique ability to cope with anything life threw at him. Again, I admired him.

Chapter 7

THE START OF THE NEW SCHOOL YEAR LOOMED. THE STREETS WERE thronging with what seemed like every parent in the country on a quest to buy school uniform… apart from me. I was totally unprepared for the boys' return to school.

Dylan seemed perfectly well but I was having trouble deciding whether to send him back after the holidays. If Deryn was neutropenic, it could be incredibly dangerous for his brother to bring something nasty home from school. At Dylan's infant school, there always seemed to be one bug or another going round, which could have a potentially disastrous effect on Deryn.

However, I had to balance it against the fact that Deryn seemed to be doing so well and hadn't been neutropenic since leaving Addenbrooke's. Encouraged by the fact that his medical team seemed more than happy for him to go back, we decided to take the plunge and allow both boys to be among their classmates once again.

Deryn was due to join the last year of junior school, Year 6, and he was looking forward to it enormously. It was also the year of the Standard Assessment Tests (SATs) so it was important for him to be there as much as possible so he could score well. Up until his diagnosis, Deryn had barely missed a day of school and he didn't want to miss any more than was absolutely necessary.

Dylan had become noticeably more quiet and subdued since Deryn was diagnosed. We kept a close eye on him, urging the staff at his school to also watch out for any signs of him getting upset. Fortunately, they were very understanding and also deeply upset by Deryn's illness. Deryn had been a pupil there and the teachers knew him very well and remembered him with great fondness. Deryn had always been very popular with the teachers and Dylan was clearly following in his big brother's footsteps.

I knew it was the right thing to do but the first day of term arrived and I felt an acute sense of dread. It was almost like dropping him off on his very first day at school all over again, a day when he waved me off cheerfully with a stoic: 'You can go now, Mummy', as I wept uncontrollably. In many ways, Deryn was even more vulnerable now than he had been at five years old and naturally, my worries were amplified.

Although I knew that he would be okay, I didn't want to let him go. I certainly didn't trust anyone else to pay as much attention to him as I would. I was gripped with a terror that they might miss something vital. My worries occupied my every thought and I sensed that if I didn't get a grip on myself, my irrational side would take over and I simply wouldn't allow him to go back.

Simon took Dylan to school and I accompanied Deryn, full of anxiety even though I had already decided to spend the whole day there with him. He couldn't get his head around the fuss I was making. We arrived at school a little earlier than the other students so that we had a chance to talk to his teacher before the rest of the children arrived.

Deryn looked very smart in his uniform but he was totally unrecognisable thanks to the bloating caused by the high-dose steroids. I was worried about how his friends would react to him, as most of them hadn't seen him since the last day of the summer term. Would he be bullied? Would they laugh at him? Would someone hurt him?

Thankfully Deryn interrupted my thoughts by asking a question.

'Can I have a bacon roll at break time?'

I didn't want to say no as I knew that he liked the bacon rolls the kitchen staff made for him. He'd told me stories about how sometimes he didn't have enough money to buy a roll so the wonderful women in the kitchen would sneak him one and they'd always put in extra bacon for him.

He approached the hatch to the kitchen, where four dinner ladies were chatting and giggling among themselves.

'Hello, lovely, what can I do for you?' one of them asked.

Deryn smiled and said he'd like a bacon roll at break time.

'Okay, no problem, can I have your name, lovely?'

Deryn seemed a bit perplexed.

'Umm, yeah, my name is Deryn.'

The lady smiled and asked how to spell it.

'D E R Y N,' he replied.

'Oh, we have another little boy here called Deryn too,' she exclaimed.

It dawned on me that these lovely women, who thought the world of Deryn, didn't recognise him now.

'I'm not new… I AM Deryn,' he corrected her with a beaming smile.

All at once, the four ladies gasped, covering their mouths in disbelief.

With tears flowing down her face, the chef at the front leaned over the counter to give Deryn the biggest hug of his life. She looked like she never wanted to let go. By now, the other three were also crying and so was I. The chef went on to tell me how wonderful they all thought Deryn was and confessed that sometimes they would indeed sneak extra bacon into his roll.

They seemed genuinely heartbroken that they hadn't recognised him and promised to look after him.

We headed off to see Deryn's teacher but the playground was

full of parents and children so there was no chance of a discreet entrance. Our efforts to blend in inconspicuously failed and it was only a matter of seconds before one child spotted him and came running over.

'Are you Deryn?' asked the little one.

Deryn didn't get a chance to answer because his mates had also spotted him and were making their way over. Before we knew it, Deryn was surround by a circle of his mates who all had a million and one questions to ask him about how he was.

Deryn said he felt like a celebrity among his circle.

'I could get used to this', he joked.

The crowd grew and the circle started to close in around him. He looked like he could handle it so I stood back and just observed.

Suddenly, a girl Deryn knew stepped forward and, without warning, poked his cheek.

'Does that hurt? Your cheeks are so big! Did it hurt when I poked it?'

I thought Deryn would get upset but he simply laughed and told her that it didn't hurt, and asked her to do it again. Without hesitation, the little girl stepped forward and gave his big shiny cheek another hearty poke. As she pushed her finger into his cheek, Deryn made a noise not dissimilar to a squeaky dog toy and the whole crowd roared with laughter.

Deryn had managed to make light of the situation using humour and his naturally relaxed reactions immediately put his friends at ease. I was bursting with pride and realised I had totally underestimated just how caring, funny and capable my son was.

All of a sudden, his best mate Joss stepped forward and planted himself right next to Deryn. Joss was larger in build than Deryn and was also very protective, even more so now that Deryn was unwell.

CHAPTER 7

There seemed to be an unspoken pact between the two of them that Joss would be Deryn's protector while he was vulnerable. It was very sweet to witness and came as a relief to feel that I wasn't going to have to worry too much and that Joss would make sure that no harm came to Deryn.

I didn't want to break up the reunion so I told Deryn I would go and see his teacher by myself and then head home.

The bell went and the children lined up in the playground to go to their new classrooms. As I stood watching from a distance, Simon came up behind me and gave my shoulders a squeeze.

'Everything okay?' he asked.

'Yes, everything is more than okay,' I replied. 'I don't think we need to worry.'

Chapter 8

LIFE WAS STARTING TO RESEMBLE A NEW NORMAL. WE WERE AWARE
that many cancer patients don't die from cancer but as a result
of an infection they simply can't fight with a compromised
immune system. We had a bag packed for Deryn and ourselves
at all times, just in case.

We were just beginning to relax when Deryn experienced his
first temperature spike of 38.5°C. He was cold, shivery and
neutropenic so we rang the hospital to tell them we were on our
way. They didn't have a room at the NNUH but said they'd
arrange one by the time we arrived as it was important that
Deryn was isolated from other children on the ward.

Once there, we were ushered into a small treatment room and
a nurse offered to make me a cup of tea and fetch Deryn a DVD
player. She returned with the tea, the player and the *Home Alone*
box set so Deryn and I made ourselves comfortable and started
watching the first film. By the time the closing credits rolled, we
still hadn't seen anyone so I popped out and asked what was
going on. The nurse said Deryn was next to be seen and we
wouldn't have to wait long.

She carried out some observations on Deryn, whose temperature had by now climbed to 39°C. He was feeling quite unwell.
We started watching the second *Home Alone* film and got through
it without seeing another soul. I poked my head out again.

'We're still waiting to see a doctor, it's been some time now,
can you tell me what's going on please?' I asked, a note of panic
creeping into my voice.

I understood the severity of an infection and was confused as to why the hospital didn't seem very concerned. Again, I was told the doctor was on his way and Deryn was next. We loaded *Home Alone 3* into the player and were about 10 minutes from the end when the doctor finally arrived and informed us he would be starting Deryn on IV antibiotics straight away.

It dawned on me just how tedious a temperature spike was going to be. I'd been told it was imperative to get Deryn to hospital within an hour but there was no sense of urgency once we arrived. Eight hours later, he was finally going to receive the treatment he needed.

Another rule of the temperature spike was that you couldn't go home until you had spent three days without a temperature. It was going to be a time-consuming scenario each time he spiked.

Blood samples were sent away to see if they grew any bugs and thankfully, the cultures grew nothing of interest. After a few hours of antibiotics, Deryn's temperature reverted to normal and three long and boring days later, I took him home.

We never did discover just what the problem was. Many times after this, his temperature would sort itself out but nonetheless, we still had to sit at hospital and wait patiently for days until we could go home.

It was only a matter of days before Deryn's next routine check-up and lumbar puncture was due. A wonderful senior nurse called him in and he took off his T-shirt so she could access the Hickman line.

Seeing my son so blasé about something so sinister was heartwarming and heartbreaking at the same time. Part of me was very proud of Deryn for adapting to this inconvenience, but I was also saddened by the fact that this horrible situation was something he had become accustomed to.

CHAPTER 8

Suddenly the nurse shrieked loudly. Deryn was howling with laughter while the nurse was in a complete fluster.

'Let me try that one more time to make absolutely sure what just happened,' she said as I stood by, intrigued.

She took the Hickman line, attached a syringe full of saline on to the end and pushed down, forcing the saline down the line. Where the line went into Deryn's chest, there was a little hole and the line was secured with a small blue stitch so that it wouldn't come out of his chest and cause problems. However, when she pushed the saline down the line, instead of going to his heart, it squirted out of the hole in his chest.

'In 15 years of nursing, I have never seen that before,' she exclaimed, shaking her head in disbelief as the saline dribbled down Deryn's belly. She explained that Deryn wouldn't be undergoing a lumbar puncture as planned. She was convinced that the Hickman line had somehow displaced from where it was supposed to be.

Minutes later, a doctor came in to see Deryn who, as usual, wasn't fussed by any of this. He thought it was hilarious that he was 'leaking' while the doctor, less amused, sent Deryn for an ultrasound scan to find out exactly what was going on.

Deryn was injected with blue dye which would reveal why the saline came out of his chest cavity. I was ushered behind a screen and stayed glued to the monitor, transfixed and forgetting for a few seconds that it was my son I was studying so intently.

I could see Deryn's lungs, heart and liver quite clearly and suddenly there was a flash of blue across the screen. Deryn's line could be seen but it was nowhere near his heart. Instead it was coiled up like a tiny sleeping snake just underneath his collarbone – a long way from where it was supposed to be.

The nurse told us that a port-a-cath would be a far better option for Deryn, given his age and level of activity, rather than another Hickman line. Made of metal and around the size of a bottle top, this port is implanted under the skin, with a line that goes to the heart. Access is made via this bottle top and the blood drawn up via a special type of cannula called a gripper. This gripper has to be pushed through the skin each time the line is accessed.

Before Deryn decided whether to go for it, he wanted to see a port and a gripper for himself – he wasn't signing up for anything he wasn't 100% sure about. So the nurse arranged for a demo on a threadbare puppet that wouldn't have looked out of place on *Sesame Street* and she showed Deryn a gripper, a 1.5cm long needle that reminded me of a stylus from a record player.

Deryn was shown where the port would be implanted, how it would be accessed and was even shown how to access it himself.

To me it looked frightening but I tried to keep my reservations hidden because I didn't want to influence his decision – he was the one who needed to make this choice. However, having watched how it would work, I could see it was a great idea. Deryn would be able to swim, take a shower and have a long soak in the bath whenever he wanted. In short, he was free to enjoy his life a little more without the worry of a line hanging down from his chest.

An extra bonus was that it couldn't be pulled by children at school. I'd already had to have a word with the mother of a younger child at school who had deliberately tried to wrench out Deryn's Hickman line.

The puppet put everything into perspective and Deryn felt it was worth dealing with the pain each time it needed to be accessed.

I watched my son take all this in with a massive grin on his face and felt enormous pride in the way he made his choice. Cancer takes away a lot of decisions so being able to make a small but important one gave him back a sense of control, something he felt he had lost since being diagnosed.

Just as we were about to leave, Dr Mike came to tease Deryn about the Hickman incident. Deryn and Mike had established a great relationship, Deryn thought the world of Mike and trusted him implicitly.

'How did you manage to do that, Deryn?' he cajoled. 'Only you could do something like this!'

'Well, you know me, Mike, I don't like to do things by the book,' Deryn quipped back with a cheeky grin.

We returned a few days later and the port-a-cath was embedded while I waited outside. Deryn came round drowsily and managed to tell me that he wanted some egg sandwiches. Fortunately, I'd already come armed with some as he had put in a food order seconds before falling unconscious.

It was heartrending to watch my child with pupils like pinpricks trying to eat egg sandwiches while still under the influence of a general anaesthetic. He could not get those sandwiches into his mouth quickly enough but, due to his lack of motor skills, it was far from easy.

Once he had finished, he was wearing most of the egg mayonnaise. He was also as high as a kite. It was the first time I had seen pupils so small since working the doors as a bouncer. I had seen people on many different drugs over the years and was no stranger to a dilated pupil but to see my 10-year-old son on another planet was a shock.

'Don't worry, it's just the morphine,' explained one of the recovery nurses.

Once we were back on the children's ward, I took the opportunity to have a proper look at his chest. The Hickman line was gone and all that was left in its place was a small red mark with a couple of tiny stitches.

On the left side of Deryn's chest was a large dressing, under which was a 4cm wound which had been glued, rather than stitched, to prevent scarring. The team decided it would be better for Deryn to have a double lumen port to allow a larger variety of drugs to enter his body at once.

A few days later we were back once again for the dressing to be removed, the port to be accessed and the lumbar puncture. As the nurse was getting her tray ready, she asked me to wash my hands, pop on some gloves and remove the dressing on Deryn's chest. Feeling useful and almost like a nurse myself, I peeled it away. Peering inside, I saw that the wound had completely torn open. On my son's chest was a 4cm gash, so deep that I could see the yellow fat and muscle.

Looking at both our faces must have invoked a guilt pang in Deryn. He told us that he had been feeling behind the dressing and getting his mates at school to feel it, too, and that all of this pressure had ripped it wide open.

I was so angry with him. What a stupid thing to do! It didn't matter how ill he was, if he needed telling off, I was going to do just that. A surgeon was called in to sew him up.

'Do you think I'll have a big scar on my chest now?' Deryn asked me.

Before I could answer, he added: 'I hope so, girls love scars!'

Chapter 9

THE WEEK AFTER THE PORT HAD BEEN IMPLANTED, DERYN HAD TO go to the NNUH to have one of his routine chemotherapy drugs, Cytarabine, infused. There were so many types of drugs that had to be administered at various times of the month and in different ways, it was quite mind-boggling keeping track.

Cytarabine had to be given at the same time every day for four consecutive days. This was frustrating as the journey to the hospital was over an hour's round trip yet the infusion only took about five minutes from start to finish.

But Deryn's uncrushable spirit in coping with everything without a murmur of complaint made me look at cancer as more of an inconvenience than a serious illness. We learned very quickly that planning ahead was something we could no longer do. Everything had to fit around Deryn's treatment schedule, which was relentless and rigorous.

We arrived at the hospital where we were greeted by a senior nurse called June, who showed us to a bed and proceeded to ask some medical questions.

She drew up the Cytarabine, only then realising that Deryn no longer had a Hickman line. She told us she hadn't accessed a port for some time and wasn't confident using one. This didn't fill us with confidence and it soon became apparent that although a port seemed like a great idea when dealing with Addenbrooke's, the staff at the NNUH perhaps weren't as proficient.

Once the dressing had been removed, we could see that the wound was healing well. There were just a few small stitches and it was neat and tidy but there was no doubt it was going to leave a cracking scar. Deryn was overjoyed!

Wary of the painful procedure, Deryn had asked to have freeze spray to numb the area. This needed to be sprayed from a distance so as not to cause a freezer burn and was worth its weight in liquid gold when administered correctly.

June was armed with a can of the spray in one hand and a gripper in the other. Deryn was a little dubious, as was I. This was the first time that Deryn's port had been accessed while he was conscious and neither of us knew what to expect. Every time Deryn had to endure pain, I prayed it would be over as quickly as possible. I hated seeing him suffer and the loss of control made it even more unbearable.

I also hated injections and blood tests and often wanted to leave the room because I felt so sick but I couldn't bring myself to leave Deryn facing it by himself. He sat on the small treatment bed, bare-chested and at June's mercy. June started to spray his skin and immediately, the skin turned white. Deryn complained that it hurt.

'You're spraying too close to the skin', I exclaimed. 'You're going to burn him.'

June assured me that she had used freeze spray many times and knew exactly what she was doing. I felt a bit silly and promptly shut up – who was I to doubt a senior nurse? After all, I was just a parent of a child who'd had cancer for a relatively short amount of time. I certainly wasn't an authority on medical matters.

With that, June pushed the gripper through Deryn's chest and into the port. Deryn inhaled sharply with pain and I realised that it was a grave mistake allowing a port to be put in. I couldn't imagine having to see him go through that each time it needed accessing.

CHAPTER 9

June tested the line and it bled back, meaning that the gripper was successfully in place, which was at least one positive. The whole affair had been an awful first introduction to having his port accessed and didn't bode well for future procedures.

The gripper was left in place so that the Cytarabine could be given every day for the next few days and June placed a transparent dressing over the top of the gripper. The effect of the freeze spray had quickly worn off and Deryn's skin was looking raw, angry and sore to the touch.

'Oh, I think I might have burnt him after all', June said dismissively.

I couldn't believe what I was hearing. A senior nurse was making light of the fact that she had burned my 10-year old son. I didn't say a word. I was angry but also embarrassed and wrestling with the notion that I had no place to judge her ability as a nurse.

Not surprisingly, Deryn was reluctant to have his port accessed again and I was in two minds about whether to ring Dr Mike and ask him to take the damn thing out. It felt like more trouble than it was worth.

I felt a pang of guilt about letting it happen. It was what Deryn had wanted, but I felt responsible. I could only hope that the pain lessened with each access.

That evening, Deryn noticed that his skin was sweating profusely beneath the clear dressing, so much so that the dressing came away at the bottom. I pushed a piece of gauze underneath to try and soak up some of the sweat and assured Deryn that we would get someone to look at it the next day. But I felt incredibly guilty and angry with myself for not saying more at the time, and for failing to stick up for my son, thereby allowing him to be hurt unnecessarily.

Guilt wasn't a new emotion. I felt a lot of it during the early days. I'd read that if you have flu during the late stages of pregnancy or while breastfeeding, it could cause leukaemia. When Deryn was a newborn, I'd had a terrible case of flu but still carried on breastfeeding him. I couldn't banish the thought that his illness might be my fault.

❖

The following morning, the gauze was soaking and the skin underneath was still sweating and looked even more inflamed than the previous day. I replaced the gauze with a fresh piece and sent Deryn off to school.

On our return to the hospital that afternoon we were seen by a senior male nurse as June was not there. He tested the line, which worked perfectly, and gave Deryn his chemo. Afterwards, I asked him to have a look underneath the dressing. He was appalled by what he saw.

He slowly and meticulously removed the dressing from Deryn's chest and immediately, we could see that his skin was red raw and had been weeping pus beneath the dressing.

I told him what had happened the previous day and he confirmed that June had burned Deryn's skin by spraying the freezing spray too close and for too long. He kept apologising as he cleaned up the mess and carefully placed another dressing over the top of the gripper. It already looked a lot better and Deryn told us it felt better, too.

The next day the kind male nurse didn't need to change Deryn's dressing as the wound had dried up quite nicely and seemed to be healing.

'I'll leave it alone today and when I take out your gripper tomorrow, I'll remove the dressing and give it a good clean,' he explained.

Day four of Cytarabine arrived but when we reached the hospital, the male nurse wasn't there. June, however, was. My

CHAPTER 9

heart sank. I was not thrilled about her being the one to remove the gripper. The male nurse had gained our trust but I no longer trusted June.

Deryn sat anxiously on the treatment bed while June gathered together everything she needed. Since the male nurse had removed the dressing carefully and slowly, Deryn decided he would do the same today. The dressings were very sticky and painful to remove at the best of times, let alone when there were stitches and tender patches underneath, so, naturally, he wanted to take his time.

'I don't see the point in taking all day to take off a dressing,' June admonished, before swatting Deryn's hands away and grabbing hold of the edge of the dressing that Deryn had managed to free up.

'Just rip them off!'

As she said the word 'rip', June tore the dressing off Deryn's chest while he yelled out in agony. I could not believe my eyes. She may have thought she was doing Deryn a favour by making it quick, but I couldn't help feeling she didn't give two hoots.

I felt sick and incredibly angry. My instincts were screaming at me to retaliate on Deryn's behalf but for some reason, I felt totally impotent and overwhelmed.

Deryn was fighting back the tears as I rushed to comfort him, gritting his teeth and clenching his fists with the pain. Not only had the gripper come out but the dressing had taken with it a large amount of Deryn's skin.

'You've ripped off his skin,' I shouted, struggling to contain my fury.

June just muttered: 'Oh yes, so I have.'

I was astonished. No apology, no remorse, nothing. I was absolutely disgusted. I didn't know what to do next. My emotions were all over the place but somehow, I managed to keep my cool and not make a scene.

Trust was extremely important and suffice to say, there was none where this nurse was concerned. June wiped the inflamed area with an antiseptic tissue and placed a more suitable gauze dressing over it.

We left in haste, thankful that we wouldn't have to go back for a couple of weeks.

Chapter 10

It was Dylan's sixth birthday and we'd planned a visit to our favourite Mexican restaurant in Norwich. We were looking forward to celebrating. It felt like forever since we'd all been out and let our hair down.

Deryn was due to go to NNUH for chemotherapy on Dylan's birthday, which was annoying timing but we'd arranged for Deryn to get to the ward later that evening so that we could enjoy a night out together first.

Leading up to the big day, we were all hoping and praying that Deryn wouldn't spike a temperature. Dylan had lost out on so many things since Deryn was diagnosed, missing many of his friends' birthday parties in case he picked up a bug. He'd had no choice but to take a back seat for the last few months. He knew that Deryn's treatment had to take priority over the rest of us and although he didn't always like it, he dealt with it unbelievably well. So it was important to me that his birthday was special.

Deryn was looking forward to tackling the same plate of enchiladas, fried sliced potatoes and salad that he'd demolished a month earlier during a steroid-induced hunger. When the food arrived, Dylan got stuck in, as did Simon and I. We were all hungry and had been looking forward to this all day. I looked over at Deryn, who was staring forlornly at his plate.

'What's up matey?' I asked.

'I can't eat it,' he muttered. 'I've tried a little bit but I feel sick.'

My heart sank. Just let Dylan have this evening, I thought, please don't take this away from him. My despondency wasn't aimed at Deryn, it was aimed at cancer. I had become sick to the back teeth of the disruption and disappointment that this disease was wreaking on both of my boys.

'Would you like to go outside for some fresh air?' I asked him. 'Are you too hot?'

'I don't know, I feel sick and my tummy hurts,' he said quietly. 'I just can't eat it, I'm sorry.'

Simon and I had worked together in highly stressful situations for many years and we had a discreet and effective way of communicating with each other without anyone else being any the wiser. It stood us in good stead at times like this.

Simon distracted Dylan, who was happily tucking in, while I walked Deryn outside for some air and took his temperature. These days, I didn't leave the house without my digital thermometer and every shape and size of dressings. His temperature was fine which meant that mercifully, we didn't have to pack up and scarper to hospital straight away.

'It's okay, big man, we won't force you to eat,' I soothed. 'Let's just enjoy Dylan's evening out and then we can head to the hospital where they can check you over.'

We headed to the NNUH hoping they could administer Deryn's drugs swiftly, but on arrival at 8.30pm, it seemed that absolutely no-one knew why we were there. Usually, it took a lot for me to lose my patience but by this time, I was fuming. Simon went to find a nurse who tried her hardest to find out what was supposed to be happening.

'Addenbrooke's has arranged for a nurse who is qualified to administer the chemotherapy to meet us here at 8:30pm,' I said curtly. I couldn't disguise my anger.

Eventually a senior nurse arrived who was qualified to give Deryn his chemotherapy. But our relief turned to dismay when she informed us at 10pm that the drug wasn't available.

CHAPTER 10

Simon rarely lost his patience or spoke sternly to any of the staff; he was very forgiving and always mindful that to err is human, but even he could no longer hide his annoyance. The pharmacy was shut and the nurse told us she was looking at other avenues to source the drug.

By 11pm, Deryn was starting to feel unwell and wanted to go home to bed. Our choice was to take him home and possibly miss the drug he desperately needed or wait in a playroom at 11pm while they tried to sort it out. Deryn slowly deteriorated and at 11.30pm, Simon snapped.

'That's it, I'm ringing Addenbrooke's myself!'

He returned a few minutes later.

'They haven't even called Addenbrooke's!' Simon fumed. 'Ward C2 has no idea what's going on, either. They thought Deryn had been given the drug!'

I was speechless. I felt cheated, lied to and utterly let down. The senior nurse reappeared.

'I'm really sorry but there's been a mistake with the drug collection,' she said, stating the obvious. 'There is no way we can get it tonight. I can only apologise, Deryn will have to come back tomorrow.'

The following day, Deryn felt pretty dreadful but his temperature was normal so we opted to wait until he had to go back for the drug before asking a doctor to check him over. The doctor decided that Deryn's bowels might be reacting to the plethora of toxic drugs he had been given. The regimen had ramped up and the breaks between treatments were shorter so it was understandable that Deryn would experience other side effects in addition to sickness and hair loss.

Fortunately, the male nurse we'd seen a few weeks earlier gave him his medication and showed us a less painful way to remove the gripper, explaining that if Deryn could pull it out while some saline was being pushed through the line, it would come out more easily as there was no suction. This was a game changer for Deryn, a world away from his earlier experience.

That evening, Deryn went to bed quite early but woke abruptly around 5am shouting: 'MUUUUUUM!'

In a blind panic, Simon and I leapt out of bed and rushed to the bathroom to find Deryn in the midst of a severe nose bleed. We had been warned this could happen as chemotherapy has a detrimental effect on the blood cells and platelets. Thankfully, the bleeding stopped after a few minutes.

Deryn was still complaining about the pain in his tummy. It had travelled down his lower right side and evolved into a sharp, stabbing pain as opposed to the dull ache he had previously complained about. His appendix was my initial concern.

'Let's get you off to hospital,' I told him while Simon rang ahead to let them know.

It was a chilly Friday morning, October 1st 2010. Summer had most definitely disappeared and I couldn't help feeling cheated as I ramped up the heaters in the car. I didn't have much chance to wallow in self-pity before Deryn gave me yet more cause for concern.

He coughed into his tissue and opened it up to show me.

'Ugh, look at this!' he exclaimed. It was a blood clot, about the size of a 10p piece.

The sickness I expected, even the nosebleeds didn't come as a surprise. But a huge blood clot wasn't on the agenda. I was terrified but, as always, I tried to hide it from Deryn.

By the time we arrived at the NNUH, Deryn was doubled over in agony. A doctor examined his abdomen and explained that it was probably an infection of the bowel called typhlitis, and not appendicitis as I had suspected. They display very similar symptoms but typhlitis was more likely as it was a side effect of the chemotherapy.

I asked if Deryn could undergo a scan to make sure the diagnosis was correct and was assured that they would start to treat him straight away. Nil by mouth and pain relief was the appropriate course.

'I'd still like a scan done, just to be sure, if that's okay?' I repeated sheepishly.

I often felt awkward and embarrassed when challenging the doctors' wisdom. I didn't like to rock the boat or cause a fuss. They were the professionals, after all.

'A scan can be done tomorrow,' the doctor answered politely.

I felt empowered. I had asked for something medical and it had been granted with no questions asked. The doctor left and the male nurse came in to access Deryn's port and give him something for the pain.

There was a rule that under no circumstances could he have ibuprofen or any other form of nonsteroidal anti-inflammatory drugs (NSAID). The risk of bleeding was too high and as oncology patients invariably have low platelets, an internal bleed could be catastrophic. So it was IV paracetamol for now until something stronger was needed.

The day flew by in a haze of daytime TV and reruns of *Top Gear* with nurses popping in and out to do observations and top up the pain relief. Deryn's consultant didn't come to see him which I thought was strange given that she was a two-minute walk away but I didn't dwell on it.

Later that evening, Deryn started to vomit and have diarrhoea so I pushed the buzzer and told the nurse what was happening, adding that he had coughed up yet another large blood clot.

It was a Friday night and as there was no doctor on the ward, we were offered the chance of seeing one from A&E as Deryn's symptoms had changed. Two hours later, a doctor duly arrived to say that this was a perfectly normal reaction for typhlitis and nothing to worry about. They would amp up the pain relief and give Deryn some antiemetics to help him deal with the sickness. There was no mention of the blood clots.

Deryn was on a saline drip to ensure that he didn't get dehydrated. He was allowed sips of water but his team was adamant that resting the bowel would allow Deryn to recover. We managed to get some sleep and Deryn was in fairly high spirits, posing for pictures with a little paper cup on his head while asking me if I liked his hat. That was Deryn, always cracking a joke when he could.

We were awoken the next morning by three large men wearing scrubs, who came to examine Deryn. They were surgeons, on hand in case Deryn needed an operation.

'Is Deryn going for a scan this morning?' I enquired.

One of the surgeons explained that he didn't need a scan as he had been diagnosed with typhlitis and the appropriate treatment was already being carried out.

'But I was told he would have a scan today because, otherwise, how does anyone know whether or not this is appendicitis?' I asked, adding: 'I would feel better if he had a scan to confirm either way what this is.'

I felt very awkward. I was pushing it, querying the judgment of a surgeon.

'Okay, we'll get one arranged', he agreed.

I felt a huge sense of relief that by the end of the day, we would know for sure what was happening. At teatime, a cleaner came into the room. It was a welcome diversion to have a chat with another adult after being isolated for most of the day. This gentleman was very easy going and we exchanged the usual pleasantries before he stopped me in my tracks.

'You have to watch them here,' he muttered to me surreptitiously. 'Keep a very close eye on them, okay?'

Before I could register what he had said, he picked up the bin bag and left the room.

Deryn was enthralled by an episode of *Top Gear* while I mulled over the comment for a few minutes, wondering what he could possibly mean by it.

Saturday night approached and still there was no scan arranged. I had been asking the nurses at regular intervals but each time, I was told that it was in hand and I should wait a little longer. Being fobbed off was becoming a familiar pattern.

Meanwhile, Deryn had been having regular blood tests and needed a blood transfusion later that evening. Before long, he was doubled over and in his worst pain so far.

'It's getting worse, Mum, not better,' he mumbled through gritted teeth.

Then he was sick again, bringing up a blood clot the size of a golf ball. I didn't bother pressing the buzzer but headed towards the nurses' station where two young nurses were idly chatting behind the desk. I thrust the bowl under their noses.

'This is not normal,' I shouted, showing them the contents. 'I want to see a doctor immediately!'

I was livid and at breaking point, having sat watching my son writhe in agony. There was no doubt in my mind that I'd been lied to many times by professionals who should know better. I immediately apologised for my outburst as I knew they weren't directly to blame but it felt like no-one was listening to my concerns.

'I want Deryn to be moved to Addenbrooke's please,' I asserted. 'I feel very let down by the NNUH. It's not your fault but please get a doctor here as soon as possible and then we can go.'

Two female doctors turned up from A&E at the same time as a nurse, who came in with a large bag of red blood cells ready for Deryn's infusion.

'Why is it you want to go to Addenbrooke's?' one of the doctors asked me sternly. 'Addenbrooke's is for very sick children, not for children with something as simple as typhlitis. Do you have a problem with the way Deryn is being treated?'

I started to stutter, my confidence sapping away. It took all my courage to reply.

'Well, it's just that we've been promised a scan for days now and he still hasn't had one,' I ventured. 'I feel he would have been scanned at Addenbrooke's by now.'

The nurse had already got the blood ready in the machine and had left the room.

'I can assure you that everything is being done that needs to be done for Deryn and that you do not need to worry, nor will you be transferred to Addenbrooke's,' added her colleague.

It was then that I noticed the blood type written in large letters across the top of the bag of blood. It was A-. Deryn was A+.

'Excuse me but is it okay for Deryn to have A- blood if he's A+?' I asked.

The doctors turned to look at one another.

'I'm not sure, is it okay that way or is it the other way that's okay?' one asked the other.

I was flabbergasted. Deryn's jaw dropped. I could imagine just how frightening it must have been for him. We sat watching the blood slowly move down the line towards Deryn's chest while two doctors tried to decide if in fact it was safe to give Deryn this blood.

'Yes, I think it is okay this way,' the other doctor responded.

I'd heard enough. I walked towards the pump and firmly pressed the off button, disabling the infusion. With that, the machine alarms started to beep.

One of the doctors reprimanded me for touching the machine, informing me that no parent should ever touch it just as the nurse returned to see why the alarms were going off.

'I turned it off because Deryn is blood group A+ and that blood is A- and neither of these doctors could tell me if it was safe for him to be given a different blood type,' I said.

The nurse calmly explained in great detail that it was absolutely fine to give A- to an A+ person, even going so far as to explain exactly why it was safe. She made sure that I was happy and understood before she asked me if it was okay for her to switch the machine back on.

I agreed, thanking her for her honesty and knowledge while the doctors nodded at each other and confirmed what the nurse had said. I was left with the overwhelming impression that the nurse's knowledge of blood groups was far superior to that of these particular doctors.

It begged the question of how on earth could I trust them with serious decisions regarding my son's health? I was close to tears, visibly shaking and absolutely terrified for Deryn's life. Perhaps I was blowing it out of proportion, perhaps he was in good hands here but everything that was happening led me to believe the opposite was true.

'I want him to go to Addenbrooke's,' I repeated.

'I will ring them and enquire but while you have a bed here and we are capable of treating Deryn, they are unlikely to allow a transfer,' said the doctor.

Deryn was given codeine for the pain and some stronger antiemetics and we were assured he would finally get a scan the following day.

As soon as the doctors left, I broke down in tears. I could feel my heart beating hard in my chest and I felt sick and angry with myself that I hadn't made more of a fuss. Why had I again just sat back and allowed myself to be railroaded?

The doctor was probably right, Addenbrooke's wouldn't let us go there just because I didn't like it at the NNUH. They were treating Deryn and he was in a lot less pain now, which was something to be grateful for, but I still couldn't shake the feeling that something terrible was going to happen if I took my eyes off the ball at any time.

Happily, the painkillers and stronger anti-sickness drugs took effect quickly and finally, Deryn and I were able to get some much-needed sleep.

Sunday arrived and I had high hopes that Deryn's long-awaited scan would finally happen. At lunchtime, a doctor came in to see Deryn, telling us he would be taken for a scan later that day. His red blood count was marginally better since the transfusion but his platelets were still incredibly low so he also had a platelet transfusion. He was extremely neutropenic yet still didn't have a high temperature which indicated to me that it couldn't be a bowel infection.

Sunday evening arrived. Still no scan. I spent most of the evening crying while Deryn slept. I felt helpless and anxious that he was not safe.

On Monday morning, Simon and Dylan came to the hospital to see us. We had agreed to give Dylan a weekend away from hospital and Simon had spent it eking out his birthday with a few extra treats.

According to Deryn's blood results, he was very low in potassium so it was decided to give him a supplement. The nurse came into the room holding a small plastic cup containing about 20ml of lurid red liquid. Deryn was told to drink it.

After four days with no food and very little water, it was no surprise that he was unable to keep the foul-tasting mixture down. The nurse reappeared with a banana, unperturbed by the fact that he was instructed to have nil by mouth.

'It's okay, the doctor has said he can have a banana to help with his potassium levels,' she informed me.

Trying to eat the banana, though, caused Deryn excruciating pain. While I knew very little about medicine, it seemed that whatever the medical team was trying was not working. We'd requested a meeting with his consultant and left him crying in the room to go and talk to her. I reiterated to her that I wanted him to have a scan.

'If it will make you feel better then we'll do a scan today but let me tell you that if we thought there would be any change in Deryn's treatment because of the results of a scan, we would have done one by now', she said.

Simon and I made our way back to Deryn's room, just as the nurse was leaving.

'Oh, hello, just to let you know that I've given Deryn a Nurofen suppository to keep his pain down while he's having his scan,' she said.

I couldn't believe my ears. Under no circumstances should this have been given to Deryn and especially not in suppository form. The risk of an internal bleed was very real and potentially fatal.

I asked if she had any idea of the damage she might have caused and she looked puzzled. She had no grasp of the serious implications of her actions, and while it wasn't an oncology ward, even I knew that giving Deryn a NSAID was incredibly dangerous.

The nurse apologised profusely and I was left reeling at the thought that after everything else that had happened, the level of incompetence could get even worse. I had completely lost all faith in the medical team at NNUH.

❖

An ultrasound scan was carried out at 2:30pm and by 3:30pm, Deryn and I were being rushed by ambulance to Addenbrooke's.

The Boy in 7 Billion

The scan showed that Deryn had acute appendicitis and the appendix itself was precariously close to bursting.

Totally exhausted, I felt vindicated – although being right didn't matter to me one jot; all that mattered was that Deryn was finally going to receive the appropriate care.

At last, we were on our way to safety.

Chapter 11

As the doors of C2 opened at Addenbrooke's, I was overcome with emotion at being surrounded by doctors and nurses who not only knew Deryn very well but who had also gained our trust and not once broken it. The relief was overwhelming and I burst into tears.

Dr Mike came to see us and said that Deryn would be going straight down to have another ultrasound, followed by a CT scan. Within a few hours, both scans confirmed that Deryn's appendix was in a bad way.

Just before midnight a surgeon arrived to see us. She was open and honest with me about just how seriously ill Deryn was and led me a little way away from Deryn so that she could explain everything very frankly, leaving me to choose what to tell him.

Deryn's appendix was on the cusp of bursting; it was incredibly swollen and seemed to be stuck to the wall of his stomach. They needed my immediate consent for emergency surgery and the worst-case scenarios were laid out for me.

While they planned to try keyhole surgery, they feared they would have to open him up in order to remove his appendix. If this was the case, there were grave concerns about Deryn's low platelets and the possibility that he could bleed to death on the operating table.

'We'll give him a blood transfusion straight away and also give him another bag in theatre, plus he'll also have a bag of platelets,' the surgeon explained.

However, it was Deryn's low neutrophil count that worried

her the most. He had virtually no immune system left so if the appendix burst while they were trying to get it out, the resulting infection could flood through his system and there would be no way for him to fight it. He might also develop a life-threatening infection from the procedure itself.

'What are his chances of surviving this?' I asked with trepidation. As soon as the words left my lips, I wished I could retract them – I didn't want to hear the answer

'It is hard for us to say,' said the surgeon's colleague. 'Perhaps 15-20%?'

'And if I don't sign the papers, what then?' I asked. I wanted to hear if there was any other way to deal with this without having to cut Deryn open.

'Then he'll die anyway,' added the male surgeon.

As much as it pained me to hear it, I appreciated his honesty. I had no choice. I signed the paperwork. It was the hardest thing I had consented to so far. I was aware that I might be signing Deryn's life away but not consenting was a definite death sentence.

It was just after midnight and the date on the paperwork read October 5th. My 31st birthday.

'We'll do our best, Callie,' said the female surgeon kindly as she put a comforting hand on my shoulder.

She and her colleague left to prepare for theatre and I walked back to Deryn's bed. I had no idea what I was going to say to him. Should I tell him everything? We had been so honest with him up until now but I didn't want to frighten him.

'I don't want to know how bad it is, just tell me what they're going to do,' Deryn demanded, anticipating that there was no good news before I had even walked into the cubicle.

That made my task a lot easier. I was thankful Deryn didn't want to know. I told him that they were taking him down to theatre to remove his appendix.

'Do you think they'll let me keep it?' he quipped.

I couldn't help smiling. His cheeky wit never seemed to desert him even at the bleakest moments.

The strong painkillers were starting to wear off as the porter wheeled him down to theatre, where the female surgeon was waiting with the anaesthetists. Deryn followed his usual routine as he started losing consciousness, his narration made the team giggle, and very soon he was out for the count.

I gave him a kiss on the forehead and stopped to watch through the small window in the door as an anaesthetist gently held Deryn's head in both hands before dropping the bed down so that he was lying flat. He pushed Deryn's jaw forward so that his mouth opened and another anaesthetist slowly pushed a large tube down his throat. A nurse rushed up and ushered me away from the window.

'You don't want to see that, Callie...', she said quietly as she steered me away.

I did though. I wanted to see it all. I wanted to make sure that Deryn was okay and that nothing bad happened to him. It was my job to do that each time he went into theatre. I felt useless and a complete failure as a mum – but this I could do.

I was given a bleeper and headed towards the canteen. I felt sick with fear, winded, as if someone had just punched me in the stomach. I couldn't breathe and feared I was going to pass out but this was not the time or place for a panic attack. I was totally on my own with no Simon to talk me down like he usually did.

'Breathe, Callie, just breathe...' I muttered to myself.

I sat in the empty café on a large leather sofa by the window, unable to eat or drink anything, willing the bleeper to go off. As I sat with my eyes shut, I could see Deryn laid out on a hard metal table. A bright orange whirlpool started swirling around Deryn's feet like an energy tornado, gaining momentum.

I felt strongly that I had to either go with whatever my mind was showing me or fight it. I decided to go with the flow and let go of everything I had been thinking about.

The beautiful orange tornado gradually moved up so that Deryn's feet were inside the whirling light. It carried on moving further up his body until it was around his chest and in an instant, the whirlpool exploded into millions of tiny stars. It was so bright that for a second, all I could see was a bright white light.

Beep beep beep beep.

I was startled out of my vivid daydream and headed off as fast as I could to the theatre. As I approached, I was gripped by terror that I might be greeted by the sad faces of the surgeons. Before I could pluck up the courage to go in, the double doors opened and I heard the beautiful sound of Deryn's infectious laugh.

My nerves were shot to shreds but the relief that he had made it through was palpable. I walked towards him feeling as if my legs were going to buckle beneath me. Deryn was sitting up in bed grinning from ear to ear, with a sandwich in front of him.

'How are you feeling, buddy?' I asked, hugging him hard, not wanting to let him go.

'A bit sore but I'm okay,' he said cheerfully.

He ate his sandwich and the female surgeon arrived to talk through what had happened in the operating room.

'Well, I don't know what to say, Callie,' she began hesitantly. 'We can't quite understand what has gone on with Deryn tonight. We were able to do the keyhole surgery with no issues which was obviously fantastic.'

Fantastic indeed. My mind started racing.

'When we finally got inside Deryn to have a good look at what

CHAPTER 11

we were facing, we were all shocked,' she continued.

Please hurry up, I thought.

'The scans showed us an appendix that was fit to burst, it was nasty and incredibly inflamed. But what we saw when we actually got inside his body was almost the exact opposite. Deryn's appendix was a little angry looking and a small part of it was stuck to his stomach but other than that, it looked relatively healthy. I was able to remove it cleanly via his belly button.'

'How could that be the case?' I asked. I was finding it hard to get my head around what had happened.

'We just don't know why the scans and what we actually found have differed so dramatically,' she went on. 'It seems to be an anomaly.'

She was smiling now and said she would be back the next day to check that his keyhole incisions were healing well. Deryn had also been listening intently.

'So how bad was it, then? What did they say my chances would be?'

He wanted to know how close he'd been to the brink. I relayed the surgeon's odds to him and he sighed.

'I'm glad you didn't tell me. I would have been well worried!'

❖

The ward was silent when we arrived back, the other children and their parents all asleep. The duty doctor warned us that someone would come in every 30 minutes to check on Deryn's three keyholes and make sure he didn't contract an infection.

The next morning, a doctor arrived to examine Deryn's abdomen and was very happy with what he saw. No redness around the wound sites, no temperature and a significant drop in pain. It seemed too good to be true.

He told us Deryn would be back on his feet within four to six weeks and needed to take it easy and rest. He wasn't due to have any chemotherapy for a couple of weeks, which meant that his blood and immune system had some time to recover. The best news was that if Deryn stayed spike-free, we would be able to go home in a couple of days.

For the next two days, he underwent rigorous checks and seemed to be out of the danger zone. The night before we were due to go home, the nurse came in to carry out observations and check his temperature

'38.5°C' she announced, sounding disappointed. 'I'll go and tell the doctor.'

A few minutes later, the doctor arrived.

'You've spiked, Deryn; you know what this means, don't you?' he asked, and even he sounded disappointed. 'Since you've been able to behave yourself so far and you're due to go home tomorrow, if you can avoid spiking again between now and leaving, we'll let you go. How does that sound?'

It was a great deal but how was Deryn supposed to prevent himself from getting a temperature? It felt like he was being given an impossible task.

'Yeah, okay,' Deryn nodded. 'I reckon I can do it.'

'Right, Deryn, you've got half an hour to get rid of the temperature. How are you going to do it?' I enquired.

'What colour is cold?' he asked. 'Blue, blue is a cool colour. I'll just imagine myself surrounded by blue light, I reckon that'll work.'

I couldn't knock his confidence or his willingness to try. It was worth a shot. I wondered if the orange light I had seen could have had something to do with the outcome of his surgery.

For the next 30 minutes, Deryn lay completely still on his bed with his eyes shut. The whole time, he told me later on, he imagined himself being surrounded by a bright blue whirlpool of light, like a tornado, he explained.

CHAPTER 11

I hadn't yet told him about the orange tornado I'd imagined so when I heard this, I was astonished. Half an hour was nearly up as the same young nurse came back in, looking apprehensive. I don't think she wanted to be the bearer of bad news and she seemed reluctant to take his temperature.

'36.5°C,' she announced with a huge grin. He was back to normal!

Deryn sat there, beaming. Whatever he'd done had worked. It could have been a coincidence – and he had to keep this up until the following morning in order to go home – but it was a great start. The nurses came in at regular intervals through the night and Deryn's temperature remained normal. The next morning, we were allowed to go home.

Six days after Deryn had his appendix out, he went back to school.

Chapter 12

Deryn's first three months of chemotherapy were intense. There wasn't much downtime between IV infusions and lumbar punctures. The idea was to hit hard with as much chemotherapy as Deryn could stand in order to get him into remission.

Once remission had been confirmed, Deryn would be able to start the next stage of chemo. Although it wasn't as intense as the previous three months, the treatment would involve Deryn spending a number of days each week at the hospital as an outpatient.

The intensity would lessen once more in May 2011 as he embarked on a 30-month maintenance programme, our hopes pinned on an immunosuppressive drug called mercaptopurine, or 6-MP, as it was commonly known.

These periods of less invasive treatment we looked forward to, as they meant more freedom to live our lives. Deryn was due to finish treatment on September 23rd 2013, which seemed like a lifetime away, but after seeing how quickly the months since diagnosis had flown by, we were hopeful that the next three years would pass quickly.

Not long after the appendix ordeal, Deryn underwent a procedure called a Minimal Residual Disease (MRD) test, to see if small numbers of leukaemic cells remained in his bone marrow.

Another bone marrow aspirate tested a sample for any signs of disease. Although Deryn had been high risk, he was well into remission and by the time the initial three months were over, he no longer had leukaemia. Against all odds, somehow the chemotherapy had worked and there were no longer any signs of the disease in his blood or bone marrow.

The feeling of complete elation when I heard this wonderful news is impossible to describe, however, it was mentioned almost in passing during one of the check ups at the NNUH. I had to ask the doctor to repeat herself as I wasn't sure I had heard her correctly.

No fanfare, trumpets or confetti? I'm not sure what I expected but I'd thought being told that Deryn no longer had cancer would come with a little more pomp and ceremony. It was fantastic news, nonetheless, and we were overjoyed!

This fraught period taught us to have a sense of perspective. Things that seem so important pale into insignificance, particularly when you meet wonderful people whose children are not lucky enough to survive.

Kenton was one such boy. His aunt Yvonne was an amazing, selfless woman who had cared for Kenton since he was very young. When he was diagnosed with cancer, she was the one who held it together for him and their family. Yvonne had incredible strength. I'd look at her and think there was no way I could ever be as strong as she was.

Kenton's death at just 14 brought it home to every parent on the ward that none of our children was invincible.

To celebrate Deryn's all-clear, we had a small low-key celebration with friends and family. The lumbar punctures dropped from twice to once a month and the longer infusions became rarer. The new regime wasn't nearly as restrictive. Finally, we felt, we could start making some plans.

We had been told about a place in Scotland called Malcolm

CHAPTER 12

Sargent House, run by the wonderful charity CLIC Sargent. A sprawling residential centre on the Ayrshire coastline, it was specifically for children who had been diagnosed with cancer and their families. We got in touch and booked to stay for a week in November. The prospect of a trip together gave us something to look forward to, instead of just looking ahead to the next hospital appointment or procedure. With a few weeks to go before our departure, all we could hope was that Deryn didn't have a temperature spike. The boys were so excited about going away, especially the prospect of an eight-hour train journey to Scotland.

With one week to go, our bags were almost packed and everything was going to plan until one evening Deryn told us that he felt cold. We knew from experience that he probably had a temperature.

The thermometer registered 38.5°C.

'Deryn, you are to be sentenced to a minimum lockdown of three days,' I joked.

Deryn rarely went to hospital with a temperature spike higher than 38.5°C, which teetered on the edge of normal but was close enough to 39°C to cause worry. It was as if the thermometer was mocking us. We knew full well that by the time Deryn got to the hospital, his temperature would have more than likely reverted to normal.

It was too important to ignore, much as I wanted to on several occasions at 3am or when we were on our way to visit friends. We simply couldn't risk it.

The whole house went into overdrive as I delegated tasks. Simon rang the hospital while I got Deryn's bag ready. Dylan occupied himself as he often had to do in these situations and kept out of the way while Deryn gathered together all of his drugs – they didn't have specialist drugs on the ward at the

NNUH so we always took in our own supply.

This would be his first stay at the NNUH since we had complained about Deryn's rough treatment at the hands of June and the lack of diagnosis when he had appendicitis. We had to ask ourselves whether it was worth pursuing a formal complaint and decided to choose our battles carefully. We also wanted to give the hospital a chance to redeem itself.

I was anxious and a little worried that we would be treated differently because of our complaint. I needn't have worried as the treatment we received was just as terrible as it had been previously.

It was a Sunday, which invariably meant fewer staff on duty, resulting in even less chance of finding someone to access Deryn's port. Deryn was shown to the small treatment room to wait until a bed became available on the ward.

I felt stronger and more capable now that I was starting to understand a lot more about his treatment and was determined to speak up when it mattered. I didn't want to keep letting Deryn down.

Two hours passed and Deryn had some observation checks.

'When will someone come to access Deryn's port to take some blood?' I asked the young nurse.

I was assured that someone would be along soon and that a doctor would follow on shortly afterwards as the IV antibiotics were on their way from the pharmacy. Maybe my complaint had made a difference after all.

Time passed and still no-one came. Deryn had made himself comfortable with a DVD player and some snacks, not at all bothered that no-one had arrived yet to poke him in the chest. I popped my head out of the door to attract the attention of a passing nurse.

'Excuse me, where is the nurse who's going to access Deryn's port?' I asked. I was assured that someone was on their way.

I knew I was being fobbed off and, bearing in mind the kind cleaner's comments a few weeks earlier, I was determined to keep my eye on the ball. I left the door slightly ajar so I could hear everything the nurses were saying to each other.

To my dismay, I heard one telling another that there were only two nurses in the whole hospital who could access a port and neither was on duty that day. I could hear them frantically calling around the hospital in the hope that someone somewhere could come and access Deryn's port.

It was a complete farce. The two-hour window had long since passed and I started to get very emotional at the thought that even if the IV antibiotics arrived, there was no-one qualified to access his port. I walked up to the nurses' station.

'No-one's coming to access Deryn's port, then?' I demanded.

One of them didn't miss a beat.

'Yes, someone is on their way,' she said again.

Life would have been more simple if the staff just told me the truth. I'd heard everything they'd been saying but still, lying was their first reaction. Inside, I was raging but I struggled to keep my composure for fear of Deryn not being treated at all – I'd seen enough posters around the hospital warning that staff wouldn't accept any abuse and in the face of such blatant untruths, I was close to saying something I might later regret.

But I couldn't keep the truth from Deryn.

'What's going on, Mum?' he asked, looking up from his film as I returned to the room.

'Lies, Deryn, more lies, that's what,' I sighed.

Five minutes later, a registrar arrived with a phlebotomist who also happened to be from Transylvania, just like the one at Addenbrooke's. Deryn couldn't believe his luck at getting two blood specialists from Dracula country and vampire jokes ensued.

The registrar asked Deryn to take off his T shirt so that he could access his line and seemed shocked to find that there was no line hanging out of Deryn's chest. He asked me where the line was and I explained that it was a port-a-cath and that he would need to access it using a gripper.

He seemed to have no idea what I was talking about, which was confirmed when he pressed so hard on Deryn's port that it made Deryn's skin go white. He was pinching it and prodding it as Deryn recoiled in pain but this didn't stop him.

With a final jab at Deryn's chest, the registrar said: 'So the port is under there and I access it with a cannula, yes?'

'No, not a cannula,' I explained. 'A gripper, it's a specialist needle for accessing ports.'

'Okay,' added the registrar. 'I'll have a go at accessing the port.'

As they left the room, Deryn looked bewildered.

'He'll "have a go", will he?' I said to Deryn who was still half naked on the treatment bed.

'Please don't let him touch me, Mum,' Deryn pleaded fearfully.

I promised I wouldn't but I was dreading having to step in and stop him. I didn't enjoy telling people in positions of authority that they were doing something wrong.

The registrar came back in, pushing a small silver trolley. On the top of the trolley was a tray and on that tray lay one antiseptic wipe, some syringes and a normal cannula.

'You can't access a port with a cannula!' I said abruptly.

The registrar ignored me, stepping towards Deryn as he tore the top of the small green packet that contained the wipe.

Just then, the phlebotomist pushed the door open.

'You don't know how to access that port any more than I do, so you are not going to access this boy's port today', she said to him firmly.

I gave a huge sigh of relief, as did Deryn. Saved at the last minute by the vampire.

The registrar looked irritated as he threw the wipe on the tray, and without saying a word, he pushed the trolley out of the door.

I told her that I was very grateful and asked if there was any way they could get Deryn cannulated short-term until someone who could access the port arrived. She agreed and finally, the IV antibiotics were administered.

A nurse duly arrived in the morning, when both ports were accessed successfully and cultures sent away. Thankfully nothing was amiss and it was just another spike with no obvious cause.

A few days later, we were all together on a train heading north. This holiday couldn't come soon enough and although it was November, not even the cold, windy climate of south-west Scotland could dampen our spirits.

The early-morning train from Norwich to London was packed but it didn't bother us as we'd booked seats for the entire journey, with a table, much to the boys' delight. As a teenager I'd always loved getting a table seat. I would travel to London on my own and spend the day walking around Camden Market before heading back and pretending I'd been at school all day.

I wasn't the easiest teenager and had given my parents plenty to worry about. They didn't have the same level of worry I experienced with Deryn, which was out of his control, and it was only as my boys grew up that I could appreciate just how waywardly I had behaved as a child.

I didn't want my children to have the same distant relationship I'd had with my parents. It was my mission to be the sort of parent they could come to with any problems, no matter how big or small.

Deryn's illness highlighted the importance of communication and the close bond that we developed was a direct result of the situation we found ourselves in. I couldn't help but see this time as a way of making up for my shortcomings as a young mother and gladly seized the chance to reconnect with my eldest child.

Days and nights spent in very close quarters ensured that there was very little we didn't know about each other. To be given the chance to really know my child inside out was a blessing and although I'm convinced there were many times Deryn didn't want me so close, by and large, he accepted me in his space around the clock.

'Here's our table! I bagsy the seat next to the window,' Deryn announced to the whole carriage.

By the time we arrived at Prestwick, it was pitch-black but our excitement was hard to contain. Luggage in tow, we made the short walk from the station to our holiday accommodation.

A large, white building with only a car park and a play area separating it from the sea, Malcolm Sargent House was a haven for cancer patients and their families. The members of staff were incredibly friendly and welcoming and we were shown to our room, which had an adjoining bedroom for the boys and a phenomenal view across to the Isle of Arran.

'Bagsy this one!' Deryn shouted as he collapsed onto the bed nearest the window.

Poor Dylan wasn't quick enough off the mark and often got the raw end of the deal but he never complained. The boys had always been very close and although they would argue from time to time, they were good friends. Dylan leapt onto Deryn's bed and started to wrestle with him. They were putting each other into headlocks and screeching with laughter. I was happy to listen to the boys' play fighting all day long.

The next week was fun-packed and exhausting. The weather

CHAPTER 12

was beautiful so the boys went out every day on go-karts or bikes. Not a day went by when they weren't out doing something. It was fantastic to see Deryn living life as a normal 10-year-old boy again.

Along the seafront ran a lengthy path that went all the way to Ayr and each morning, I went for a run along the coast path as the sun was coming up. I was in heaven. Malcolm Sargent House was working its magic.

Each day, we rode bikes along the same path, cycling a little further away from our base. One day we decided to try and cycle all the way to Ayr. Deryn went ahead on his mountain bike, while Dylan and I hung back a little. Simon was ultra competitive, as was Deryn, so he put his foot down and soon caught up with Deryn.

Deryn was eye to eye with Simon when all of a sudden, the chain came off Simon's bike and he flew straight over the handlebars, landing with a sickening thud on the path. Deryn howled with laughter while Simon lay spread-eagled on his front with his bike in a crumpled heap next to him. Dylan and I were a short way behind but we saw it all and before we could even ask if he was okay, we started laughing too.

By the time we reached them, Simon had picked up his bike and thrown it down on the path in anger. Deryn was crying with laughter and Simon was unimpressed at the fact that none of us could stop laughing for long enough to ask him if he was all right.

'Are you OK?' I eventually asked, still trying hard not to laugh. He was fine apart from a bruised ego. Nevertheless, we put off going to Ayr and Deryn's brilliant re-enactment of the crash that evening had even Simon laughing despite his hurt pride.

We decided to visit Arran on the ferry the next day. The crossing was very windy and the boys thought it was hilarious to stand out on deck trying to hold themselves upright in the wind. Hanging on to the railings as the wind blasted them, the skin on their faces resembled something from a G force experiment and they couldn't stop giggling.

Deryn had been wearing his favourite hat but a sudden forceful gust whipped it off his head and flung it into the air.

'My hat!' Deryn shouted, laughing uncontrollably. He tried to catch it but it blew under the railings and into the sea below.

'Well, some shark is going to have a new hat today,' Deryn laughed.

I fell in love with Arran as soon as we set foot on the island. There was a chocolate shop where you could watch chocolates being hand made, a small cheese producer and a wool shop full of proper Arran jumpers.

We made the most of our visit, walking up to Brodick Castle and back through the grounds. It was stunning, the autumnal orange glow radiated throughout the arboretum and we stumbled on numerous small streams with beautiful waterfalls.

I was impressed that Deryn was able to walk so far that day. He had been inactive for four months and I'd noticed the detrimental effect being incapacitated had had on his body in that short time scale. His muscles were depleted and his weight had fluctuated so much that he was covered in stretch marks.

By the end of our day trip, we had managed to walk to the bottom of Goat Fell, Arran's highest peak, before heading back to the port to catch the ferry.

It soon became apparent that we had totally underestimated how long it would take us to get back to the port. As we walked across the beach back towards Brodick, we saw a ferry in the distance.

'Is that our ferry, Dad?' Deryn asked.

Simon checked the timetable and discovered that it was indeed ours – and by the looks of things, it was going to get to the port a lot quicker than we were.

Hopping through gardens and over fences, we hurried across the beach, giggling as we went. Simon grabbed Deryn and threw him over his shoulder, I tried to do the same with Dylan and we made a run for the ferry but we were still leaping through people's gardens as we watched it turn around and leave Arran.

It gave us all a good chuckle. Laughing together at this mini catastrophe was therapeutic. We eventually arrived back at the house – heavily laden with chocolates and fridge magnets – later that evening, tired and ready for bed.

The week went far too quickly but we were thrilled to learn that we could visit twice a year for up to four years after Deryn finished treatment. It was a tonic and we all agreed we would arrange another trip there the following summer.

Back home in Norfolk, normal life resumed and the boys were soon back at school. Deryn's Disability Living Allowance had finally been processed, which was a lifesaver. It meant that the pressure was off Simon finding a job, something which was proving inexplicably difficult.

Since signing on for the Jobseeker Allowance, he'd had a few interviews but as soon as he revealed his son was going through cancer treatment and that he might need time off to look after his youngest child, the job in question would disappear into the ether. Understandably, prospective employers were brutally honest with Simon and told him they couldn't risk taking him on knowing that he might be needed elsewhere for the foreseeable future.

Christmas was a few weeks away and although we couldn't lavish expensive gifts on the kids (nor did we want to), one thing we were determined to do was to make it the best Christmas ever, with all of our friends and family together for lots of food and memory-making moments.

Deryn turned 11 on the 1st December 2010. It was a highly emotional day given that, on several occasions, we had been told that he possibly wouldn't live to see 11. Deryn had proved them all wrong. We took him to celebrate at his favourite Mexican restaurant, where he was adamant that this time, he was going to finish the entire meal.

'Damn you, enchiladas!' Deryn muttered as he glared at the few leftovers on his plate. 'I'll get you next time.'

Chapter 13

It was 5am on December 23rd and everything was prepared for Christmas. The food was bought, most of the presents were wrapped and ready to go under the tree and we were good to go.

Or so I thought.

Deryn woke up screaming the house down. Simon ran into his room and saw Deryn writhing in bed, clutching his stomach and screaming that he was in agony.

'It feels like someone's stabbing me!' he cried.

It couldn't be his appendix but could it be typhlitis? Autopilot kicked in once again and Simon offered to take Deryn to hospital so that I could finish the final preparations for Christmas. We hoped and prayed that whatever it was could be dealt with quickly.

Simon whisked Deryn off to NNUH and it wasn't long before they were dispatched to Addenbrooke's, which pleased and worried me in equal measures as it became clear that something serious was going on.

I knew Deryn would be in the best hands but it was frustrating that this was happening so close to Christmas. I carried on with my last-minute jobs regardless, trying to stay positive. However, by teatime, our eagerly anticipated family Christmas had been cancelled.

Deryn had pancreatitis brought on by a combination of the chemotherapy drug PEG asparaginase (or PEG asparagus, as Deryn called it) and the steroid dexamethasone. The chances of getting pancreatitis from this combination was one in 500.

Typically, Deryn was that one in 500.

The pain was unbearable and Deryn's medical team rapidly placed him on some high-dose painkillers but nothing helped to ease the discomfort so, for the first time, he was put on a morphine drip.

The pinprick pupils and incoherent speech I had first witnessed a few months previously would become all too familiar. I absolutely hated seeing Deryn so drugged up.

The drip had a button which was placed within Deryn's reach so he could administer the opiate whenever he needed it. This was a novelty which would rapidly wear off once he realised that only a certain amount came out, no matter how many times he pushed the button. The copious amounts of morphine coursing through his body ensured that he could no longer stay awake.

There was no treatment strategy for pancreatitis, apart from nil by mouth and pain relief. Because of the morphine, he also largely slept through the treatment. It was a case of waiting it out until things improved.

On Christmas Eve, Simon seized the opportunity while Deryn was comatose to come and collect Dylan and I so that we could all spend the festive period together as a family, even if it was in hospital. The ward was eerily quiet as everyone who could get home for Christmas had been discharged.

Despite this, the staff put in a huge amount of effort to make the ward look as festive as possible. There was an enormous, beautifully decorated tree and Christmas music was playing behind the nurses' station. A large table was overloaded with Christmas cakes, chocolates and biscuits and, with barely a soul there to tuck in, Simon, Dylan and I made sure it didn't go to waste.

The nurses were in fancy dress, some sporting elf costumes while others were dressed up as Christmas trees and puddings. Life on a children's ward at Christmas was an education and I was impressed at the lengths to which the staff went to make it special for the unfortunate souls who had to remain in hospital at this special time of year.

Many of the staff had children themselves and would rather have been at home but those amazing individuals never let on. They were in high spirits, utterly determined to make it memorable for every one of the children in their care.

Simon and Dylan went home late on Christmas Eve and were due to return on Christmas morning. It was the first time in nine years that we hadn't woken up together on Christmas morning. I always wanted to try and make the holidays perfect but there was no way of doing that this year.

I woke up to find a large sack full of presents on the end of Deryn's bed. I had no idea where they'd come from until I looked at the label on the sack. It was an incredibly thoughtful gesture from a local charity.

I couldn't believe what was inside: there were board games, puzzles, card games and craft kits. I was overwhelmed by the generosity of people who didn't even know us and as I sat looking at Deryn, who had been fast asleep since Christmas Eve morning, I cried. I could easily have wallowed in self-pity for hours, if not days, but then I remembered Kenton and Yvonne.

No matter how frustrating it might feel to be in hospital over Christmas, at least Deryn was still here. I knew someone who would have an empty chair at their table that day and I couldn't imagine how hard that was going to be for Yvonne's family.

While waiting for Simon and Dylan to arrive, I checked my Facebook feed, which was full of pictures of my friends' children as they opened their gifts. It was so lovely to feel connected to people. Far from making me feel down, it brought me a lot of comfort and cheered me up.

I posted my own status, wishing my friends and family a merry

Christmas and posting a picture of Deryn still unconscious, wearing a paper hat from a Christmas cracker that had been put in the sack of gifts.

The messages that came back were naturally sympathetic and sad in tone.

'I'm so sorry that you're in hospital over Christmas, life isn't fair,' commented one friend.

'Oh my God, you've had your whole Christmas ruined. I'm so sorry,' said another.

I wrote back insisting that I was one of the lucky ones. My son was still here, the surroundings didn't matter, nor did the fact that he was asleep, all that mattered was that he was still alive and that meant we were the fortunate ones.

Simon and Dylan arrived later that morning with a couple of presents from under the tree, one each for Dylan and Deryn. When I asked Dylan if he'd opened his other presents, he told me that he hadn't.

'Oh, why not, darling?' I asked him.

We hadn't told him to wait and I'd thought he would have ripped through them like a child possessed.

'I want to wait for Deryn to come home so that we can all have Christmas together,' replied my sensitive and considerate son. 'So I'm not opening anything else until he is home.'

Having felt immense pride at the way Deryn handled life's plan, I had a deep sense of respect for Dylan too. He was also a very kind soul and I was reminded once again just how lucky I was.

Christmas lunch was served on the ward and as a special Christmas treat parents and siblings were allowed to eat, too. We tucked into a delicious roast turkey lunch with lashings of gravy, pigs in blankets and stuffing galore. Deryn was nil by mouth so he couldn't have anything and I was relieved that he slept through lunch so that he was at least spared the torture of seeing everyone else eating.

After the festivities came to an end, Simon took Dylan home and promised to return early the next morning. I made the most of the peace and quiet, watching Christmas films and YouTube videos, researching on the internet and chatting to friends on Facebook.

I was awoken the following morning by Deryn nudging me in a panic. He'd slept right through to Boxing Day morning and as he came round groggily, he didn't have a clue what was going on.

'Mum, Mum,' he whispered. 'I don't like the drugs, I don't want them anymore.'

'What's the matter, Deryn?' I asked. 'Why don't you want the morphine anymore?'

'You're not going to believe me,' he continued haltingly, still whispering. 'I think they've done something funny to me… I saw a giant Christmas pudding by my bed in the middle of the night!'

I couldn't help letting out a giggle. With that, Deryn's nurse came back into the cubicle to do routine observations, still in festive fancy dress.

'Oh… I see!' Deryn added as he too started to laugh. 'Is it Christmas Day yet?'

I had to break it to him that he'd managed to sleep right through Christmas. To make the news more bearable, I passed him his large sack of presents.

Boxing Day passed in a blur with the boys playing board games, watching TV and listening to music while we went to the parents' room for some time on our own. Although Simon had always worked nine to five, we had also worked together over the weekend as bouncers and were used to spending a lot more time together. We were mindful that our relationship was just as important as Deryn's cancer treatment.

Nine more days would pass before Deryn was well enough to go home. His daily diet consisted of ice lollies and sips of water for several days after Boxing Day. In typical Deryn style, he took all this in his stride although he was miffed at missing out on pigs in blankets.

New Year's Eve arrived and we had reluctantly decided that Dylan and I wouldn't visit Simon and Deryn at the hospital for a few days as the fuel costs for daily 100-mile round trips were horrendous. My best friend Penny asked me what I was doing for New Year's Eve and when I told her that we wouldn't be at the hospital, she insisted that I use her car.

'Don't worry about the fuel, just go and surprise those boys of yours,' Penny insisted.

I couldn't say no.

That evening, I spoke to Simon and Deryn on Skype. They had no idea that we would be driving over later that evening to see in the new year with them both. I'd made some mince pies and bought a bottle of alcohol-free bubbly.

The ward was as quiet as you'd expect it to be at 11:30pm on New Year's Eve. We crept down the long corridor and approached Deryn's cubicle. The long, blue paper curtains had been drawn all the way around and there wasn't a peep coming from the other side.

I hoped that Simon wasn't asleep already and pulled back the curtain to see Simon sitting in a chair reading. Deryn was dead to the world. Simon's surprised face was a picture.

'What are you doing here, darling?' he said with a grin. 'How did you get here? Actually, just come over here and give me a hug!'

We left Deryn asleep in bed and made our way to the parents' room to watch the Big Ben countdown on TV. As it struck midnight, we had a group hug and a kiss followed by a mince pie and some bubbly before saying our goodbyes.

I was filled with hope that this year, things would turn a corner for Deryn. Being nil by mouth and on a fluid-only diet, his weight had crashed dramatically and in the space of two weeks, he'd lost more than 12 kilos in weight. He looked skeletal, his bones were poking through his skin and his face was gaunt. It was awful to see him in such a skinny and fragile state.

Out of everything that Deryn had already endured, the dramatic weight loss was by far the hardest thing for me to witness. I remembered vividly just how strong and fit Deryn had been before his cancer diagnosis and to see him look so frail reduced me to tears. It was truly heartbreaking and I knew that it would take a long time to get him back to how he used to be.

The hospital decided that a nasogastric (NG) tube and a feeding pump were the answer. Deryn was not pleased at the prospect of an NG tube. He'd seen other children on the ward with them and they looked uncomfortable. I didn't relish the idea either but there was no alternative.

A specialist nurse came to see him and showed us how to use the feeding pump, which was going to be supplied with six weeks' worth of 'food'. I thought I'd seen Deryn in enough discomfort to last a lifetime. I didn't think it could get much worse than watching your child recoil in pain while being cannulated or writhe around in agony with stomach cramps. I was wrong.

Watching an NG tube being inserted for the first time was one of the most horrifying things I have ever seen. As one of the nurses started explaining what would happen, Deryn looked terrified but he knew there was no other way to start gaining weight and getting better.

The nurse opened the packet and gave Deryn a drink of water and a straw. The idea was that the drink would help Deryn swallow the tube as the nurse pushed it down into his stomach via his nostril.

'Are you ready Deryn?' she asked gently.

'No. Okay, YES, do it now!'

The nurse started to feed the tube into Deryn's nose and down the back of his throat while another nurse held the cup of water and encouraged Deryn to drink through the straw. He was trying so hard but he couldn't stop gagging, his eyes were streaming and his face was turning scarlet.

I wanted to look away but I carried on holding his hand and waited for it to be over. Deryn finished the cup of water but the tube still wasn't quite in place. He retched again and again until the nurse was happy that the tube was where it should be. Inside the tube was a metal wire to stop it being too pliable, which made it easier to insert. The nurse pulled out the wire from inside the tube and Deryn retched again.

The NG tube was stuck to Deryn's cheek to prevent it from coming out. The line had to be far enough inside his stomach to work but they also needed to ensure that it hadn't gone into his lungs. The nurse took a syringe and undid the small cap on the end of the line, pushing it into the end of the line.

She pulled on the plunger and a few seconds later, the syringe was half-full of the contents of Deryn's stomach. The nurse squirted a tiny amount on a litmus paper to make sure it was acidic, which it was. The procedure had gone to plan.

Deryn wasn't fazed by the syringe of his stomach contents – he just thought it was pretty cool to be able to see what he'd just drank.

'What do you reckon it would look like if I drank some Ribena?' he mused.

'We'll try it when you get home if you like,' Simon replied with a grin.

We would need to aspirate his stomach via this tube each time we wanted to use it for feeding, for it was imperative that the tube was correctly positioned or it could result in the liquid feed going into his lungs during the night. We would also have to raise him up on a huge stack of pillows.

Armed with the pump and instructions, we were discharged on January 4th 2011 and celebrated Christmas Day belatedly on January 5th, surrounded by our dearest friends and family who came to share the day with us.

In a state of high excitement, Deryn eagerly piled his plate up with food but he could only eat one thing… a pig in a blanket!

Chapter 14

DERYN ADAPTED TO THE NG TUBE REALLY WELL, EVEN GOING SO far as to aspirate his stomach himself. Dylan wanted to learn how to use the machinery, too, and after being shown a couple of times, we put Dylan, with some supervision, in charge of the nightly feeds.

Sometimes, in the middle of the night, Deryn would lose the NG tube. I'd find him hunched over the sink with the nose tube stuck to his face and the rest of it no longer in his stomach but hanging out of his mouth.

'Cool, huh?' Deryn quipped as best he could with a tube in his mouth.

The first time it happened, we were due at hospital for chemotherapy the next day and Deryn knew he would have to have another put in as soon as he got there. We were all relieved that it was helping him progress with some weight gain. Once it had done its job – five or six tubes down the line – I was glad to see the back of it while Deryn was more ambivalent.

'I don't mind the tube so much,' he told his nurse. 'But it's the food, it tastes rank.'

I wasn't sure how he knew this as every bit of nourishment went straight into his stomach, bypassing his taste buds.

'I can taste it when I burp,' he explained with a grin.

As he was constantly neutropenic, neither of the boys went back to school until the end of April. By the time Deryn's immune system recovered, it was time for his next maintenance programme to start. As he no longer needed a line in his chest,

Deryn was able to have his port removed in a simple procedure. The surgeon who removed it had also removed Deryn's appendix and announced that she had 'tidied up the port scar' afterwards.

'What? You've made it all neat and tidy?' Deryn mock-grumbled. 'I was hoping to have a massive scar, not a neat one!' he continued, trying his hardest to look annoyed.

❖

Meanwhile, the SATs were approaching and Deryn wanted to achieve the best marks possible despite his prolonged absences. The teachers at school were incredibly supportive, sending work home for him and keeping in touch with us on a regular basis. They were very understanding about Deryn's absence, as was Dylan's school.

He was a tough kid and believed his autism had helped him get through the tougher times. He spoke of feeling disconnected from what was going on around him, which made it easier to simply switch off from what was happening to him. This gave me a great feeling of relief, to know that Deryn wasn't suffering as much as I'd imagined.

Two weeks before the SATs, Deryn's teacher brought round some workbooks for him to revise from. She didn't expect him to get both books completed as there was six months' work inside them and simply hoped he would do a little to give him a better chance in his exams.

Deryn spent hours revising each day and finished both books by the time exam day arrived. I'd never seen him work so hard. Unfortunately, he was still neutropenic and therefore unable to sit his exams in a hall with 100 other children.

After some deliberation with the teachers, we agreed that Deryn would sit his tests in one of the school offices by himself, accompanied by a designated teacher. It was a good compromise.

CHAPTER 14

'I get to sit on my own?' he asked.

'Not quite, Deryn, someone will be with you, so don't get any ideas about cheating,' Simon joked.

'I don't need to, I'm going to get full marks with all my revision!' he retorted confidently.

I drove him to school and we went in via the back entrance. He loved his VIP status and special treatment as he made his way to the office and took his place at a small table inside.

'Good luck, Deryn,' I called out as I left the building.

A few weeks later, we were back at Malcolm Sargent House in Ayr enjoying a second wonderful break when we got a call from his teacher.

'Hello Mrs Blackwell, I have Deryn's SAT results here. Just to let you know that we've also worked out his attendance for the year, which was 36%.'

This obviously wasn't great, and only made the next piece of news even more difficult to believe.

'However, Deryn did very well in his exams,' the teacher continued cheerfully. 'In fact, he was just one question away from scoring 100%!'

I couldn't believe it! His confidence wasn't misplaced at all, it had been spot on.

'How did I do then, Mum?' Deryn asked me as soon as I put down the phone.

'Ah, you did alright dude. You didn't get 100% though...' I teased him. 'But you were only one question away from it!'

This called for a celebration. We had discovered an authentic 1950s Italian ice cream parlour nearby so that afternoon, we took the boys along and Deryn chose the biggest sundae he could find to celebrate his stupendous achievement.

❖

A poster on the noticeboard at Addenbrooke's had aroused

interest from Deryn. The Ellen MacArthur Cancer Trust was looking for children to go sailing on the Isle of Wight.

This wonderful charity, set up by round-the-world record-setting sailor Dame Ellen after she'd spent some time with young oncology patients, was working towards rebuilding the confidence and joie de vivre of kids like Deryn.

'Mum, can I go?' he begged us now.

Having read through the details, I was amazed and surprised that Deryn was so keen to take part. He had become very reclusive during the previous 12 months of treatment, isolated from his friends due to lengthy stays in hospital and his confidence had taken a battering. Now he was volunteering to go away with a group of kids he'd never met.

The children would spend five days at sea on a racing yacht, learning how to sail, cook and look after themselves. More importantly, they would also be spending time with others who were, pardon the pun, in the same boat.

It felt like a little breakthrough, a way back into normal life for Deryn.

'Yeah, I can't see why not,' I enthused.

We filled out the application form and sent it off. I was concerned that his initial excitement might subside and we'd be left red-faced, explaining why Deryn couldn't go on the trip. So when a place was offered to him, I was thrilled when he jumped at the chance to take it.

A few weeks later, I drove Deryn to Cambridge where we met up with the rest of the group and their parents to await the arrival of the minibus. Deryn recognised one young lad from C2. Dawson had been an inpatient for six months during 2010 and the boys had played pool together one evening.

Dawson had been given the all-clear and looked incredible. Looking around at the faces of these excited youngsters, no-one would have guessed how much they had been through.

Deryn and Dawson sat next to each other, chatting and laughing away together in no time. It was lovely to see Deryn goofing around and acting like a regular kid. This group might all have had the same thing in common but their banter and conversations were just like any other kids might have in the playground.

Like me, Dawson's mum Cheryl was terrified about letting her son head off without her by his side. We both noticed how well they were getting on and how happy they seemed, although it wasn't enough to stop us and the rest of the parents shedding a few tears as the minibus departed.

Driving myself home, my first thought was: 'How am I going to cope for the next five days without Deryn?'

In some ways, I was going to worry even more, handing over his medical care to someone I hadn't even met after a year of being in charge of a major part of it myself. I had been administering the cytotoxic drugs intravenously for a few months before his port had come out and my level of medical involvement had surpassed handing out pills.

Arriving home, the house seemed eerily quiet. Deryn had a big presence which filled every room. Without it, I felt my mind wandering to a place that I never dared let it go.

'This is what it would be like if Deryn died,' I thought to myself as I made a cup of tea. I hated thinking like this but I was powerless to control it. My mind liked to torment me and shine a light on my weak spot.

'Stop it!' I muttered under my breath.

'Pull yourself together, woman.'

Deryn wasn't dead and I should be grateful for that, not moping and feeling sad because he was away enjoying himself.

❖

The week whizzed by and we barely had time to spoil Dylan

before it was time for us to collect his big brother from Cambridge. I couldn't wait to hear how he got on and how much he'd enjoyed himself sailing.

As soon as Deryn got off the minibus and said goodbye to his new friends, he raced over and enveloped me in a huge hug. He was on a high, which was fantastic to see, and didn't stop talking about the trip all the way home.

He proudly boasted that he had personally made Ellen MacArthur a bacon sandwich and that while she was onboard visiting the children, Deryn had been at the wheel and Dame Ellen had commented on his outstanding sailing ability.

'There was this one boat that pulled up beside us, and it was full of old people,' he continued. 'We all started shooting at them with our high-powered water guns and some of the kids filled up water balloons and threw them at the boat – it was AMAZING,' he chuckled.

'Oh no! What did those poor people do?' I asked.

'They didn't care – they all had water guns too and started firing back at us! It was hilarious… we won, though, we were the best pirates.'

I hadn't seen Deryn so animated about anything before, apart from jujitsu, which he hadn't been able to do for quite some time. He had discovered a new passion and it was heart-warming to listen as he trilled on about what fun he'd had.

'I'm mega good at it too, Mum!' he proclaimed.

I felt silly for all the worry I'd put myself through. I was wrong to be concerned. Deryn had been given the opportunity to have the most incredible experience thanks to Dame Ellen's wonderful charity and had grabbed it with both hands. I was so proud of him – yet again. I could learn a lot from his positive outlook. It can't have been easy for him but he didn't hesitate when offered the chance to take a major step back to normality.

CHAPTER 14

The boy I sent away on that minibus – a boy with no confidence, a shadow of his former self who was too scared to go outside in case he caught a bug or hurt himself – was certainly not the same boy they delivered back to me five days later.

The Ellen MacArthur Cancer Trust gave me back my son.

Chapter 15

HAVING HAD HIS FIRST TASTE OF INDEPENDENCE AND ADVENTURE ON the sailing trip, Deryn was keen to strike out alone again. We'd heard about a charity called Over the Wall, based on actor Paul Newman's charity camp, Hole in the Wall Gang, at a beautiful old castle called Barretstown in the Wicklow Mountains near Dublin.

Hundreds of young cancer patients visited each year from all over the world and were treated to a magical week of activities. Deryn's newly discovered thirst for excitement led to me applying for a place at their summer camp and he was lucky enough to be invited to the centre for a week.

It seemed to be karma that Deryn's treatment fell right in the middle of the two trips and would resume a few days after his return from Ireland. At last, the gods were working in our favour for a change.

Deryn was ecstatic, me, not so much. It meant leaving him once again in the capable hands of a stranger who would fly with him to southern Ireland for the week. At least his general health seemed good and his treatment seemed to have balanced out with regular periods when he wasn't neutropenic.

The thought still terrified me but I'd been broken in by the sailing trip, which he had enjoyed so much that there was no way I could prevent him from taking part in yet another amazing experience. Putting aside my concerns, I was really pleased for him. Cancer had wreaked so much heartache but it also brought Deryn the opportunity to have some awesome experiences.

One week after returning from the Isle of Wight, and following many talks with the charity's medical team, we were driving him to Heathrow Airport, with Deryn chattering away excitedly while I tried to hide my apprehension.

More than anything, he was looking forward to the flight. He had always loved flying but we hadn't even been allowed to leave the county without first getting the green light from the nearest hospital to wherever we were planning to go. It made visiting family and friends outside Norfolk such a logistical undertaking that we didn't bother.

However, Deryn's team was happy for him to go away under the care of cancer charities because they had everything in place for any eventuality. I felt reassured knowing Barretstown had its own team of doctors and oncology nurses. Deryn would also have a blood test while he was away and a close eye would be kept on him.

There was nothing to worry about but I could feel my stomach start to churn the second we walked into the airport. Three smiley young women wearing bright pink Barretstown T-shirts approached us with a pink helium balloon. They were the chaperones for Deryn and two other children on the trip.

As I hugged and kissed him goodbye and watched him walk towards security, I had a sudden panic.

Did they have his meds?

Had I forgotten anything really important?

Had I forgotten to tell him I loved him?

What if he didn't like it there?

What if he needed me?

My mind went into overdrive so I tried to shut out all the negative thoughts and worries by concentrating on just how well Deryn looked as he walked across the terminal. Not so long ago, he was painfully thin and frail and before that, incredibly bloated from steroids. He looked more like his old self, his face no longer resembled the moon and he no longer had tubes in him.

I watched as he walked through security. Deryn turned and looked dismayed to see me still standing there like a lemon. He started waving his hands at me, not to say goodbye but as if he was shooing away a fly. I wasn't leaving until he had disappeared from my sight.

That summer was epic for all of us. Dylan had been to stay with his grandparents in Telford, while Simon and I spent some much-needed quality time together. For me the icing on the cake was being invited on a trip to Ibiza with my best childhood friend Kerry.

I'd never been on a girlie holiday or even away with a friend before. I lived quite a solitary life when it came to close friends. I'd been bullied for many years as a child and didn't really trust anyone outside my immediate circle. But when Kerry asked me to go away with her, Simon pushed me to say yes.

'It'll be good for you, Callie, you need a break after the year we've just had,' he assured me. 'You'll have a great time.'

I wasn't convinced as I hadn't ever left the boys and Simon before, but Simon was relentless and reassured me that everything would be just fine at home without me. He was more than able to cope, he was an amazing father and I knew he could do it.

So I took Kerry up on her kind offer and for four days, I was carefree and felt young again. It felt like a regeneration for my soul. I hadn't realised just how much I needed to be Callie, not a wife or an oncology mum, just for a few days.

Simon was right, it was a fantastic tonic for me.

❖

Simon had also had a wonderful 2011, having been chosen from more than 3,000 applicants to star in BBC1's second series of *The Great British Bake Off*.

My man is an incredible baker and often turns to the kitchen in times of despair. When Deryn was sick Simon would spend hours making sweet treats in the hope of tempting him to eat during the tough times.

I urged him to apply but none of us really expected him to make it through the selection process. So we were ecstatic when he reached the second stage and was invited to London to meet its stars Mary Berry and Paul Hollywood.

In the third and final round of tests, he had to follow one of Paul's bread recipes. Simon excels at bread in particular so he was on fire. We travelled down to London together and while he was being put through his paces in the kitchen, I took the boys to Hamleys in Regent Street for some retail therapy. By the time we got back, Simon had finished and we got to meet Paul and Mary, who were both lovely.

We were blown away to hear that Simon had made it through to the final 12 and would be appearing in the series.

'How on earth did I blag my way into this one?' he joked as he packed his bag for the first of many trips to London for filming.

The boys and I thought we'd surprise Simon during the filming of episode two and arrived at the set to watch. It was fascinating for the boys to see the huge cameras and lots of people frantically running around all over the studio. They were mesmerised by the whole affair.

But by far, the highlight for the three of us was being able to tuck into the copious amounts of delicious food made by all the contestants. We were in heaven. Deryn and Dylan had also made some treats of their own to give to Paul and Mary. Deryn had made cheese straws from scratch, spending hours the previous day rolling and folding his own puff pastry while Dylan opted for blueberry muffins. Both boys were extremely proud of their efforts, as were Paul and Mary.

CHAPTER 15

For the final episode, we were invited to a street party where the three finalists baked for all the contestants' friends and families. It was an amazing day, one we will never forget. The boys loved knowing who the winner was three months in advance and having to keep it a secret.

When the series started airing on TV, we had a little celebration of our own, inviting friends and neighbours over to watch with us and sample the same cakes Simon had baked for his episode. Any criticism of our star from the judges was met with boos and cries of: 'He doesn't know what he's talking about, these cupcakes are amazing!'

After the previous year, it really felt like 2011 might be the upturn in fortune we all needed.

Deryn's week in Ireland was a roaring success and he came back full of stories about the lads he'd shared a dormitory with. They'd enjoyed all sorts of high jinks; late-night pillow fights, canoeing, rock climbing, discos, limousine rides and hanging off high ropes.

'Can I go again next year?' he pleaded.

With each trip away, I noticed Deryn was becoming stronger and more confident. The sheer brilliance of these charities and the role they play in the recovery of children who have suffered so much is undeniable.

The idea of him continuing to strike out and try new sports and different hobbies with other children his own age was something I could only hope and pray for. To have something to look forward to outside of chemotherapy and hospital stays was doing Deryn the world of good.

And it was beautiful to see all the good things that were coming his way.

Chapter 16

THE START OF HIGH SCHOOL WAS LOOMING AND I HAD MIXED feelings about Deryn launching into his secondary education.

I had attended the same high school 20 years earlier and had not enjoyed my experience there. I was bullied so badly that from the age of 12 I was playing truant regularly and only attending one or two days a week. I was worried about my children being bullied but both my boys were very popular and well-liked by everyone who met them and I hoped this would be their saving grace.

While Deryn hadn't experienced any more nastiness, apart from the line-tugging incident, Dylan had had to endure some unkind comments from a couple of his classmates. One little boy had approached him in the playground to say he hoped his brother died of cancer. Dylan was obviously devastated but he didn't let it change the person he was and remained kind and considerate.

I needed reassuring that things at my old school had changed and that my son would be well cared for. I met with the headmaster and was given a tour of the school. It felt very strange being there again after so many years. A lot had changed but it still held horrible connotations for me.

'You need to convince me to send my son here,' I told the teacher showing me around.

The staff members patiently answered my questions. After a day there, I felt it was the right place for Deryn after all and that he would flourish. All his friends were also going and Deryn was really looking forward to becoming a high school student.

Before term started, he was assessed by a child psychologist to determine whether or not he needed extra support given his autism and Tourette's, as well as the fact that he had missed an extraordinary amount of schooling due to his illness. The psychologist quizzed Deryn at length on a broad cross-section of topics before putting down his pen.

'I can't assess him any further,' he announced. 'Deryn is being tested at the level of a 17-year-old and he's got everything correct so far. I don't think he is going to get assistance at school because he's too intelligent.

'If he was behind or slow at learning, he would get funding but as it stands, he's excelling and I can't see them helping him unless he starts struggling.'

'Whoop whoop, I always knew I was a genius!' Deryn chipped in with a laugh.

'Modest, too,' I added.

I felt relieved and proud that despite his prolonged absences, Deryn was still ahead of the game. Maybe he wouldn't fall behind after all. And maybe I should just stop worrying. Children need to experience the rites of passage of adolescence and starting secondary school is one of them. I was looking forward to watching him mature and find his place in the world.

We bought Deryn's uniform but didn't bother with a PE kit as he had been advised not to do physical education due to the drop off in his fitness levels. He was quietly relieved that he wouldn't look silly in front of his friends as his physical deterioration was a source of great frustration and sadness for him.

'I'm not like I used to be,' Deryn confided in me sadly on a rare off day. 'I used to be the fittest and fastest boy in my whole school. Now I'm slow and weak. I'm never going to get back to how I was.'

CHAPTER 16

Witnessing the changes that cancer had wrought on his body made him annoyed and ashamed of the boy he had physically become.

'I just want to be normal,' he explained.

I enveloped him in a hug and tried to soothe him with the little knowledge I had about how he was feeling. I had been overweight for most of my life until I managed to lose eight stone in 2009. Once I reached a healthy weight, I started training hard and it became a passion.

Working out saved my sanity during the tougher times and provided an escape from the hospital. The staff thought I was mad when I headed out at 10pm clad in bright pink high-visibility lycra. Sometimes, if I couldn't get to the gym, I'd work out at the end of Deryn's bed, in hospital corridors, even in the bathrooms on the ward late at night, occasionally giving the night staff a surprise when they walked in to find me mid-squat!

Altering my body beyond recognition wasn't just for my benefit. I knew I had to lead by example and show Deryn that no matter how bad things get, you can change anything if you try hard enough. I wanted him to see me persevering in the hope it would encourage him not to quit, either.

'There's no such thing as normal, darling, we're all different,' I told him. 'We all have different versions of normal – this is your normal but it won't be forever, I promise you that.'

A lot of my friends seemed upset that their children were heading off to big school. They didn't like seeing their children getting older. I was ecstatic to see both boys growing up. It was an honour and a privilege, one that I was aware not everyone was so fortunate to be granted.

❖

The first day of term arrived and Deryn could hardly contain his excitement at putting on his new uniform and shiny new school shoes. Rucksack on back, he strolled into school with all the confidence in the world. The two fabulous summer trips had prepared him well for this day and he owned it.

I watched children bounding out of the school gates at the end of the day. Deryn soon emerged surrounded by his friends, chatting and laughing. It was like he'd never been out of the fold. He got in the car beaming from ear to ear.

'It was awesome!' he declared.

The new term seemed to herald a fresh start. Simon and I were desperate to get back to work now that we had more time on our hands and Deryn's health had stabilised.

Simon set up his own business making bespoke cob pizza ovens and built up a small clientele. He was no threat to Richard Branson but thoroughly enjoyed running his own company. I also decided on a new direction – joining the Territorial Army. I'd wanted to be a soldier since I was young. My dad had been in the army and I had wonderful memories of being with him when he worked on military vehicles.

At that particular moment, life was fabulous.

Deryn was in a quandary. The Starlight Children's Foundation had been in touch, inviting him to make one of his dreams come true and he didn't know what to ask for.

'Shall I get my bedroom kitted out with gadgets, spend the day somewhere amazing or ask to meet someone?' he pondered.

In the end, it wasn't a tough decision. Deryn had been obsessed by the Royal Marines since he was tiny but having had cancer in addition to his other problems, there was no way he would ever be able to make that particular career a reality.

So he asked for the next best thing – the chance to spend a day behind the scenes at the Commando Training Centre Royal Marines in Devon. Rather amazingly, the charity got in touch to say his wish had been granted.

The boys, Simon and I were invited to spend not one but two days at their Lympstone base, getting a feel for the 32-week elite training course, which involves huge physical challenges and advanced weapon training, leading to the ultimate prize of a cherished green beret.

I was overjoyed. Military service had been a big part of both our lives when we were children and it seemed our boys were just as 'army barmy'. Indeed, Deryn admired the green berets immensely and aspired to be as tough as they were.

We arrived at the beautiful Devon hotel that was to be our base to a warm welcome from the staff. We polished off pizza from room service before falling into bed, although we were so excited that none of us slept very well.

The following morning, we headed down to have breakfast with the Starlight team and a journalist, photographer and TV cameraman who would capture everything and turn it into a DVD for Deryn to keep.

Deryn was presented with an enormous box and asked to open it. He cut through the tape and a huge smile spread across his face as he spotted the contents. He joyfully held up a pair of combat boots, trousers, jacket, military issue socks and some Royal Marine T shirts… he'd been given the whole shebang, including a black training beret with a red flash at the front. He was overjoyed.

He put on the uniform and emerged dressed from head to toe in green, looking incredibly grown up and desperately keen to get to the training camp. Not to be left out, Dylan was also ready for action in a Royal Marines costume that we'd bought him for his birthday.

We signed in at the camp guard room and Warrant Officer 1 Richard Edge greeted us warmly and chaperoned us around, showing us the swimming pool, the mess, accommodation blocks and the gym, where we were faced with 40 young men doing press-ups.

Standing in front of them was a physical training instructor who told us that these lads were on week seven of their training programme and were just starting to understand how hard this was going to be for them. I felt for them, some were not much older than Deryn and they were being pushed to their limits in front of us.

Next up was a visit to the infamous assault course made up of two parts; the top field and the bottom field. The top field isn't attempted until a recruit has 16 weeks of training under his belt. Deryn was invited to get stuck into the obstacles on the bottom field, much to his delight, and threw himself inside tunnels, over a six-foot wall and across balance beams – although he sensibly declined the chance to swim in the freezing cold outdoor pool.

Next stop was the heavy weapons section to watch a group of specially trained marines operating Javelin Portable anti-tank missiles. Two Javelins were set up on computers for the boys to practice on and Deryn and Dylan were straight in there. Simon and I stood quietly in the doorway, soaking up the sight of them being put to the test by some pretty amazing gadgetry.

'Can you see the tank through the sights?' one of the marines asked Deryn.

'Yep, I've got it; it's moving but I can follow it,' Deryn replied, sounding every bit the rookie soldier.

'When you're happy you've got the target, press this button here,' explained the marine.

'WOOOO WHOOOO!' Deryn yelled as he activated the button. 'I hit it!' I thought he was going to burst with excitement.

'Yeah, I hit mine too!' shouted Dylan.

Deryn now had his sights set on a second target, a bicycle,

about a mile away. Within a few seconds, he'd locked onto it and hit the bike. The weapons experts were impressed with Deryn's aim and confidence and outside the room, we were stopped by a sergeant. This man had some serious scars on his face and having heard how well Deryn had performed, he wanted to chat.

'If you successfully operate a Javelin while under fire in an operation, they give you a special coin,' he explained as he showed us a large gold coin in a plastic case. 'Not many marines have this coin because it's very hard to use a Javelin under fire. This one is mine.'

He handed Deryn the coin to admire. Deryn was in awe, turning it over in his hands. As he went to hand it back to the sergeant, the veteran shook his head.

'No, it's yours, fella,' he said with a wink. 'I want you to have it.'

Deryn was totally dumbstruck as this selfless soldier shook our hands and went back to his work. A ride in an open-top Land Rover laden with machine guns was next and the marines on board allowed both boys to get behind the heavy weaponry.

The following day, we returned to the camp dressed up as instructed to dine in the officers' mess before witnessing a passing-out parade along with the families of the latest bunch of successful recruits.

A grand room tastefully furnished with oversized leather Chesterfield style chairs was occupied by some distinguished gentlemen sporting large moustaches and with chests full of medals.

The boys were also dressed to impress in white shirts, black trousers, waistcoats and ties and were each given Royal Marine pins to wear, which they did with utmost pride. They were invited to watch a video film of the new marines while sitting next to the camp commandant, the most important person in the room, who treated the boys as his equals.

After the film, we made our way to the Falklands Hall where 18 new marines – from an intake of 53 – were presented with their green berets. We felt so privileged to sit there alongside the parents and siblings of these lads.

At the passing-out parade, Deryn sat next to an elderly ex-Royal Marine whose chest was adorned with many medals. He couldn't stop smiling. After the ceremony, Deryn was introduced to the Rear Admiral, who paid tribute to Deryn's amazing courage in a speech before presenting Deryn with a beautiful framed photograph of him on the Land Rover with the rest of the marines.

My spine tingled as he spoke of Deryn's strength and spirit in the face of adversity, a strength that Royal Marines need to possess if they are to get through their arduous training. He told Deryn that from now on, he was an honorary Royal Marine and if ever he needed their help, he had only to ask.

I could no longer contain my emotions. Tears ran down my face as I struggled to regain my composure before chatting to the Rear Admiral about Deryn's journey through cancer.

The final flourish was the chance to visit the Royal Marines shop on site where the boys were given lots of memorabilia to remind them of this special visit. They were both blown away and struggled to carry their new hoodies, cufflinks, wallets, mugs, pens, pencils, notebooks and bookmarks as we walked towards the main gate.

Reluctant to leave, they asked Warrant Officer Edge if they could come back.

'I want you to go off and get a good education and some life experience and come back when you're 21,' he told them. 'The best marines are those who come here with a good idea of the world.'

CHAPTER 16

We shook hands and thanked everyone for their kindness and generosity. It had been a truly amazing 48 hours which none of us would ever forget. And in the same way that Deryn had been inspired by those dedicated new recruits and battle-scarred veterans, so some of the toughest men in the armed forces had also been inspired – and reduced to tears – by Deryn's courage.

Chapter 17

Wɪᴛʜ ɢᴏᴏᴅ ꜰᴏʀᴛᴜɴᴇ ꜱᴇᴇᴍᴇᴅ ᴛᴏ ʙᴇ ꜱᴍɪʟɪɴɢ ᴏɴ ᴜꜱ, ꜰᴏʀ ꜱᴏᴍᴇ ᴏꜰ our dear friends, life had just taken a turn for the worse. Tiegan, the wonderful, smiley little girl we'd met during Deryn's first stay at Addenbrooke's, had been given the all clear. This was wonderful news, but shortly after being discharged from hospital, Tiegan's mum found a lump. The cancer had returned.

She was sent to Bristol Children's Hospital for a bone marrow transplant but unfortunately, it didn't work and she returned to Addenbrooke's to spend her last weeks close to her family. Deryn had made friends with quite a few children who had died and although he cared, he never showed that he was upset.

'It's all part of life, Mum,' he told me one day when we were talking about it.

Tiegan was different. Deryn had a real soft spot for her. This bubbly, irrepressible two-year-old had taught him more about life than he could ever imagine. I didn't know how to broach the subject of her death but it was something that had to be done so I took a deep breath and sat down with Deryn in his bedroom.

'I have to tell you something Deryn, it's about Tiegan,' I said quietly.

Deryn began to cry. We cuddled as he sobbed for the toddler who had lit up so many lives and touched his own.

We celebrated Deryn's 12th birthday with friends and family and Christmas was another big celebration at home, a marked difference to the previous one spent in hospital with Deryn barely conscious. This time he managed to eat more than one pig in a blanket – it was wonderful to see him enjoying life and feeling like his old self again.

The return of his appetite happily coincided with an invitation to the BBC Good Food Show at the NEC in Birmingham as a result of Simon's participation in The Great British Bake Off.

It was a wonderful day for all of us, but especially Simon, who was asked by a young fan for his autograph. What touched him even more was that this young girl was blind. She asked to put her hands on his face so that she could know what he looked like. He was very moved by the encounter.

We hung out backstage with Paul Hollywood, Mary Berry and many other famous TV chefs and personalities. The boys loved being VIPs behind the velvet rope. Having worked at events like this in my bouncer days, it was also a revelation for me to be on the other side of the rope for a change.

Seeing the boys standing shoulder to shoulder with DJ Chris Evans, *MasterChef*'s Gregg Wallace and ITV's *This Morning* star chef Gino D'Acampo was surreal and I was struck by the kindness of the celebrities we met. Simon was also being recognised by dozens of *GBBO* fans and watching him sign autographs made me giggle.

For Deryn the highlight was being able to sample food made by all the top chefs at the event. He tried a little of everything on offer and seemed to be developing a real passion for cooking. He was in awe of the TV chefs and went from stand to stand trying different recipes from around the world and watching their every move as they chopped and prepared ingredients expertly in seconds.

After such a fraught relationship with food, it was a pleasure and a relief to see him taking such an interest. Enjoying a family day out brought it home to me how lucky we were and I couldn't help feeling blessed.

Deryn was in remission and all his tests were clear. He was being monitored closely with weekly blood tests and regular lumbar punctures, so if something did occur, it would be caught quickly. The future looked bright.

However, with the loss of Tiegan still playing on my mind, fears of a relapse were never far away and would creep up whenever we heard bad news about our oncology friends and families. I tried to banish the bad thoughts – the less we focused on what could possibly go wrong, the more time we had to focus on what was going right which, at the moment, was everything.

❖

As New Year 2012 dawned, it felt like the right time to start looking towards the future. Simon had applied to become a nurse once before but due to finances, it hadn't been feasible. Now, it looked quite possible that both of us would be in a position to embark on a career in this field.

I wanted to be on an equal footing with the nurses, to understand what was going on with more confidence. So far, it was Google, a keen ear and intuition that had served me. I wanted more. When I was younger, I'd joined the Royal Army Medical Corp as an army reservist. I'd been thrown into the deep end of the medical pool and loved every second of it.

Neither Simon nor I had the appropriate qualifications to enrol on a degree course so we both applied for a year-long higher education course, which would eventually allow us to apply to university. To our astonishment, we were both accepted and enrolled for September.

Towards the end of January, Deryn started to experience a tickly cough. He was a few days off his monthly oncology check-up at the NNUH and as most of the kids in the neighbourhood had had colds and flu, I didn't panic.

Deryn's consultant took one look at his throat and declared there was absolutely nothing to worry about. But it didn't improve and when we went back the following month, the tickle was still there. Deryn was no longer coughing but said it felt as if something was stuck in his throat. I was concerned.

'Deryn's tonsils look a little inflamed but there's nothing to suggest there is anything to be concerned about,' his consultant told me.

'Could this be a secondary cancer?' I asked hesitantly, not wanting to hear the answer.

She told me the idea of a secondary cancer was 'ridiculous'. I was worrying unnecessarily.

Was it ridiculous? I didn't think so – secondary cancers can occur as a result of chemotherapy. Deryn's team had told me as much. But the doctor dismissed my concerns, telling me I was worrying about nothing.

Everything else was clear and Deryn's blood tests were looking great. I was torn between believing the consultant and trusting my instincts.

The following month, Deryn's throat was still bugging him. A different doctor looked him over and noticed black spots on his tonsils but decided to check them again at the following month's appointment and arrange for a specialist after that.

I wasn't reassured and told the doctor so. I asked if Deryn could see a specialist earlier as the problem had started three months earlier and showed no signs of improving. My intuition had served me well so far. I had known that leukaemia wasn't glandular fever, that appendicitis wasn't typhlitis… and I knew that this wasn't something that should be brushed off as over-anxiety.

Deryn's April appointment arrived and while he was still able to eat, the obstruction in his throat was really starting to get him down.

'It feels like there's something scratchy, like a crisp, permanently stuck in my throat,' he complained.

I told myself I was not going to leave the hospital this time until I had an appointment with an ear, nose and throat specialist.

Blood tests came back absolutely fine, with everything as it should have been. The cytotoxic drugs were given with no problems and all that was left to do was the physical examination.

The same consultant as the previous month examined Deryn as our usual consultant was on holiday again – 'I'm going to rename her Judith Chalmers, she's away so often,' I joked.

The consultant took her little wooden stick and pushed Deryn's tongue down while shining a bright light into his throat.

'Yes, the black spots have gone now and there appear to be some white marks which have changed shape slightly from last month,' she remarked.

Alarm bells rang. Surely he would be referred to an ENT specialist now?

'But I don't think it's anything to be concerned about, and it's certainly not a secondary cancer,' she continued. 'Deryn's blood count is absolutely normal.'

I begged her to refer him anyway and she told me she would arrange for an ENT appointment. It was made for two months' time.

My relief turned to anger. With his history, a speedy appointment was not too much to expect. I was sure that he had only been given the appointment to shut me up and send me on my way. I couldn't shake the feeling that something was seriously amiss.

The May appointment saw the same clear blood results but when I insisted the consultant look at Deryn's throat again, she finally conceded that something might be wrong.

'Deryn's tonsils do look quite different from the last time I saw them,' she said. 'First they had black spots, then they had white marks and now they seem to have some holes in them. I think I'll call the ENT surgeon to see if he can take a look.'

Frustrated but relieved, we were given a 1pm appointment with an ENT surgeon. Finally, my concerns were being taken seriously. We went into Norwich to kill some time and returned to the surgeon's office, buoyed by the fact that we would finally get an answer to this itchy, scratchy throat.

Deryn sat in the chair with his head back and mouth wide open as the surgeon shone a torch into his mouth and took a long look at Deryn's throat.

'Deryn's tonsils are swollen and need to come out as soon as possible,' he said. I detected a note of concern in his voice.

'I am quite concerned as they don't look like anything I have seen before.'

I felt sick. I had tried so hard not to be pessimistic but I knew better than to dismiss my gut instincts.

'Can I keep them once they come out?' Deryn asked. 'They wouldn't let me keep my appendix, so can I keep my tonsils please?'

Deryn sat there smiling at us.

'Well… can I?'

Chapter 18

THE TONSILLECTOMY WAS BOOKED FOR JUNE AND THIS TIME, AFTER five months of intense discomfort, Deryn couldn't wait to get back into hospital. I was anxious to see the surgery over and done with, too. It was distressing knowing that Deryn was in constant pain and there was nothing I could do to help.

He woke up after the operation in complete agony. Usually, he would be tucking into egg sandwiches and making the recovery team giggle but even he couldn't put a brave face on it this time.

His mouth was covered in dried blood, his teeth were coated red and he could barely speak above a whisper. I had a quick look inside his throat and was shocked to see it looking sore, swollen and bloody.

I felt awful for him. The aftermath of surgery was far more traumatic than the sore tonsils had been. We knew that Deryn had a high pain threshold and could only imagine the agony our poor lad was going through. The ENT surgeon arrived to talk us through the operation and from his demeanour, I knew it wasn't good news.

'I have to admit that I've never seen tonsils quite like Deryn's before, Mrs Blackwell,' he began. 'They were incredibly hard, almost rock-like, and tremendously difficult to remove. The reason Deryn is in so much pain is because I had to literally pull them out. Deryn's throat is badly bruised.'

Like rocks and incredibly hard to remove. I needed to know why.

'I have no idea why and for that reason, I have sent them away for testing,' he added. 'They looked very different to how they should have looked.'

'So, I can't keep them then?' Deryn interrupted, in a hoarse whisper.

The surgeon cracked a smile.

'No, I'm sorry Deryn, I'm afraid you can't.'

It was deeply concerning news but we didn't dwell on it and concentrated on helping Deryn to feel better. For several days, the wounds in his throat continued to open up, causing him to lose mouthfuls of blood at a time. He wasn't able to talk properly for well over a week and was horribly sore.

The only upside was that he was on doctor's orders to have ice cream for breakfast, lunch and dinner with snacks of ice cream in between. Deryn was overjoyed about having his favourite dessert all day every day for two weeks – heaven on a plate!

He was due back at Addenbrooke's for a routine lumbar puncture and another bone marrow aspirate to check for any signs of leukaemia returning. It was a sensible move considering the poorly state of his tonsils and my concerns that he might have a secondary cancer.

Somehow, we managed to stay upbeat and positive. His blood tests had been fine for months, he'd displayed none of the symptoms he'd had when he was first diagnosed and he looked really healthy. He had breezed through the last few months of treatment and chemotherapy.

If this was a secondary cancer, I reasoned, it would probably be localised, as any spread of the disease would have shown up in his blood tests by now and he would have been deteriorating health-wise.

As we arrived at hospital for the procedure, James, a sarcoma consultant, introduced himself and asked if he could speak to just me and Simon privately. My heart started racing and I felt

CHAPTER 18

heady and faint.

'I'll be alright out here, Mum,' Deryn told me breezily as Simon and I walked towards the consulting room. My heart was pounding out of my chest and I tried to convince myself that perhaps James liked to consult with parents rather than having younger ears in the room. Simon looked desperately worried, too. Was he also talking to himself like I was and trying to hold it together?

James cleared his throat.

'The initial histology reports have come back on Deryn's tonsils,' he said gently. 'I'm sorry to be the one to have to break this news to you but it appears that this is in fact a secondary cancer.'

I can't remember which emotion I felt first but I was hit by a tsunami of anger, sadness, fear and uncertainty.

Anger that I hadn't been listened to all those months ago when my suggestion of this very scenario was deemed 'ridiculous'.

Sadness that Deryn would have to go through hell again after he'd already been through so much. I felt distraught for Dylan and Simon, too.

Fear that we would lose Deryn after feeling so confident that he would pull through.

And uncertainty. Life had been going so well for all of us. What did this mean for Deryn's future, for Dylan and for Simon and I and our dreams of a nursing career?

Physically, I felt winded. A maelstrom of emotions was spinning around my head but I'd had a lot of practice at pretending I was fine when all I wanted to do was cry, shout and destroy the planet around me. I somehow managed to stay calm.

I glanced over at Simon. He, too, looked cool and collected, having also honed the skill of hiding his true feelings. But however hurt and angry we felt, we couldn't allow our emotions to take over and lead us down a path of despair.

'Is it leukaemia?' I asked in a voice that didn't sound like mine.

James told us it wasn't leukaemia, but confirmed it was a secondary cancer. They could tell the tonsils had somehow turned into malignant tumours, possibly a sarcoma – a malignant tumour of connective tissue.

Slices of Deryn's tonsils had been sent to leading oncology specialists in America, Australia and beyond. It felt momentarily reassuring to hear that no stone would be left unturned in determining what type of cancer this was. But if the UK specialists were stumped, it must be incredibly rare… so how would anyone know how to treat it?

I started to worry that Deryn would be worried as it felt like we'd been in that room for hours. We hadn't, of course, and had only been in there for a few minutes, but the news had come as such a blow that all concept of time had disappeared.

'What do we tell Deryn?' I asked Simon.

Going against our own honesty policy, Simon and I decided not to tell Deryn the truth, not yet at least. Our son was waiting to go in for his lumbar puncture and bone marrow aspirate and we couldn't break this news to him just before he underwent a general anaesthetic.

I took a deep breath, straightened myself and put on my poker face as I walked over to Deryn, who was happily sitting playing on the Xbox in the waiting room.

'Okay, so what did he tell you that you don't want to tell me, then?' Deryn demanded, staring straight at me. 'I can take it, you know.'

What? I wasn't prepared for this! I'd tried to hide it but Deryn and I had spent so much time together that he could see right through me.

I turned to Simon who simply nodded.

'It is cancer, they don't know what type yet but your tonsils had turned into malignant tumours,' I told him, my voice

CHAPTER 18

breaking. 'I'm so sorry.'

'Oh well, I kinda knew it anyway,' he shrugged as he turned back to the Xbox.

Had he understood what I'd just said to him? Knowing Deryn the way I did, I knew he comprehended everything. He wasn't in denial; he was reacting the way he always did, with an acceptance that blew me away.

Seconds later Deryn was called through to theatre and just as the anaesthetic kicked in, he looked at me.

'It'll be alright, please don't worry about it,' he whispered before losing consciousness.

The nurses offered us a quiet room so that we could have some privacy and as I walked in, I felt like my heart was exploding into a million pieces. My facade slipped away, I was broken. I slumped in the chair and sobbed my heart out.

Simon, my big, strong, rugby-playing, ex-military husband, also cried out as if his heart was breaking. I had never seen or heard any man cry like it before and the sound of his world falling apart tore at my heart.

'Why him? Why now? Why can't cancer just leave him the fuck alone!' Simon screamed. He fell back into a chair with his head in his hands and quietly wept.

Throughout the previous two years, Simon had been the strong one, my rock. Neither of us had broken down since that fateful day in July 2010 but this second diagnosis hit us hard. It was my turn to be there for Simon now. I put my arms around him and we stayed in the room for what felt like an eternity, holding one another and sobbing.

❖

The first diagnosis had been devastating but to hear it a second time was even harder. We were about to be thrust into the world of the unknown once more but it was a world we were now familiar with and that scared me.

I had seen just how horrendous cancer treatment could be. Many of the saddest things I'd ever seen didn't even happen to my child but to other young patients.

However, I'd seen Deryn vomit until his throat bled, in agony and not be able to do a damn thing about it. In a matter of months I'd watched him change from my healthy strong 10-year-old boy into a bed-bound bag of bones. I'd held his hand through more general anaesthetics and painful procedures than I could count.

Now I had to put on a brave face for my children. Neither Simon nor I wanted the boys to see us break down. It wasn't about trying to be superhuman but how could we expect them to keep positive and strong if we gave up?

I'd been in a place where each day brought a new uncertainty and a new worry. A place where I had to dig deep inside my soul to find the strength to carry on. I didn't want to go there again. I couldn't go there again, I had nothing left to give.

As I stood in Simon's arms, these thoughts ran through my mind and then something changed. I realised that, yes, I could carry on, I had to. I couldn't just stop here and now. Where would that leave any of us? I had no choice but to pick myself up and think of the positives.

We knew the team, we knew the hospital and we knew most of the parents. We knew that no matter what, we would have the most amazing support network from our oncology friends. Knowing that we were not alone and that there were many who had walked this path before us somehow made it easier to bear. We didn't need to shoulder this burden by ourselves.

As if we had read each other's mind, Simon and I broke away from our embrace. Still holding hands, we looked at each other and smiled.

CHAPTER 18

'We're better than this, we can do this, we HAVE to do this – like Deryn said, it will all be all right and we mustn't worry about it,' Simon said as he wiped my tears away. 'Deryn is always right!'

There was a quiet knock at the door. Deryn had come out of theatre and was waiting in the ward. We were told not to rush as he was still asleep. He woke up and felt well enough to demand some food. He wasn't dwelling on this new setback, and we shouldn't, either.

James came to tell us that they would run a lot more tests and were relying heavily on the other oncology specialists to come up with some answers. Deryn's tonsils had made their way around the world and people with expensive microscopes were examining the tissue. We had to wait to find out what type of sarcoma it was and until then, they couldn't even contemplate a treatment plan.

It was time to go home and face the terrible task of telling family and friends the news. This was not the time to be breaking down or feeling hopeless and sorry for ourselves. It was up to us to stay strong for the sake of everyone else. We had to lead by example.

Chapter 19

Life is precious. This setback reminded us of that and we vowed to make the following days and weeks full of joy and, finances permitting, give the boys everything they wanted.

We had been gifted some free tickets to Alton Towers. Deryn had wanted to go for a long time but we had been putting it off until he was stronger. Now, however, seemed like the perfect moment to take the boys away from everything.

Deryn suffered with mobility issues so we were given a disability badge which allowed us to jump the queues for the rides. The boys were ecstatic and not even the miserable English summer could dampen our spirits that day.

Times like these, all together having fun, were how good memories were made and no matter what we faced in the future, nothing could take these moments away from us. The smiles on the faces of all three of my boys were priceless. We had a wonderful time and didn't want the day to end.

Deryn had an MRI and CT scan to establish whether there were any more tumours in his body. Fortunately, the results came back saying he was clear.

The good times continued. Our friends owned a holiday cottage on the Norfolk coast – with an outdoor hot tub, much to the boys' delight. They offered us a week there while we awaited the results of Deryn's biopsy. We hired a tiny boat on the Norfolk Broads, packed a picnic and spent an entire day cruising around.

After his week away with Ellen MacArthur, Deryn was now a

competent sailor. The boat was the size of a small car and Simon was making a hash of mooring it near a large patch of grass where we wanted to have lunch.

'Let me do it, Dad,' Deryn pleaded.

'Go for it, dude,' Simon nodded, stepping aside to let Deryn get to the wheel.

Within a couple of minutes, Deryn had effortlessly turned the boat around and parked it parallel to the jetty. We stood gazing in wonder as he stepped on to the jetty where he tied the boat up like a professional.

'Come on, then, let's go and get some lunch,' he grinned, thrilled that he'd remembered exactly what to do.

'Well done, mate, that was quite impressive,' I beamed.

'Nah, that's nothing,' he chuckled. 'I had to moor up a 40ft yacht on the Isle of Wight – this was easy compared to that.'

That afternoon Deryn again took the wheel and was in his element.

Sailing was something he loved, it made him feel alive and he looked and felt very comfortable in a yacht or dinghy. The Ellen MacArthur Trust had invited Deryn to sail again with them in Essex and he couldn't wait to be back on the water.

'I hope I can do the Round the Island race when I'm older,' he told me after his trip.

'With you onboard, they'll be bound to win,' I replied.

I loved the fact he was not afraid to line up ambitions and think about the future. He knew he had some tough times ahead of him and he wanted to make the most of every opportunity while he could.

He also returned to Barretstown with the blessing of his medical team, who were happy for him to keep active while he felt so well. He came home buzzing about befriending many of the Russian children on the trip.

CHAPTER 19

'I really want to go to St Petersburg, Mum,' Deryn told me. 'The Russian kids were ace, more crazy than anyone I've ever met!'

A few days after he returned, we went to court to finalise Deryn's adoption by Simon. Once the legalities had been dealt with, the judge shook Deryn and Simon's hands and wished them the best of luck for their future. It was very touching. Afterwards, we held a small party to celebrate. Finally, our family was complete.

The last few weeks had been everything we'd hoped for, packed with amazing memories and good times with friends and family. They were also a distraction from the fact that we still had no more news about what kind of cancer Deryn had. A sore throat flared up and once again, alarm bells rang and an appointment with an ENT surgeon was hastily arranged.

Deryn's throat had healed nicely but the tonsillectomy had left a large void at the back of his throat. Thankfully the site looked clear of lesions and obvious signs of tumours. However, right at the back of Deryn's throat, there appeared to be an ulcer.

To the right of this was another, much smaller one. They didn't look sinister but required investigation, nonetheless. The ENT surgeon wanted to remove the ulcerated area and surrounding tissue just to be safe and send the tissue off for further tests to determine whether or not it was cancerous.

Sadly, this meant further surgery, a prospect which, after the last painful procedure, filled me with dread. A PET scan was also scheduled to search for pre-cancerous cells as, following Deryn's tonsil removal, there was a possibility that some cancer cells had travelled around his body via the lymphatic system.

The mere mention of this scan terrified me. We had gone from an all-clear through the rest of his body to the possibility of further cancerous cells lurking and waiting to turn into malignant tumours.

But at least we were inching closer to some kind of diagnosis. Nothing was definite but after what felt like a lifetime of testing, cross-referencing and discussions, scientists in labs all over the globe had crossed every cancer known to man off the list.

All except one.

Langerhans cell sarcoma.

Chapter 20

James, the sarcoma consultant, called me to explain that a scientist in London had been working on Deryn's tissue samples for weeks, studying the cancer cells in great detail on a molecular level.

Working around the clock and having investigated the DNA of the cells, she could finally confirm that it was indeed Langerhans cell sarcoma.

I had never heard of this condition and Deryn's medical team didn't know much about it either, so I Googled it and discovered that LCS is a very rare subtype of sarcoma – so rare that fewer than 50 cases have ever been recorded worldwide and treatment is experimental. It is not to be confused with Langerhans cell histiocytosis, a more common illness that occurs mainly in children.

We finally knew what we were dealing with – one of the rarest illnesses known to man. The diagnosis came as a relief, even though no-one knew just yet what the best course of treatment would be.

I decided to begin documenting Deryn's journey so we started a blog called Chief Cancer Collector to allow friends and family to follow our story as well as put LCS on to the web so that if anyone else Googled this rare condition, they would find us and get in touch.

As for Deryn, he was impatient to get treatment started. He wanted to get on with it and get it over with.

'I still know that I'm going to be okay, Mum,' he said cheerfully one morning. 'I know that this isn't going to kill me.'

I wanted to believe that he wasn't just trying to make me feel better but that he had some sort of sixth sense about his destiny. Once again, I could only admire his positive and optimistic outlook at a time when my own intuition seemed to have gone into hiding.

'We will have to wait for the results of Deryn's upcoming PET scan to see whether or not it has spread,' James explained. 'After that, we can start making decisions. We have got a lot of people on Deryn's case and we're all working together to come up with the best treatment plan we can.'

His assurances gave me a glimmer of hope that we could get through this. Information was key and I resolved to research long and hard to come up with as much documentary evidence as I could gather on LCS. After a fairly hit-and-miss education, I was turning into a geek with a huge thirst for medical knowledge.

I learned from my research that there was a very small number of people living with LCS. I came across one woman in Australia called Maria, whose son Daniel had been diagnosed with LCS in 2009 at the age of 18. I wrote to Maria telling her about Deryn and received a swift reply filling me in on everything she had found out about the condition.

The tumour in Daniel's stomach had been the size of an orange and only been treated with radiotherapy. Maria had taken Daniel to see a doctor specialising in Chinese medicine and on his advice Daniel stopped eating meat, sugar and dairy. He'd had no chemotherapy and had been cancer-free for more than 18 months. This was very promising news.

Maria also told me of two other LCS sufferers she had heard of in Texas but she hadn't found anyone else. I spoke to James to relay my findings and he confirmed that they had similarly limited knowledge of this rare condition. He told me a

55-year-old British man had recently been diagnosed, making Deryn one of only five people worldwide who had the disease.

I was hoping that Deryn, like Daniel, might also get away with radiotherapy alone, but unfortunately Deryn had to continue chemotherapy for ALL.

I felt quite uplifted after the conversation with James. It helped that he embraced my desire to contribute to the discussion and treated me less like a patient's mum and more like an equal fighting for a common cause.

I got in touch with the LCS sufferers in Texas but no-one could tell me much more than I already knew. However, I discovered that none of the other patients were children and none of them had been diagnosed with cancer before LCS. Some patients – all now deceased – had gone on to develop leukaemia after the LCS diagnosis.

We knew how much Deryn liked to mess with the order of things and it bemused me that he had to get two cancers the opposite way around. I interrupted him midway through a game on his PlayStation to give him this news.

'Wow!' he exclaimed. 'So just five people in the whole world have what I have?' he said with something approaching pride at being unique.

When I explained that every one of the other patients only had LCS and that he appeared to be not only the youngest patient in the world but also the only one fighting ALL and LCS, he grabbed his phone and started scrolling manically through the menu.

He soon found an app that allowed him to see the world's population in real time and started making rapid calculations about just how special this made him.

'That makes me one in seven billion, 600 million, 358,000… oh, it keeps changing!' he laughed. 'One in 7 billion, 600 million,

362,000… nope, that's not right either.

'Mum,' he exclaimed finally. 'It makes me one in seven billion!'

❖

Deryn was officially a one off, a medical mystery, totally unique, one in seven billion. It was a badge he wore with pride. While I was worrying about the unknown, Deryn was relishing his newfound individuality.

'So there are doctors all over the world who know my name?' Deryn asked Dr Mike.

'I'm afraid not,' he said. 'We couldn't use your real name so you are known as Patient X. But yes,' Dr Mike added with a grin. 'Your tonsils are very well known throughout the medical world.'

Deryn needed a cannula fitted so that the nurses in the nuclear medicine unit could inject his veins with an irradiated substance that would allow them to pinpoint any areas of cancer throughout his body.

A radiologist arrived to take blood so that Deryn's sugar levels could be tested. She returned wearing a lead apron to protect her from exposure to the radioactive materials she would be handling. Deryn and I watched with fascination as she placed a metal box on the table and carefully opened the lid. Inside lay a large syringe containing what looked like thick treacle.

With a syringe of saline in one hand, to help the 'treacle' pass through Deryn's veins, and the syringe of the black liquid in the other, the nurse asked Deryn to look away while she injected him.

'Now Deryn, you mustn't talk for at least 90 minutes because your vocal chords might try to use the fluid and this may inadvertently show them up as cancer cells and then the ENT surgeon might whip them out,' she told him jovially.

'What exactly was in that syringe?' I asked the nurse.

'Irradiated glucose,' she answered. 'Our functioning organs

use glucose in a similar way to how cancer cells use it, however it's very different from how all of our other cells use it.

'The scan will pick up where all of the glucose has headed. The heart, lungs and other organs will show up as dark areas but nowhere else should. If there are dark areas elsewhere, this would suggest that there are cancer cells hard at work,' she explained.

'Glucose? As in sugar?' I asked.

'Yes, just like normal sugar,' she explained, handing me a small device. 'Sugar feeds cancer quicker than anything else. It is a cancer cell's favourite form of energy. Without glucose, a cancer cell cannot function.

'This is a Geiger counter,' she continued. 'You need to keep this on you and if the number starts to increase, you must move away from Deryn. I will be back in about 90 minutes and please, Deryn, no talking.'

We sat there in silence for 90 minutes with me staring at the Geiger counter to see if the number was increasing. If it was unsafe for me to be too near Deryn, what on earth would that stuff do to him?

The thought of him being injected with yet another dangerous substance made me feel sick but there was nothing I could do. And maybe, just maybe, it would help to kick cancer to the kerb.

Deryn clicked his fingers at me from time to time to get my attention, before acting out some request that he had in a very one-sided game of charades. It was quite amusing and helped us pass the time.

After what felt like a lifetime in that tiny room, it was time for the PET scan.

'Come on then, Deryn, let's go ride that funky Polo mint!' I laughed. This was a nickname we had come up with for the large, white, circular scanner.

Deryn shot me a grin before climbing on to the rigid table in readiness and I left to wait outside the room. Mike had told us that once the scan results came back, the team would hold a meeting to discuss the best way to proceed.

At home, Deryn went straight to his room, delighted by the instruction to avoid his little brother for six hours while he was still full of radiation.

We joked about how he might turn into the Incredible Hulk overnight or end up with a permanent Ready Brek glow – I had to make light of it because the idea of harmful radiation coursing through Deryn's damaged body that could also harm Dylan from a distance was too much to take in.

It was only when I was back at home making dinner that the radiologist's explanation fully registered with me. I played it back through my mind, over and over, to make sure that I had heard her correctly.

'Sugar feeds cancer quicker than anything else. It is a cancer cell's favourite form of energy. Without glucose, a cancer cell cannot function.'

Without glucose a cancer cell cannot function…

On top of the fridge was a colossal, now almost empty, tub of Maxijul, a food and energy supplement that I had been giving to Deryn in everything he consumed during the months leading up to his throat problems. The hospital dietician had prescribed it to help Deryn put on a few much-needed kilos in weight.

Tears welled up in my eyes as I turned the tub around to read the ingredients on the label.

There it was in black and white on the back of the container. Ingredients: 100% glucose.

Chapter 21

THAT EVENING, AFTER SIMON WENT TO BED, I STARTED RESEARCHING glucose and its effects on cancer. I felt so ashamed that I might have contributed in some way to Deryn's disease. To my horror, I discovered that what the radiologist had told me was accurate.

I had been giving Deryn seven or eight scoops of Maxijul in every drink and meal, in the hope that it might build him up a bit. What had I done? Had I fed the cancer?

And why did a radiologist know that glucose feeds cancer quicker than anything else yet a dietician on a children's oncology ward was prescribing a supplement that was 100% glucose? I'd been told that diet had absolutely nothing to do with cancer but this new information seemed to contradict that.

If sugar feeds cancer quicker than anything else and without it, cancer cells can't function then surely sugar was the absolute antithesis of what I should be giving my cancer-fighting son?

I felt utterly lost, confused and overwhelmed. I tossed and turned all night long, haunted by the radiologist's words. I was reeling with guilt but I knew I had to let it go. Everything I had done up until that day, I'd done with the best of intentions. I couldn't blame myself for something I'd had no prior knowledge of.

Now that I knew better, it was easy to stop buying sweets, chocolate and sugary drinks. I had always been proud of the efforts I'd made to regulate the boys' sugar intake and now I had the best reason to impose certain restrictions.

I started buying sugar-free drinks and checking the labels on processed foods for hidden sugar. To support Deryn, I decided all of us would have to stop consuming these foods. It was a superhuman challenge for Simon as he was a sugar addict, but he was keen to do whatever he could to help.

Meanwhile, I found myself hoping and praying that the cancer was localised to Deryn's throat. How did it become normal to hope that my son only had cancer in his throat?

A few days later, the ENT surgeon and two of Deryn's oncology consultants got together to discuss the outcome of the latest scan and what course of action should be taken. Simon called Addenbrooke's and one of the team read him the transcript from the meeting over the phone.

I stood nearby, trying my hardest to decipher the news from Simon's expression.

'So, has it spread?' I heard him ask eventually.

I saw Simon's shoulders drop as he sighed with relief. He knew how worried I was and he was kind enough to put me out of my misery.

'There is NO activity anywhere else in his body,' he announced with a smile.

The relief was palpable. A localised cancer we could deal with. The scans revealed that there was activity in the area of the right tonsil, where the ulcer was situated. However, because there may have been an infection in the area, they concluded that they would wait for the ENT surgeon to remove some more tissue for further analysis.

❖

Deryn couldn't be operated on until the beginning of October, which gave the boys a little more time to enjoy themselves. They had just gone back to school but we whipped them out for a trip to Disneyland Paris.

The boys had a wonderful time. The two-day adventure

passed in a blur of fantastic food, stomach churning rides, warm sunshine, great company and many memories. They made friends with other families in a similar position and – flying in the face of my new clean-eating family-food regime – they all developed an addiction to pain au chocolate.

While Simon and the boys were making their way to France thanks to the Leukaemia and Lymphoma research charity, I was making good use of the time to pursue my own path and I headed to Grantham Barracks in Lincolnshire to start a fortnight of TA training, after which I would be a fully fledged army reservist.

I made it known to my corporal that I needed to be in a position to take a phone call at any time and asked if I could give Simon his number. But it was clear from day one that I wasn't going to get much sympathy from him.

'What makes you so special, Blackwell?' he sniped.

I had tried to avoid the whole platoon hearing my request but my corporal wanted an explanation.

'My eldest son has recently been diagnosed with cancer for the second time and I am waiting to hear what course of treatment they plan to put him through,' I told him.

There was silence. He wrote down his number and handed it to me.

The two weeks of training was fun, demanding, terrifying, painful and – above all – hugely rewarding. The family came to my passing-out parade and I felt incredibly proud that I had made it.

Back in Norfolk, the boys had returned to school and Simon had started his nursing course at college. I would have to catch up, having missed the start of my course,

We arranged for the boys to go to the school breakfast club every morning so Simon and I could go to college and be back in time to pick them up. My TA career was mainly focused on one or two weekends a month and now that I had qualified, my commitment was just 23 days a year which was manageable.

Life was continuing at full pelt, as normally as possible in the circumstances.

❖

Deryn, meanwhile, was relishing the chance to hang out with his friends and ride his BMX. He was so happy to be able to lead a normal life again in between chemotherapy treatments.

At his next infusion, in the waiting room we bumped into Dawson, Deryn's sailing partner from the Ellen MacArthur trip. Unfortunately, Dawson had relapsed and needed a bone marrow transplant. He was a shell of the exuberant boy we'd last seen two years earlier. He was incredibly thin and fragile, had a nose tube inserted and was still suffering side effects from the operation many months later.

Being confronted by such a dramatic change in Dawson's appearance made the very idea of a bone marrow transplant frightening to me. I prayed that Deryn wouldn't need one. Tiegan had passed away just after her transplant and to see Dawson looking so frail following his operation was a huge worry.

Like Deryn, though, Dawson still possessed a wicked sense of humour. The boys found some dressing up clothes and promptly put them on, prancing about like something out of *Harry Potter*. No matter how harsh the treatment these boys went through, it couldn't strip them of who they really were. It might change their appearance and damage their insides but their inspirational light always shone through and Dawson's light was blinding.

❖

The date for Deryn's surgery arrived and the ENT surgeon told us he planned to take away more of Deryn's throat tissue in the hope of eliminating any remaining cancer as well as the possibility of it spreading further.

But while I was dreading this – we knew that the pain and discomfort would be even worse than the tonsillectomy – Deryn was trying not to dwell on it and concentrated instead on getting the rest of the cancer out of his body. I took a few days off college so that I could stay in hospital with Deryn and he was given a bed on the children's general surgery ward, C3, instead of C2, where no bed was available.

The surgeon explained that it would be tricky to cut out a lot of the tissue from the back of the throat so he planned to focus on the right side of the throat and the small area to the left with visible ulcerations. Hopefully, this wouldn't affect Deryn's speech or ability to swallow, nor be too disfiguring.

Deryn was concerned about the pain afterwards – and there was no getting away from the fact that this was more invasive surgery than before, which would mean an increase in pain and recuperation time.

'We'll make sure you have enough pain relief to see you through, so please try not to worry too much,' the surgeon reassured Deryn. 'Do you have any more questions?'

'Just one,' he said. 'Can we please hurry up and get on with it?'

While he was waiting for his op, a young teenager called Max was ushered into the next cubicle. His leg was in plaster and Max's mother hurriedly pulled the curtains across, which was fine by me as we would often keep the curtains drawn between beds for privacy. However, there was usually at least a polite 'Hello' or similar acknowledgement.

I could hear Max's mother on her mobile phone telling friends and family that Max had fallen off his bike and now needed surgery to fix his broken leg. Within an hour or so, Max had his first visitors and his mother greeted them with tears. I was mindful of the fact that what is normal for the spider is chaos for the fly but as the day wore on, I found myself getting more and more frustrated and upset.

'Poor Max is supposed to be going out with his friends on his bike at the weekend,' I heard her say. 'I just feel so sad that he isn't going to be able to have a normal, happy life for the next few weeks. Life is so unfair. Why did this have to happen?'

I understood that Max wanted to be out with his mates and it was sad that he wouldn't be able to ride his bike for a few weeks but I found this mum's 'woe is me' attitude insulting. I had to fight the urge to take her by the hand and lead her across the corridor to C2 where she would see just how unfair life could be.

The porters arrived to take Deryn into theatre and I accompanied him. I was full of trepidation as I walked towards the recovery ward an hour or so later, dreading what kind of pain he would be in. To my delight, Deryn was sitting up in bed, smiling and making polite requests for food. Just like old times.

'Can I have sausage, chips and beans, please?' he asked.

I shone a little torch into his mouth. The surgeon had used heat to cauterise the wounds and the entire back of his throat was burnt. It was the most brutal-looking laceration I had ever seen but it didn't seem to be causing Deryn too much pain, and was certainly not enough to put him off eating.

'Can I take a picture of your throat, Deryn, I want to show it to your dad?' I asked.

Deryn chuckled and nodded. He was used to my strange requests as I had been taking pictures and videos to document his journey since diagnosis.

Back on C3, Max and his mother had yet more visitors. In our absence, another young couple had arrived with a two-year-old boy with a cleft lip. I gave the little boy a wave and his mum prompted him to wave back.

Within a few minutes, the ENT surgeon came back to see Deryn and tell us how well the surgery had gone. I noticed that next door, Max's mum fell silent once the surgeon started to go into detail about Deryn's operation.

'I managed to remove all of the cancer in Deryn's throat,' he said with a smile, 'but it wasn't easy and I also had to take out a reasonable amount of the soft palate at the back, more than expected.'

He added that you could now fit a golf ball into each wound, which went back as far as the muscle in Deryn's throat. Part of the roof of his mouth was also missing, leaving a gap for food to accidentally slip through into his nose.

'Am I going to have any problems eating?' Deryn interjected, anxious to tuck into his first post-op meal as soon as possible.

'You can eat, Deryn, if you feel up to it,' the surgeon replied. 'Just take it easy and don't eat anything that may irritate the wounds. And in the nicest way possible, I really hope I don't see you again.'

The cubicle next door remained silent. The young mum opposite apologised for listening in and started to tell me about her son. He had been born not only with a cleft lip but also a cleft palate and the majority of the roof of his mouth was missing. He was 18 months old and was about to undergo surgery number five.

She talked me through some of the difficulties they had experienced in terms of eating and drinking, giving me a valuable insight into what may loom for Deryn.

'I can't even remember the number of times I've been feeding him milk and the milk has started to pour out of his nose,' she revealed. 'It was frightening at first but after a while it becomes funny and then it's just a nuisance.'

She and I shared a matter-of-fact approach which comes from living with a child with a serious condition over a long period of time. It becomes your life and you can't operate at a highly emotional, charged level every day without giving yourself a nervous breakdown. Our conversation was interrupted by a nurse who arrived to take the little boy down to surgery. I wished him good luck as they wheeled him out of the ward.

I felt a pang of guilt that Max's mother had overheard our entire conversation but there were lessons here for us both. I had to learn not to take offence at things that had absolutely nothing to do with me and I hoped she had learned that things could always be worse.

Deryn could not hide his glee when we were told there was a bed free on C2.

'Yaaaay – going back to my people,' he laughed as he was pushed down the corridor. He made short work of his sausage, chips and beans – a rare treat since our healthy food regime kicked in – and we bumped into Dr Mike.

'Hi Deryn, you're looking very well. When are you having your surgery?' Dr Mike asked.

'I've already had it, Mike – would you like to see?' Deryn asked, opening his mouth as wide as he could. Dr Mike recoiled in horror while Deryn could only laugh at his reaction.

'You're a doctor, Mike, how can you be grossed out?' he grinned.

'I deal with blood, Deryn, not things like this!' Mike answered with a laugh.

All of a sudden, Deryn started to snort and coughed a whole chip into his hand. Without missing a beat, he popped it back into his mouth and ate it, causing Dr Mike to go into meltdown.

Deryn's infectious laughter rang out through the corridor. It was a beautiful moment.

Chapter 22

Deryn's remarkable chip trick prompted Dr Mike to fill us in on a possible treatment plan following in-depth discussions with the world's leading oncologists, all of whom were fascinated by his unique case.

A lot was riding on whether or not the ulcers were cancerous and whether they too were Langerhans cell sarcoma. Dr Mike assured us that everyone was keen to get something started for Deryn but that his team would first need to establish whether this was, in fact, a relapse rather than a secondary cancer as first thought.

When leukaemia relapses, it tends to show itself in the same form. Very rarely, it can return in a different form. LCS is so closely linked to the bone marrow that Deryn's doctors felt this may be what was happening.

An emergency plan was put in place as the team felt it was too dangerous to simply carry on as before. Maintenance was to cease and intensive chemotherapy with a different drug that treated leukaemia as well as sarcoma would start with immediate effect. It was a completely experimental treatment regime and nobody knew for sure if it would work.

My heart sank. I had hoped that Deryn would simply carry on his ALL treatment, with some radiotherapy added in for good measure. The notion of more intensive chemotherapy filled me with sadness that my poor son was going to have to go through the horrors of toxic drugs all over again.

An ultrasound would determine whether or not the veins in

his neck were viable enough to put in another Hickman line – yes, it was coming back. Fortunately, Deryn had amazing veins so there was no issue.

The following morning, I woke up in Addenbrooke's – on my 33rd birthday. I couldn't resist a joke about whether birthdays in hospital really counted... could I not just keep saying I was 30?

A friend suggested that I set up a Facebook page to document Deryn's treatment. She made a very good point that as his cancer was so rare, Facebook had far more reach than my blog and more people would be able to find out about Deryn and his progress.

My friend also recommended that we sell wristbands to raise awareness of LCS as well as raising some much needed funds for ourselves. Times were going to get more difficult financially and wristbands were a great way to raise money. I felt apprehensive about taking money from people but my friend pointed out that I would be selling something rather than just asking for donations.

'People want to help you, Callie, please let them,' she insisted.

I agreed to going on Facebook; the wristband idea was something we could implement in the future. Another friend, Jen Haigh, came up with the genius idea of incorporating Deryn's name into the page. And so the DoEveRYthiNg Facebook page started, which led to us expanding it into a charity.

Deryn loved the idea. We had spoken about using our experiences to help others. Hopefully, DoEveRYthiNg would grow into something big in time but for the foreseeable future, we had to concentrate on Deryn and what he was about to face.

I went to see Dr Mike alone to find out more about the proposed treatment plan. As soon as he looked across the desk at me, I could tell by his face that this wasn't going to be good news. We knew each other well enough to be open and frank with one another.

The histology report on Deryn's throat tissue indicated that, as the team had suspected, this was in fact a relapse and not a secondary cancer after all. The ulcerations were indeed cancerous. On a genetic level, the cells also shared some strong similarities with the original cells present when Deryn was first diagnosed with leukaemia.

I felt dizzy with panic. Yet again, life was going to be a rollercoaster of hospital stays and nasty side effects, with unknown twists and turns along the way. However, my biggest fear was that Deryn would be put forward for a bone marrow transplant. This was the big bad wolf of cancer treatment, another level altogether.

I was terrified. I thought about Tiegan. Her relapse had also presented in a different way, in the form of a lump, and the transplant couldn't save her. What if the same happened to Deryn? Then I heard the words and it was real, there was no going back and there was no way to pretend that this wasn't happening.

'We have opted to give Deryn a bone marrow transplant,' Dr Mike said gravely. It sounded as if he, too, would have preferred to avoid this outcome.

'This means that Deryn will undergo intensive chemotherapy but this time, there will be no breaks for at least 14 weeks. If a donor can be located after the treatment period, Deryn will be transferred to Bristol Children's Hospital where he will be prepared for the transplant.'

Dr Mike explained the procedure in more detail. They would effectively strip Deryn's bone marrow away to make room for replacement tissue. The 14 weeks of intensive chemo and further 12 days of chemotherapy and radiotherapy were required to kill off all of his bone marrow. If they left any behind, the rogue cells could overpower the newly donated tissue and the transplant would fail.

The worst-case scenario was laid out for us: Deryn might have to stay in Bristol for up to five months, depending on how well he responded to treatment and whether or not he picked up any infections. Much of this time would be spent in total isolation as even a tiny bug could be potentially fatal.

Ideally, they would have liked a sibling to donate the marrow but as Dylan was not Deryn's full brother, he wasn't a suitable match. The next best chance of success was marrow from a totally unrelated person, requiring a search through the national database. If they couldn't find a suitable donor in a reasonable time frame, I would be the last resort.

I was reeling with sadness about the prospect of Deryn enduring further pain, sickness and lethargy. I didn't want him to have the transplant, I wanted them to leave him alone. The leukaemia hadn't returned in its original form and the cancer had been cut out of his throat. Was there really any need for this?

On the other hand, how do you tell a highly qualified oncology team that you don't want your child to have a particular treatment regime if that is his best chance of pulling through? I was in no position to argue.

In the early days of Deryn's treatment – having heard about the vile side effects and long-term damage chemotherapy can wreak – I'd asked what would happen if I said no to any of the drugs or therapies. The answer wasn't what I expected to hear.

'Unfortunately Mrs Blackwell, if you say no to treatment of any kind, Deryn will be made a ward of court and the treatment will be carried out in your absence,' a doctor told me. 'It is much better for your son that you are there beside him, supporting him while he goes through this.'

My hands were tied. Even if there was another, less invasive way forward, I had no choice or say in the matter. I was mindful of that conversation as Dr Mike was telling me about the transplant procedure.

I had to ask the question.

'Do we have a choice about the transplant?'

'Yes, you do,' Dr Mike answered, to my surprise.

I shared my fears with him. Would I be taking Deryn to Bristol as a healthy looking boy only to bring him back a mere ghost of his former self? What if I couldn't bring him home at all?

Dr Mike explained that while there was a risk, the working relationship between Bristol and Addenbrooke's was fantastic and complications and problems were extremely rare.

'Please don't use the R word when talking about Deryn,' I added with a rueful smile. 'You know he doesn't ever like to do things the easy way.'

Dr Mike was doing his best to put my mind at rest but I needed to discuss everything with Deryn and Simon before we committed to it.

I called Simon, who listened intently as I relayed everything to him.

'What should we do?' I asked him.

Simon's view was that Deryn needed to make the decision and Deryn alone. He was right, of course. While the procedure would have a massive impact on us all, Deryn should be the one in the driving seat.

My heart was in my mouth at the thought of breaking the news of the transplant to him. I talked him through all the options, including the possibility of saying no, and asked if he wanted to go through with it. Deryn answered without hesitation.

'I haven't lost anything yet, have I? I'm very competitive and I don't intend to lose this either. If I don't try then I'll never know, will I?'

I was amazed and humbled by my son every day but this was beyond what I'd expected. He really was the most amazing person I had ever met. Nothing fazed him, he seemed fearless.

I wished I could be more like him.

❖

The day arrived for the Hickman line to be inserted and Deryn was keen to get it over with as quickly as possible. As the anaesthetist was preparing to cannulate Deryn so that they could put him under, Deryn started issuing instructions.

'Not this vein, or this one,' he said, pointing to two blue lines on the back of his hand. 'This one is better and I think you'll find that it also bleeds back much better than the others.'

'Remind me again why we can't go into the peripheral vein on the inside of your arm, Deryn', asked one of the anaesthetists politely.

'Because I have Tourette's and one of my tics is to quickly bend my elbows,' he explained patiently. 'As soon as there is a cannula in there, the tic comes back and I can't control it.'

The anaesthetist accepted his reasoning and said that they would go into the back of his hand as usual. A trainee would be performing the procedure. Deryn didn't mind, he knew that trainees had to learn somehow and was always open to helping students but being as knowledgeable as he was about his body, he wasn't afraid to offer up some guidance either.

'I've told you which veins work and which one's don't work, so go for this one here, please,' he said with a note of authority in his voice. This seemed to make the trainee rather nervous.

'I prefer the look of this vein Deryn,' he said sheepishly. 'Is it okay if I try this one?'

Deryn didn't mind being a guinea pig but he certainly wasn't going to put himself through unnecessary pain for the sake of some training.

'It won't work, I'm telling you,' he insisted. 'You need to go for this one here.' This time Deryn's tone was more agitated as he pointed out the fleshy blue vein on the side of his hand.

I knew Deryn was right; the veins on the back of his hands had been scarred from so much access that they barely worked any longer – it was the big one that ran just under the thumb that they needed to get to. However, the trainee decided against Deryn's advice and went for the back of his hand. No sooner was the cannula in than the vein collapsed, causing a nasty stinging sensation.

'I bloody told you!' Deryn blurted out angrily.

The poor trainee looked devastated and immediately apologised. I felt for him but couldn't help thinking that when a patient as seasoned as Deryn tells you which vein to access, maybe you should just listen to them. One of the other anaesthetists stepped in and quickly and successfully accessed the preferred vein. There was no harm done and Deryn recovered his composure before slipping under.

Now that we knew what the treatment plan would be, it became blindingly obvious that it wasn't feasible for both Simon and me to continue our nursing training. We had to decide which one of us was going to give it up.

Neither of us wanted to deprive the other: I wanted Simon to have the chance of a career I knew he would excel at while Simon wanted me to have the same opportunity. After discussing it endlessly, Simon pointed out that as I was also training as a medic in the TA, it was better for me to carry on as it would complement my army career. I wasn't comfortable with the idea of him stepping aside for me but he was insistent.

We arranged that I would spend every Monday to Thursday at college while Simon would be at hospital with Deryn. Then we would swap over and I would stay at the hospital until Sunday night. Dylan would be at school and I wouldn't be able to see him at weekends but with two boys to care for who were five hours' drive from each other, it seemed like the most sensible way forward.

❖

The intensive chemotherapy was booked in, and rather than wait for the distressing moment when his hair would start falling out, Deryn asked me if I would shave it all off in advance. He was sick of watching it fall out in clumps every time he moved his head.

'Tell you what, Mum,' he said with a huge grin as he had one of his brainwaves. 'You can do mine if I can do yours!'

'All right then,' I sighed, watching him brandish the clippers. 'Why not?'

I was eager to do whatever I could to make this less frightening and more doable. I'd had my own hair trauma in 2007, when I suffered alopecia as a result of taking slimming pills. I was clinically obese at the time and opted for the easy way to lose weight. But losing 90% of my hair for over two years was enough to see me shed my excess weight without any further need of pills and potions.

Saying yes was easy; it was only hair, after all, and although my hair was my defining feature, I wasn't sad to see it go. If Deryn could lose his hair umpteen times and not be bothered, what was I worried about?

I shaved Deryn's head and then it was my turn. Deryn couldn't disguise his excitement, digging the clippers in enthusiastically as he tried to find the right angle. I felt as though I was being scalped. Deryn was doubled over with laughter as I made whimpering sounds each time he touched me with the clippers.

Actually, it didn't hurt much but knowing that I was making Deryn laugh was more than enough reward for me to keep up the pretence of being terrified. I didn't get to hear that beautiful belly laugh very often. Shaving your head is liberating. I would recommend it to everyone. Just the once…

I'd arranged for some of our dearest friends and family members to go out for a Chinese meal in Norwich. Deryn loved Chinese food and the fact that this was an all-you-can-eat buffet made it a million times better.

'I'm going to eat myself into a coma before they lock me away in a room on my own for months on end,' Deryn joked as he went up for his first round.

He made the most of it and, five plates later, was fit to pop.

'I won't need to eat hospital food for at least a week now,' he announced cheerfully.

I could feel so much love in the restaurant that evening and as I thanked everyone for making the effort to come to Deryn's 'last supper' for a while, it occurred to me that this really could be his last experience of a normal life.

We were heading into the unknown yet again. No matter how many times we made that journey, it didn't get any easier. As we drove home along the quiet country lanes out of the city, Simon and I chatted about how we were going to keep all the balls in the air. Our lives felt like a game of pick up sticks… no sooner had we picked up the sticks than they were tossed violently into the air again.

'It's not going to be easy,' I said, trying to fight the feeling of despair that threatened to engulf me.

'Hey, it's no fun if it's easy,' Simon replied with a wink.

Chapter 23

THE CHANCE OF DERYN COMING HOME DURING HIS 14-WEEK intensive chemotherapy period in hospital was incredibly slim – everything depended on how well he reacted to the new regime. We hoped that by Christmas, he might be allowed home for a couple of days but, if not, the highly festive C2 was a worthy alternative.

While Deryn was being checked over, I asked the doctor whether they planned to adapt a well-known regime or play it all by ear.

'There is no protocol for this situation so we will be using experimental treatments,' he explained. 'We don't know how much chemotherapy it will take to treat Deryn's types of cancers so we have decided to give him everything we can without killing him.'

It really was going to be all or nothing.

A nurse was waiting in the treatment room and Deryn hopped on to the bed and lifted his T shirt to reveal his brand new Hickman line. He lay there, twiddling the line between his fingers like he didn't have a care in the world until he noticed the bag of liquid on the nurse's trolley.

Deryn had been given some funky coloured drugs in his time – the first chemotherapy drug he had was a burnt-orange colour – but this one was a vivid, bright blue, reminding me of those vibrant slush puppies I'd drunk as a kid. Nothing wholesome or good ever came in shades like that.

'Whoa! Look at the colour of it!' Deryn gasped. There was no fear, only bemusement.

It was very odd to see the nurse hooking Deryn back up to an infusion via a Hickman line. It felt like such a long time ago that he'd been hooked up to anything and I had gotten used to seeing him without any restrictions or lines poking out of his skin. Watching the infusion start and seeing the bright blue liquid dripping down into the transparent line felt surreal to me. Deryn, on the other hand, seemed totally unbothered by it all.

'It's happening so we've just got to get on with it,' he shrugged, as the nurse cleared away the packaging.

I followed Deryn as he pushed his robot into the waiting area, walking as if in a daze. Then I spotted Dawson and his mum Cheryl, who had arrived for a check-up. We hadn't seen Dawson since getting the news that Deryn would have a transplant and seeing his face immediately lifted my spirits. If anyone would be able to tell me exactly what to expect for the next few months, it would be Cheryl.

Leaving the boys to catch up together, Cheryl and I talked in great depth about Deryn's upcoming bone marrow transplant.

'It's not going to be easy but Deryn is tough like Dawson, and he'll be just fine,' she said, patting my hand. 'And you're strong so you'll be okay too.'

Cheryl gave me some wonderful hints and practical tips to prepare us and help things go smoothly.

'Take a big plastic box with all of Deryn's stuff in it,' she advised. 'You have to wash and tumble dry all of his clothes and put them in individual plastic bags to guard against contamination. I use resealable freezer bags and roll the clothes because that gives you more space – and trust me, you don't get a lot of space in a bone marrow transplant ward.

'Take some slipper socks, too, they come in handy as you have to take your shoes off and it's nice to have something to put on,'

Cheryl continued as I wrote each nugget of wisdom in a notebook.

She urged us to take in DVDs, books, games and a PlayStation to keep Deryn occupied. Everything had to be wiped down or washed and nothing would be allowed into the BMT room unless it was spotlessly clean. If it couldn't be cleaned, it wouldn't be admitted.

'And laminate some pictures to put up on the wall,' Cheryl added. 'They really helped Dawson when times got hard.'

Last but not least, she told me to take care of myself. It might have been Deryn going through it but it wasn't going to be plain sailing for any of us. Just then, Deryn came bounding over, robot and Dawson in tow with a massive grin on his face.

'Mum, come with me, you need to see this!' he beamed as he led me to the lavatory. 'What does blue and yellow make?'

'Green,' I answered hesitantly.

'Yeah, well look at what that blue stuff has done to my wee!' Deryn chuckled, pointing down the loo.

Sure enough, the water was now a vibrant shade of green. Cheryl and I looked at each other.

'You're both going to be okay,' she said with a reassuring smile.

The infusion finished and once Dawson had had his check up, we said our goodbyes and headed to the car to get Deryn's things. Simon and Dylan came to help carry virtually the entire contents of Deryn's room to his new home on the ward. Duvets, pillows, DVDs, teddy bears… it was going to be cosy.

'Well if I'm going to be here for over three months, I might as well make myself at home,' Deryn laughed as we struggled up the corridor with all our things.

The nurses welcomed Deryn back with open arms and showed him to his room. Simon and Dylan said their goodbyes and left

– for the next few months, Simon and I would only see each other on a Sunday night and a Thursday afternoon.

As a now unfamiliar face on C2, I was offered advice by other parents who had been there for some time. They had no idea that I was a seasoned oncology mum who knew the ward as well as I knew my own home. It was encouraging to see that nothing had changed and although the people were new, the old camaraderie was alive and kicking.

That first week was very tough on all of us but our friends rallied around, making the whole shift a little more bearable. Some looked after Dylan while others sold wristbands on our behalf. A few mentioned arranging fundraising events to help. Their generosity and that of strangers who didn't even know us was heartwarming and overwhelming. Without their support and input, life would have been very much harder. Thank you didn't seem to cut it.

However, a fellow oncology parent made it clear how disgusted she was at the fact that we were accepting help from friends and well wishers. She was very vocal about how it was our job to provide everything for Deryn and not go sponging off our friends. I didn't know anyone else who shared her opinion but her words taunted me on a daily basis, nonetheless.

A few days after Deryn's admission, a woman I knew vaguely approached me in the supermarket aisle. After swapping pleasantries, she pushed a £20 note into my hand.

'Do whatever you need to do with that my love, I just wish I could do more to help you all,' she said as I stood there, lost for words. I told her that I couldn't possibly accept the money but she insisted I take it. It was almost as if she could read my mind.

'I don't mind what you spend it on, my dear – go and get your nails done if you like – it's for you to make your life a little bit more bearable. I think you deserve a bit of a treat.'

CHAPTER 23

Her words and extraordinary gesture allowed me to feel so much better about accepting the help that so many of our friends wanted to give us.

'One day,' I thought, 'I will treat myself to a manicure.'

❖

So began the new regime, with different drugs and renewed hope that everything would go to plan.

Deryn was obsessed with all things scientific and we filled our days writing essays, drawing diagrams of electrons and wading through the books he had brought in to keep himself occupied and his studies up to speed. Before long, my head was spinning with organelles, transmission electron microscopes and analysing onion skin at close quarters.

When Deryn was asked if he'd like to share a room with another lad of his age on C2, he jumped at the chance. The pair of them spent hours enthusiastically putting up posters and customising the clinical-looking room to look more like a typical teenager's bedroom. Both boys had a games console and the nurses managed to find a huge TV for them to play on.

It was wonderful to see Deryn in his element and also share a chat and a laugh with another parent. Each evening, we would sit and have a good chinwag while the lads played games or watched DVDs. It was a very special time and we all bonded.

A month or so into treatment, Deryn picked up a bug and had to be put into an isolation room away from everyone else for a couple of weeks. Being hidden away at the back of the ward and left undisturbed had its advantages: Deryn spent his days watching *The Big Bang Theory* and I was able to concentrate on my studies.

To alleviate his boredom, he created a wishlist on an internet shopping site, browsing through books, DVDs and games and adding all the things he liked the look of. The idea was that people could look it up and send things to him in hospital. I was horrified as well as concerned about how greedy or spoilt he might look.

'Deryn, you can't just put everything you want on there!' I chided, flabbergasted at the sheer amount of things he had listed.

'I don't expect anyone to buy anything off this list, Mum,' he retorted. 'It's a wishlist so I'm just putting on things that I wish for. I'm just dreaming.'

Who was I to stop him?

Our routine over the ensuing weeks varied very little. Simon and I would swap shifts on Thursdays and Sundays, grabbing a quick coffee and a catch-up chat together about how Deryn was progressing before going our separate ways. I was trying to focus on my college studies as well as make time for Dylan, who would come and see his brother once a week on a Thursday when Simon and I did our handover. We were like ships passing in the night.

The oncology team was keen to put Deryn back on a drug combination of PEG-asparaginase and dexamethasone – the same drugs which had caused him to contract pancreatitis and suffer a dramatic two-stone weight loss.

I was vehemently against the idea and shared my concerns with the consultant – but he stopped me in my tracks.

'The last time Deryn developed pancreatitis, it was a 1 in 500 chance, and for him to suffer the same consequences again would be 1 in 1,000 chance,' he said. 'It's not very likely and we feel it is worth the risk.'

'You are aware that this is Deryn we're talking about,' I said, trying to remain calm. 'The chances of him having the two cancers he has is 1 in 7 billion so those odds don't mean anything to me.'

The course went ahead and, as I had feared, within a couple of days, Deryn was once again in agony with acute pancreatitis, leading to two weeks of nil-by-mouth and sudden weight loss. To stabilise his weight, he was placed on total parenteral nutrition, a form of liquid feeding containing vitamins, minerals, glucose, salts and amino acids which fulfilled his daily requirements and bypassed his stomach straight into his bloodstream.

Carrying an increased risk of kidney and liver damage, it was a short-term solution I was not thrilled about, but at least the pancreatitis deemed this particular drug combination no longer worth the risk and to our relief, the next course was crossed off the flow chart.

Deryn's nasogastric feeding tube needed replacing whenever he was sick so the team thought it would be a better idea to replace it with a much longer nasojejunal tube, which would bypass his stomach and go straight into the intestines. Deryn was not amused.

'I wish you'd have a tube put in, Mum, so you know what it feels like,' he told me one day. Simon had been brave enough to have one fitted to help him understand how Deryn felt but I was quite happy not knowing, I could imagine just how awful it was and didn't need to go to that extreme to empathise with him.

This time around the large doses of regular chemotherapy were hitting Deryn much harder. He couldn't eat much and even when he was in the mood for food, his mouth was so sore that he couldn't face the pain and discomfort. Despite this, he meekly accepted everything that was happening, telling me there was no point in him fighting against the unpleasant treatments and side effects.

Many times, I just wanted to cry but Deryn's courage and acceptance didn't allow me to weep or complain. Instead, I threw myself into my studies, wishing the next few months away.

❖

As Christmas approached, Deryn was pretty much confined to the ward. We did manage to fit in one last hurrah, a cheeky visit to Nando's and a game of bowling, before Deryn became too ill to leave his room. He was placed on methotrexate, a drug which caused terrible ulcers, and to combat the side effects and possible organ failure, he was also infused with a whopping nine litres of saline.

Within 24 hours, the whole of Deryn's mouth was completely ulcerated and blistered as far down as his throat, making eating and drinking impossible. One evening, blood started pouring from his mouth, the result of all the ulcers bursting simultaneously. His mouth was red raw and full of craters where the ulcers had been.

I felt like a failure for not being able to take the pain away. I would have taken every single blister in my own mouth if I could. I couldn't imagine how much it hurt and this was only the first course of methotrexate; there would be more rounds to come.

The following week was hell on earth: vomiting, diarrhoea, stomach cramps, ulcers, nosebleeds and headaches which crippled Deryn and left him weak and bedbound. He was placed on a drug to treat the fluid build-up caused by the enormous saline dose, which led to bedwetting every few hours. His temperature skyrocketed and he looked like he was going to die.

I couldn't take it any longer. I called in one of his doctors.

'Deryn has no cancer present, is that correct?' I asked.

'Correct.'

'And he is still in remission from leukaemia and all the Langerhans cell sarcoma cells were cut out of his throat. Is that correct?' I continued, fighting back the tears.

'Correct.'

'So what on earth are we doing all of this for, then?' I railed.

'Why are you giving so much chemotherapy to a child who doesn't even have cancer? You are poisoning him and I'm allowing you to do it. I can't allow it anymore. I want to stop the treatment.'

I was distraught and the doctor allowed me to finish my rant before calmly answering my concerns.

'You are right in everything you're saying, Callie,' he said gently. 'We believe that the surgeon removed all of the cancerous cells and yes, the leukaemia hasn't returned.' He continued softly: 'We are not worried about what we can see on the scans or in the blood tests but we are extremely concerned about what we cannot see. This is why we are treating Deryn in this way.'

I slumped back down in the chair. I felt totally despondent. I couldn't even consider stopping any of his treatment because of what may be lurking around out of sight.

Deryn was fast asleep, having been given a very high dose of morphine, and I was alone; trapped and without a choice in the matter, yet again. I couldn't argue with what the doctor told me. He knew what he was talking about. Could I risk stopping any of this if there was even a small chance that cancer may rear its ugly head once more? I was being held hostage by the dreaded C word.

Within 10 days, though, Deryn was back to as normal as he could be. His mouth was still full of ulcers and he knew they would still be a problem by the time his birthday came around.

'No cake for me, then,' he joked feebly. Even he was struggling to see the funny side.

But he was soon distracted from the pain by a few surprises...

Chapter 24

If there was ever a good time for a wish to come true, it was now. One of our friends had asked Deryn for a link to his internet wishlist. Unbeknown to us, she had shared it with all of her friends, who also shared it with their friends.

Pretty much overnight books, DVDs, games and puzzles began arriving at the hospital, often anonymously sent, without messages attached. Deryn was overjoyed and spent his time putting up posters and watching films that kind wellwishers had bought from his list. My only sadness was that I couldn't personally thank each one of these amazing people for brightening up a little boy's life just when he needed it the most.

One of the gifts was a brand new PlayStation. Deryn's was quite old – Simon had won it in a competition several years earlier and Deryn had cheekily put a new one on the list. Neither of us had expected any of his wishlist to materialise, least of all the PlayStation. It was donated by someone called Victor, who instantly became Deryn's hero.

One oncology 'friend', however, was unimpressed that people had been so generous and ranted to a friend of mine about the unfairness of it all. I was astonished that anyone could be jealous of the smattering of good times you might have following a cancer diagnosis.

I could understand it from children, who don't fully understand that the good times are far outweighed by the bad and that children who are critically ill deserve something to look forward to.

I could also understand why some adults didn't get it. I had tried to keep my updates and Facebook posts as upbeat as possible. The raw, horrible things that go on behind closed doors rarely make it as far as the outside world.

My oncology 'friend' had a son who had been diagnosed with ALL at the same time as Deryn and they were the same age. Thankfully, her son hadn't relapsed so, although she had first-hand experience of how awful a cancer diagnosis was, she had no idea how hard it was the second time around.

Jealousy was one of the stranger sides of having a child with cancer. Going sailing, having a Starlight wish and spending time at Barretstown were all wonderful experiences, perks that wouldn't have been possible if Deryn had not been diagnosed with cancer.

I can only say that we would have gladly swapped lives with anyone who begrudged Deryn some small pleasure in what had become a very limited life. No amount of financial help or thoughtful gifts were worth the pain and suffering he was enduring.

❖

We heard about a scheme called Beads of Courage, which rewards critically ill children for enduring different treatments and helps them own their stories of courage.

The idea is simple; for each procedure a child endures, a coloured bead is given to them. At certain points – for instance, when a line is removed or something monumental happens – larger and more vibrant beads are presented. Deryn liked the idea of a keepsake to show all of his procedures at a glance, the only problem being that he'd had so many that it was tricky to backdate them all.

We made some rough calculations and worked out that, so far, Deryn had undergone approximately 1800 separate procedures relating to blood tests, surgeries, bouts of neutropenia and nights in hospital. Everyone deserved a bead and Deryn had almost

2,000 beads owing to him. He would have easily cleaned out the hospital's stock so we decided that for every 100 procedures, he would receive a large, brightly coloured bead instead.

Deryn was very proud of his 18 beads and was already eager to see just how long the string would be once he'd had his bone marrow transplant.

'Can you imagine how many beads I'm going to have after that?' he chuckled. 'Millions, I reckon!'

With some weeks of treatment still to go, my dearest friend Jovan was beavering away trying to arrange a fundraising event at the supermarket she worked at in Watton. Her husband had designed some posters and the people of the town got right behind it. Although Deryn and I were many miles away, the love from our hometown was keenly felt by us both.

Jovan did an amazing job at running the event, which involved volunteers cycling on exercise bikes, raffle prizes, collecting donations in buckets and selling wristbands. We were blown away by everyone's generosity.

We were hoping to take Deryn home for a couple of days to celebrate his 13th birthday but it wasn't looking likely as he was suffering terribly from the effects of methotrexate and wasn't in any fit state to be leaving the hospital.

Within the grounds, however, was a building called Acorn House, which was designed as accommodation for parents of children who were in Addenbrooke's for long term treatment or serious injury. The wonderful staff agreed to allow us to use their kitchen and communal area to throw a surprise party for Deryn. If he couldn't go to his party, we would bring his party to him.

While we carried on with the preparations to celebrate his teen milestone, Deryn was having fun experimenting with what little hair he had left.

He had always had very thick hair and during previous chemo treatments, it had thinned out but never disappeared completely. This time, the more powerful drugs in adult doses were causing his hair to fall out more quickly than before so he and Simon decided to get creative – pulling tufts of his hair out and leaving a smiley face shape on his scalp.

By the time his birthday week dawned, Deryn was sporting a 'bone dome': the smiley face had disappeared and he was a bald as a boiled egg.

A couple of days before his birthday, a huge parcel arrived from America. My friend Kat had held a yard sale and used the proceeds to buy the boys a box of fabulous presents which she shipped over.

Their faces were a picture as they pulled out brightly coloured trainers, slouch beanies, hoodies, belts and stickers galore. Kat hadn't forgotten us, either, sending me a beautiful angel carved from wood with a candle in her hands. The accompanying card contained a message so heartfelt that I shed a tear. I was so lucky to have friends like these.

Deryn wore his trainers nonstop, they became slippers as he wasn't allowed outside. The staff and other patients were full of compliments about how cool they looked and Deryn would proudly announce that they had come all the way from America.

The surprises didn't end there and the day before his birthday, Jovan came over to see us at Acorn House where we were staying in the lead-up to Deryn's surprise party. She arrived with three massive bags and two large balloon sculptures.

I was already overwhelmed but then Jovan dropped the bomb.

'With the money we raised from the fundraiser, we were able to buy you everything else from your wishlist,' she told Deryn happily as she started to pile gifts up on the table in front of him.

Deryn's eyes nearly popped out. There were so many boxes, each wrapped in bright pink paper. For the first time, Deryn was speechless as he tore through each piece of wrapping, reluctantly at first in case he appeared ungrateful, then with growing enthusiasm as he uncovered a treasure trove of DVDs and PlayStation games. It was priceless to watch and we saw the sparkle return to his eyes that we'd feared we might not see again. I felt completely overwhelmed by the generosity and love coming from our hometown. For the first time in a very long while, I felt like part of the community.

Later that evening, Simon and Dylan came over to help make the final arrangements for Deryn's party. It was lovely to have them both there and for the first time in an eternity I was able to share a bedroom with my husband. The rare opportunity to spend longer than 15 minutes with Simon over a cup of coffee twice a week was enough to make me very happy.

The big day arrived and Simon and I started blowing up balloons and cooking the party food we'd bought. Unfortunately, Deryn couldn't manage any breakfast as his mouth was still too sore and ulcerated but there would be all his friends to feed.

We set the large dining table with plates, napkins and copious amounts of confetti as well as party poppers and crackers. Content that everything was perfect, I headed off to the ward to try and get Deryn up and looking half decent before his party guests arrived.

It felt strange to be the mother of a teenager. Time had passed so quickly since Deryn was first diagnosed almost three years before and to me, he still looked like a 10-year-old as the chemotherapy and high dose steroids had stunted his growth.

I wondered again about his chances of having children in the future. It had crossed my mind before and I'd asked the question when Deryn first started chemotherapy but the answers weren't clear cut. Because of Deryn's young age when he'd first started chemo, it would have been impossible to take a sperm donation for his future. Now that he'd been diagnosed again and faced even more treatment at an important stage of his development, the chances of him being able to produce sperm were marginal at best.

Before I got bogged down in negative thoughts, Simon texted to say that Deryn's guests were arriving.

His schoolfriend Kim, who had been spending more and more time with him and had become his girlfriend, was the first there and the three of us made our way to Acorn House. In the hallway, Kim stood behind Deryn and put her hands over his eyes. Walking like this they tentatively made their way into the party room, which was full of balloons, decorations, cake… and friends trying hard not to give the game away.

Kim whipped her hands away and a huge roar of 'Happy Birthday' went up. Deryn beamed from ear to ear, totally blown away by the number of people who had come to celebrate with him.

It had been eight weeks since he'd seen any of his friends apart from Kim and he had a lot of catching up to do. As I watched him chatting away with his friends and showing off his new trainers, I thought back to the day I'd left Chelsea and Westminster Hospital carrying a cumbersome car seat containing a tiny little boy who would change my life in more ways than I could ever imagine. I remembered his first breath, his first cry, the very first time he looked at me, the love I felt for him. I remembered it all.

We were living a life that many parents would describe as their worst nightmare but I could only feel fortunate. I was grateful that he was well enough to enjoy his party, even if he couldn't eat a single morsel of his three birthday cakes.

We made the most of a wonderful few hours with friends and family before waving them off just before lunch so that Deryn could go back to the ward for further chemotherapy infusions.

It wasn't long before he was back in his usual position, bolt upright in bed, attached to a robot, sucking up the WiFi and the drugs.

That night he fell asleep with an enormous smile on his face.

Chapter 25

Two days after Deryn's birthday, he picked up the viral lung infection respiratory syncytial virus. To protect the rest of the kids on the ward, back he went into a single room.

Happily, this proved to be only a minor setback as, otherwise, he was making big leaps. His appetite had returned with a vengeance and he had made friends with three other boys on the ward. When he wasn't confined to his room, he would hang out with them, playing games and kidding around like any other teenager. Seeing him mobile and sociable made me very happy.

The ward was starting to feel very festive. A huge Christmas tree had been beautifully decorated by the parents, homemade robins hung on the wall and we bought a smaller tree for Deryn's room. Kim helped Deryn decorate it with baubles and three small stars which he hung in prime position, each one in memory of his friends on the ward who sadly hadn't made it.

In the doctors' opinion, he had dealt with the latest round of treatment really well and, as he posed no threat to anyone apart from the kids on C2, it was agreed that he could come home for up to three weeks. We were elated. As long as he didn't have any other issues, he would be home for Christmas.

This recuperation period would allow the body some crucial recovery time before the next round of treatment started. He was touching distance away from the end of the 14-week preparation period prior to the bone marrow transplant, a thought which still terrified me.

His temporary discharge could not have been more perfectly

timed. Deryn's high school had arranged a fundraising day for him, and the children and teachers were astonished and thrilled when we arrived with him in tow.

Nine weeks in hospital had given Deryn mobility problems and the muscles in his legs were emaciated and withered. But his friends pulled up a chair for him and spent the whole day entertaining him and keeping him occupied. School friends manned tombola stalls whilst others enjoyed themselves on the inflatable bungee run, they'd even got a DJ playing Deryn's favourite tracks.

The following day, a friend held a bake sale for Deryn and once again, we were reminded of the fantastic support and generosity of our local community. It was an amazing morale boost. Everyone was trying so hard to keep our spirits up, which made it easier to stay positive.

With a boot full of cakes, we pulled up at our house and Deryn, tired from so much excitement, announced that he was feeling cold and shivery. He was still in the car when I whipped the thermometer out and placed it in his ear.

Beep beep. 38.3°C..

'Argh, fuck,' I muttered under my breath. Three weeks had been wishful thinking but we'd assumed that Deryn might last a bit longer than 36 hours.

Operation 'sort it all out' was thrust into action and within 10 minutes, our bags were packed for the night. With no bed available at Addenbrooke's, we were told to take Deryn to the NNUH where he would be stabilised until a bed became free.

I did not want to go back there but we had no choice. Simon had attended a meeting with some of the staff we had complained about a week or two earlier. He received something approaching an apology but with June merely moved to another department so that she wouldn't come into contact with Deryn again, our trust in them was gone and I wondered if we were now known as 'that nightmare family'.

At the hospital the antibiotics were administered quickly and efficiently and I allowed myself to feel confident that things would be okay this time. But it didn't take long for that feeling to evaporate. The senior nurse assigned to Deryn was coming and going from his room without washing her hands. She bumbled about, making silly errors with the machinery and despite the importance of Deryn being barrier-nursed to prevent his infection spreading, she kept leaving the door to his room open.

Over the course of the evening, she made other elementary mistakes, including not clamping the bag of saline effectively so it poured out all over the floor at my feet. It stayed there for an hour until I cleaned it up myself. I was desperate for us to be transferred to Addenbrooke's but with no bed free, we were told we would have to spend the night at NNUH.

At 7am the next morning, a different nurse came in to remove the empty antibiotic fluid bag from the Hickman line, clean the bung and place it back on the line and flush the Hickman. I watched as he turned the machine off and flung the line over the top of the robot stand.

Two female doctors arrived mid-morning to examine Deryn. He moved his Hickman line out of the way for them and a look of horror descended on his face.

'Mum, I don't have a bung,' he yelled.

I felt sick. The nurse had taken Deryn's bung off and left it there, hanging on the end of the antibiotic line for the last three hours. Deryn looked absolutely terrified. We both knew that his actions in leaving Deryn's line open could have potentially fatal consequences, as did the two doctors, who looked equally terrified.

Suddenly, the nurse reappeared with a tray of IV drugs. I

admonished him for leaving Deryn at the mercy of the elements for three hours. He tried to cover his tracks and make light of his mistake, then hurried out and returned with a syringe with saline and a new bung attached having walked through the ward with it unprotected.

I had been told that it was imperative that the line be bled back before administering anything because if there was anything nasty brewing inside the line, it could be drawn out with the blood and not pushed further into the heart.

The nurse used a sterile wipe to thoroughly clean the end of the now open Hickman line, attached the syringe, gave it a twist and quickly flushed the saline down the line before I had a chance to ask what he was doing.

'Oh my God! What the hell have you just done?!' I cried out in horror. 'If there was an infection in Deryn's line from it being open for almost three hours, you have just pushed it into his heart!'

The doctors apologised profusely and told the nurse not to put the new bag of saline on as Deryn would soon be transferred to Addenbrooke's. My relief at finally being able to leave for a safe haven was tempered by Deryn's worried little face.

'I knew something bad was going to happen,' he said quietly. 'I don't feel safe here.'

At Addenbrooke's he was placed in a barrier-nursing room where he had culture and blood tests to determine exactly which bugs were in his system and he received the crucial platelets and blood transfusions that he desperately needed.

After urgent discussions with his team there, they announced they would take full responsibility for Deryn's primary care. I was overwhelmed with an enormous sense of relief that finally, it wouldn't be just down to me to watch out for glaring errors and recklessness at the hands of nursing staff who were clearly out of their depth.

Two very fraught days later, we got the results of the culture tests. They indicated that as well as the RSV we knew about, Deryn also had two different types of bug in his Hickman line. One strain was most commonly found in the gut so to have it in his line – and potentially his heart – was of grave concern.

For the next week, we watched as Deryn battled with raging fevers of over 40°C.. His team at Addenbrooke's was struggling to get on top of the infections and none of the usual antibiotics seemed to be working. Both infections were resistant to traditional medicines but after seven days of steadfast attempts with many different drug combinations, they found one that worked.

It was only after Deryn recovered from the two infections that Dr Mike told us just how close we'd come to losing him.

'It was touch and go there for a while,' he revealed with typical understatement.

Deryn had been incredibly lucky. And so, for the sake of every other child who might follow in his footsteps, I wrote a long letter to the head of the NNUH and tried to put this sorry episode behind us while we focused on the challenge ahead.

Now that Deryn was out of the woods, Dr Mike wanted to prepare him for the next stage of treatment and the bone marrow transplant at Bristol.

Following a barrage of tests to assess the correct dosage and how well Deryn might cope, he would start 7 to 10 days of conditioning – an extremely intensive course of chemotherapy and radiotherapy to strip him of his own bone marrow cells and bring his entire immune system to a standstill. Dr Mike explained that once conditioning was complete, the bone marrow would no longer fulfil its usual function of producing blood cells and fighting infection.

The conditioning protocol targeted the entire body with several rounds of total body irradiation radiotherapy, something I hoped that Bristol would decide against. Deryn no longer had any visible cancer cells present, and what little I had read about radiotherapy filled me with horror – I knew that it could cause cancer.

No-one can live for very long without bone marrow. Transplant patients are more susceptible than a newborn baby to illness and the only way to survive is to have regular transfusions of red cells and platelet cells. Unfortunately, they can't give white cell transfusions so the only way to keep Deryn safe was to isolate him from anything that could cause him harm for a minimum of four weeks.

After the conditioning period had elapsed, the transplant would then 'rescue' Deryn with the donated bone marrow of another person. I was awestruck at the thought of an anonymous donor being able to save Deryn's life. Whoever this mystery person was, they were already a hero in my eyes.

It was a relief to hear that the transplant procedure would be painless, no worse than a blood transfusion, and with pretty much the same immediate risks – usually simple issues such as allergies.

The donor, on the other hand, would face some discomfort. Dr Mike explained that the bone marrow would be extracted in one of two ways. The first method involved the donor being given drugs to force their bone marrow to produce many more cells than they usually would, before the marrow is removed through the hip ball joint by a large needle.

The second, less intrusive, method involves marrow cells being collected in a needle in much the same way as a blood donation. A third option – completely painless – is to use donated stem cells from a bank of frozen umbilical cords.

During this period, Simon and I would be Deryn's only permitted visitors. Dylan wasn't allowed because of his age and despite his tender years, he understood.

All being well, we were hoping to see signs that the transplant was working in 20-24 days. Deryn's medical team expected to see blood cell production start around day 21. Those first four weeks were the most crucial to his recovery. If he was unlucky enough to pick up a bacterial or viral infection – even a common cold – it could prove fatal. We had everything crossed for our boy.

The best news was yet to come. Deryn had to eat a completely clean diet. This was music to my ears. I had learned a lot about food and nutrition since his diagnosis as well as the effect of sugar on cancerous tumours and I was really looking forward to getting Deryn on a decent, clean diet at last.

While he was in hospital it had been an impossible task getting good quality, nutritious food into him. In truth, his diet had been terrible. But when your sick child will only eat Burger King or McDonald's, you give in just to see them eat. The thought of a healthy food plan which would educate his taste buds was wonderful.

However, the hospital's idea of clean eating did not tally with mine. No organic fresh fruit and vegetables. No salads because of the risk of bacteria. Everything had to be microwaved so that the heat could kill any possible chance of food poisoning. The menu, we learned, would include pizza and chips, even crisps and chocolate. To drink, there would be sterile water – tap water could also carry bacteria – plus fruit juice and even Coke.

And Bristol was about to sound worse still. As soon as the new marrow engrafts and starts to produce blood cells, an immunosuppressant drug called cyclosporine is introduced to prevent the body from rejecting the new marrow, a very real and grave concern.

Deryn would also be at risk of developing graft versus host disease, a sign that the new immune system is attacking the host's body. GvHD commonly affects the skin but can also manifest in the gut, causing extreme diarrhoea.

As Dr Mike told us all this, Deryn was listening intently. At the mention of diarrhoea, he chipped in with, 'Oh that sounds like fun, I hope they give me a bucket because one of those chamber pots is never going to be big enough.'

Mike and I burst out laughing. His ability to lighten the mood never ceased to amaze me.

The day of the transplant would be the start of our countdown – day 0. After 100 days, as long as there were very few complications, Deryn would be able to come off his clean diet and interact with people again.

'Can I have a takeaway on day 100?' he pleaded. 'I will finish that plate of enchiladas!'

While no-one knew for sure what the outcome would be, Deryn was insistent that he should go through with the operation as it was the only way to ensure that cancer did not return. And if there were some rogue cells lurking, they would also be banished for good.

It was going to be a tough journey for all of us but if anyone could walk through Hell with a smile on his face, it was Deryn. He was born to succeed, to fight and conquer everything that challenged him.

Whatever the transplant was going to throw at him, I was confident he could deal with it. I had to believe that he wasn't going to die in Bristol otherwise I could not have let him go.

As I listened to Dr Mike outline the side effects of a bone

marrow transplant, my thoughts wandered to our friends who had been here before us. It was a blessing that Deryn was 13 because he could understand why the doctors were making him feel so poorly. He could see the bigger picture and come to terms with why all of this was necessary. I couldn't even imagine how hard it must have been for my friends with much younger children.

Poignantly, Tiegan's mum Emma came to see me to offer me her support. It was barely a year since she lost her beautiful little girl and there she was, back in the same hospital, sitting with me, trying to make me feel better.

As we chatted over a coffee, she told me that I shouldn't compare Deryn to Tiegan as she had been very poorly before she went to Bristol, while Deryn was in a much stronger position. I loved her for that – after all that she had been through, her priority was to alleviate my concerns.

Chapter 26

Meanwhile, Christmas came and went in a flash. There was still no news of a donor for Deryn. I'd seen many people appealing for a suitable donor online and while I always shared their plight, I had never felt anxious about whether we would find one for Deryn. I just assumed someone, somewhere would be a match for him.

There was a young girl in the isolation room opposite Deryn who had been searching for a donor for years. She was being kept alive with cells derived from horse or rabbit blood. It was amazing what could be done but nothing could substitute a bone marrow transplant and there are many risks associated with severely mismatched marrow.

The perfect donor would be a 10/10 match with Deryn's protein markers, which means less of a chance of the transplant failing. In his own inimitable fashion, Deryn had quite rare markers and the rarity of his marrow would make finding a 10/10 donor increasingly unlikely. However, the team were very optimistic that they would be able to find at least a 9/10 match.

In mid-January, I received the call I had been waiting for. A donor, at last. Our first visit to the Bristol Children's Hospital loomed and I was filled with trepidation about the procedure but also a sense of excitement at the idea of living in a bustling city for several months, exploring new sights and sounds whenever Deryn's health might allow it.

Simon drove us down and in a matter of hours, we were a long way from the familiar flatlands of Norfolk, skirting an undulating landscape which became more built up and urban until we approached the funky, multicoloured hoop sculpture which marked the hospital's cheerful, brightly decorated entrance.

We were greeted warmly by an enthusiastic elderly receptionist who directed us to the oncology day ward. The lift had a running commentary from Wallace, of Wallace and Gromit fame, telling kids to hold on tight as it went between floors. Thoughtful touches like this along with the welcoming smiles from staff gave me confidence that Deryn was going to be in excellent hands.

We made our way to the day ward to meet Charlotte, the transplant coordinator, who would be in charge of the smooth running of all tests and prep meetings. Deryn was looking a little green around the gills and no sooner had she arrived than he was hunched over a paper bowl vomiting. It wasn't much of an introduction.

She had arranged a meeting with Deryn's consultant to discuss his forthcoming treatment, the 'chat' I had been dreading. Deryn and Dylan stayed in the playroom – a relief as at this stage, I wanted to relay everything Deryn needed to know in my own way rather than have him listening in on every torturous detail.

Deryn's new consultant stepped out of her office to greet us and I was speechless at how glamorous she was. Clad in the most exquisite dress, her hair and make-up were flawless and she was dripping in elegant gold jewellery. I felt underdressed and a bit awestruck in her presence.

Dr Glam introduced herself with a firm handshake and a warm smile and immediately put me at ease as she invited us into her office. Simon gave my hand a squeeze, sensing how nervous I was about what we were about to hear. I was too consumed in my own thoughts to wonder if he was as nervous as I was. As we sat down, still hand in hand, she introduced us to another woman at the back of the room who was writing up notes on a large whiteboard.

'This is Dr Ponni, she will be heavily involved with Deryn's bone marrow transplant and she's here to help me explain all about the procedure,' she added.

A petite woman who had the kind of smile that could light up a room, Dr Ponni had the most wonderful energy about her. I liked her immediately.

Dr Glam started the meeting. 'So, as you know, Deryn was diagnosed with T-cell acute lymphoblastic leukaemia, one of the hardest types of leukaemia to treat successfully,' she began.

I felt a wave of despair sucking the energy out of me.

'Obviously his second, much rarer cancer has not been seen by any of us before so a bone marrow transplant is experimental treatment at best,' she continued. 'We have no idea if the procedure will prevent Langerhans cell sarcoma from returning.'

Dr Glam carried on talking while Ponni wrote information on the whiteboard in front of us. Very soon the board was covered in notes, the odds of certain things happening and the remedies to every potential issue and risk factor.

They seemed to have every eventuality covered. The side effects to the drugs they would pump into Deryn sounded severe and horrendous but I appreciated them warning us of all the horrible possibilities and allowed myself to hope that maybe it wouldn't be as scary as I had imagined after all.

As well as graft versus host disease, there were other short-term risks associated with the transplant. Hair loss, muscle wasting, liver, kidney and heart failure, brain damage, nausea, loss of appetite, weight loss, fluid retention and the nasty, ulcer-causing mucositis, to name just a few.

Deryn would be infertile after the bone marrow transplant – if he wasn't already – and he had accepted that he would never be able to have biological children of his own.

Then there were the long-term side effects of the drugs to consider: bone weakness, muscle damage, avascular necrosis – death of bone tissue – heart, liver and kidney damage, stunted growth, delayed puberty, cataracts. Oh, and cancer, again. Many of these issues could affect Deryn, even years after the treatment ended. And last but by no means least, the transplant could fail to engraft and we would be back at square one.

I struggled to compute the logic behind trying to stop cancer coming back by using treatments that could cause cancer. Surely there had to be a way to target cancer cells without damaging the cells around them? But it seemed that this was our only option, our only chance of preventing cancer coming back for the foreseeable future. For now, it was all about trying to make sure that Deryn had some kind of future at all.

Before the conditioning could start, Deryn had to give a large donation of his own bone marrow, a rescue donation which would be kept in cold storage in the event that he may need it later on.

The whole idea of the transplant was to eradicate his marrow and fully replace it with someone else's but it was reassuring to know that if the donor marrow failed to engraft, there was another way to keep him alive.

It felt like we had options, quite a few of them. The best option of all was that a suitable match had been found in Germany. A 44-year-old man – rated at 9/10 – was willing to go through an extremely uncomfortable procedure in the hope of saving the life of a complete stranger.

I was intrigued, but we wouldn't be allowed to know any more about him other than his age and country of origin until Deryn was two years post-transplant. And if Deryn didn't make it, we would never be allowed to know his identity.

Deryn could die because of an infection, an adverse reaction to one of the drugs or a serious side effect. But we had a lot of faith in the team at Bristol as their success rate showed just how capable they were at performing bone marrow transplants.

Dr Glam told us that the conditioning would push his body to the upper limit of what it could contend with and in order to assess how far they could push Deryn, they had to carry out invasive tests to establish exactly what condition his body was currently in.

It tore me up inside knowing that they were going to put my courageous son through such a hard time. Deryn had already been through more than enough in his short life but there was some small comfort in knowing that every test would ensure that each move was as calculated as it could be.

We headed off for the first of many sets of tests to determine Deryn's starting position. His teeth were thoroughly checked to establish the damage caused by the drugs and constant vomiting. I was astonished when they gave him the thumbs up, confirming that no fillings were needed and his enamel was still in good condition.

The rest of the tests were taking place in the old part of the main hospital, where brown walls and dated furniture adorned the long and twisty corridors. The lifts looked like something from an old movie and I half expected a bellboy to be inside when the doors opened.

'I really hope that their equipment is a little more up to date,' Deryn quipped cheekily.

He had an echocardiogram on his heart, a CT scan and a couple of ultrasound scans of his internal organs. Every test came back clear and some of the medical team commented on how amazing it was that Deryn had come this far with absolutely no sign of any lasting organ damage.

It was wonderful to hear that he was still very healthy inside, even if that in turn meant that they could now administer much harsher treatment. I was undecided as to whether this was a good thing or not.

Our final appointment that day was at radiotherapy. This was the bete noir for me. There was no way to avoid it and, while Deryn seemed unbothered, I was quietly fearful of the risks associated with this particular therapy.

The radiologist talked us through, adding that Deryn would be subjected to far more radiotherapy than most adults could withstand, let alone children. He would also undergo several sessions of total body irradiation as well as multiple sessions of directed radiation to his throat. He was likely to develop cataracts within 10 years and the radiation could cause permanent damage to his salivary glands, vocal chords and thyroid.

Deryn had to be fitted for a mask designed to pin him to the table so that he remained completely still throughout the radiotherapy on his throat. The very idea of being so confined was making him feel unwell and he became tearful and started to panic that he was going to be sick during the fitting.

I reassured him, advising him to think only about breathing in through his nose and out through his mouth as a calming technique. I had done this myself on many occasions, and it seemed to work.

I gave his hand a little squeeze. Deryn and I hadn't ever had much physical contact. I wasn't a tactile person and neither was he. We didn't feel the need to cuddle each other to show that we cared about each other but since his diagnosis, we had both become more demonstrative and benefited from the odd hug or hand squeeze. Just this once, I wished I'd spent more time hugging him as a child.

✣

Deryn was called through to a room where he had to climb onto a large, rock-solid bed with a hard plastic block at the head of it. This went under Deryn's neck, forcing him to look absolutely straight upwards. The mask was made from plastic that was malleable when soaked in hot water and once it was soft and floppy, it was draped over Deryn's face and sank around his eyes and chin, fitting perfectly to his face. It hardened up quickly and we were left with a perfect recreation of his features.

We returned to the radiotherapy department so that Deryn could have some small test doses to measure accurately just how much his body could withstand. The first thing I noticed was the sheer thickness of the door, which looked like it belonged in a bank vault.

Lying on another bed in his underwear, he had sensors attached to him so that the doctors could read the radiation levels. The sensors were held on by what looked like large elasticated nets – one on his head and one around his chest – as well as a cold pack around his throat to protect it from the radiation. Lasers shone across Deryn's body and I was shown where the radiotherapy would be directed before leaving him there alone to be zapped, all trussed up like a turkey.

Deryn breezed through with characteristic good humour and a few jokes with the team before we headed off to have another dry run with the direct radiation team and the chilling mask. It was clipped on to him, securing him to the table so that he couldn't move one whisker. There were no tantrums or resistance, he took it all in his stride regardless of how rotten he was feeling.

I watched on a monitor as the nurses lined up green lasers, aiming the rays exactly where his tonsils had once been. Seconds later, the nurses were back in the room and had unclipped Deryn from the table.

The test run was hard enough to watch and made me feel like saying: 'Stop, this is a mistake, I've changed my mind,' but it wasn't about me. Deryn had made his choice and I had to respect that.

The final test to see how well his lungs were functioning was the most fun. He was asked to sit inside a large glazed box and blow out five virtual candles on the computer monitor.

'Are you going to fill it with water?' he chuckled. 'Do I have to escape like Houdini?'

After being given the cleanest bill of health anyone in his position could wish for, we headed home to Norfolk for two precious weeks of as much fun as we could fit in before his return to Bristol, including a cheeky Mexican supper where yet again, Deryn was defeated by his enchiladas.

Simon and I had been talking about having some professional family photographs taken and a photographer who happened to be a friend's sister kindly stepped in and offered to shoot some carefree, relaxed portraits for free. We were humbled by her gesture. I didn't want to be maudlin but I needed some wonderful photos of all four of us together as an insurance policy that Deryn was going to be okay.

One soggy February morning, we met the photographer in Wayland Woods to have a lark about in front of the lens. Deryn had always been photogenic and had done a photo shoot for an advertising campaign when he was just four. Unfortunately, the worsening Tourette's Syndrome and uncontrollable tics put paid to any subsequent shoots but he had always fancied his chances.

'When I've stopped looking ill, I'd like to have another go at modelling,' he announced after posing for a few shots.

The change in his appearance was one of the hardest things for me to come to terms with. I'd witnessed him at both ends of

TOP Callie with a 'fit and healthy' baby Deryn in January 2000. 'He was a dream baby and made it easy for me to be a good first time mum...'

LEFT In September 2010, with his brother, Dylan. Deryn became bloated from the water retention caused by the steroids, so was given a new nickname, 'Moonface'

TOP Sailing round the Isle of Wight with the Ellen MacArthur Cancer Trust, June 2011

RIGHT Action man! The Starlight Children's Foundation arranged for Deryn to spend a day behind-the-scenes at the Commando Training Centre Royal Marines in Devon, October 2011

BOTTOM Happy together in January 2013. But by the end of the year they had all moved into the Charlton Farm Hospice

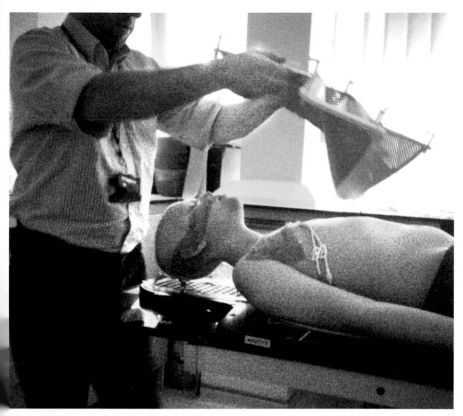

ABOVE Deryn in January 2013, having his mask made – before being 'zapped' by the radiation therapy

LEFT Just before receiving his bone marrow transplant in February 2013

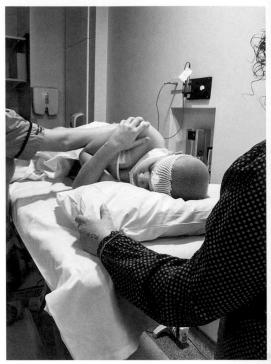

ABOVE In June 2013 with Simon, who always kept such a postive attitude: 'He'll be alright, you know...'

RIGHT In one of his radiotherapy treatments in February 2013

BOTTOM March 2013 and a much-needed visit from actress Linda Robson that lifted their spirits. Deryn wasn't allowed out of his room after his bone marrow transplant, but he still managed to communicate!

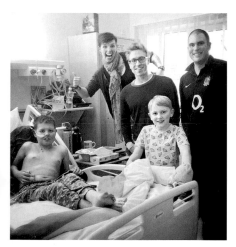

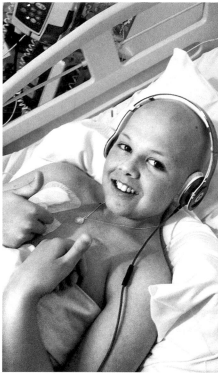

CLOCKWISE FROM TOP LEFT The marvellous Russell Howard dropped by to say hi to Deryn and stayed for hours; Deryn watching a movie after his bone marrow transplant in April 2013; The post arrives with one or two birthday cards in December 2013; The 'last' Christmas with Deryn in the hospice in 2013; Deryn's favourite actors Simon Pegg and Nick Frost surprised him with a visit in November 2013 - he was thrilled!

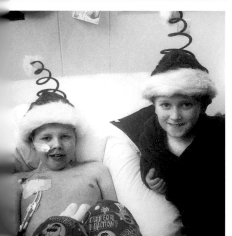

RIGHT October 2013 and off to a Cancer Charity Ball. From left to right; Penny, Callie, Marcie, Deryn, Dylan, Simon and Joss.

BELOW LEFT January 2014 after a bone marrow aspirate

BELOW RIGHT The boys sharing a moment together in January 2014.

BOTTOM LEFT Deryn with his little cousin, Isla, in January 2014.

BOTTOM RIGHT Finally – in February 2014 – the line comes out and it's the end of treatment!

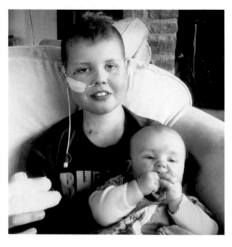

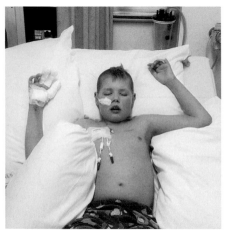

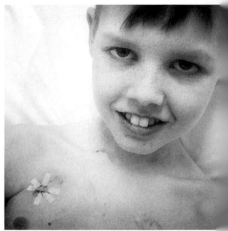

ABOVE A thin but healthier looking Deryn sailing again with the Ellen MacArthur Cancer Trust, this time in April 2014; **LEFT, TOP TO BOTTOM** With Dylan on a family break to Spain in June 2014 – Deryn's struggle to eat clearly visible; **BELOW** June 2016, suited, booted and off to his prom!

TODAY 'Deryn has been through so much – we all have. But now we're stronger than we've ever been. As we look optimistically to our own future, we hope that with this book, something good can be learned from what we've been through, too.'

the physical spectrum and at times, he was totally unrecognisable to me – except for his smile, which never changed.

With just a few days left before heading to Bristol, Dawson's mum Cheryl arranged a party for Deryn. She gave him a small kneeling golden bear with its hands clasped together in prayer, the 'Hope Bear' that Dawson had inherited from another child who had also had a bone marrow transplant. It became his lucky charm and he was hugely touched by Cheryl's gift. Emma also gave Deryn the same 'Hope Bear' that Tiegan had taken with her to Bristol. Double the hope.

Deryn's story had touched the hearts of many, not just those who knew him but thousands of people who had never met him but had heard about his plight through social media. Our local newspapers had also followed his story from the very beginning and before long it was picked up by the national press, aided by his 'one in seven billion' status.

In addition, Simon had stayed in touch with Paul Hollywood after The Great British Bake Off as well as many of the celebrity chefs he met along the way and when Paul started tweeting about Deryn, we saw his Twitter following shoot up, which amused us all no end.

Suddenly life went crazy. I was getting emails and calls from media outlets, journalists and radio shows all wanting to hear about Deryn's story. Knowing that people cared and wanted to cover what was happening to him somehow gave the whole awful situation some meaning. Deryn truly revelled in his newfound fame.

While he had no interest in talking about himself or his illness, he was happy to play the part of the main character with me as his narrator.

My blog was attracting visitors from as far afield as America, Australia and more surprisingly, Iraq and Afghanistan, which moved me immensely. It wasn't long before we saw Deryn's story on the BBC news website. And after seeing his name appear in a headline on Fox News, Deryn burst out laughing.

'This is ridiculous!' he giggled. 'I can't believe they know who I am at Fox News!'

It was surreal but, in my view, any publicity was good publicity. Spreading awareness of this rare cancer so that anyone else who found themselves in a similar situation could get in touch was my main aim. I wanted to pass on what I had learned so far and perhaps learn from others, too.

It was also my hope that bone marrow donation would become more common. I knew many people who had never even heard of it and with so many needing donors, if Deryn's story could inspire people to sign up, that would be wonderful.

I felt very strongly that everything I'd learned had enabled me to move on and cope with the next step with far less fear and much more power.

Chapter 27

Before we left for Bristol friends and family came to wish Deryn emotional goodbyes and good lucks. They were far more upset and anxious about the impending transplant than we were. Incredibly, I felt no fear as we set off on the morning of February 14th 2013. As for Deryn, he was looking forward to what the future had in store for him once all this was over.

'The sooner it starts, the sooner it's over and the sooner I can get back to living my life,' he told me matter-of-factly as we set off for Bristol a day ahead of the conditioning programme.

The transplant coordinator had arranged an apartment for us to stay in during Deryn's treatment at Bristol and we were looking forward to exploring it. But breaking the news that his trusty four-legged friend Ozzy wouldn't be able to come with us was the only thing which elicited a tear from Deryn. A friend stepped in to help look after him but as the pair of them had been inseparable ever since we rescued Ozzy when Deryn was just five years old, this was a bitter pill to swallow.

Happily, Deryn's spirits lifted when we arrived at the apartment. It was a lovely, airy space in the heart of the city with a balcony overlooking the street below and a bedroom for each of the boys. He was over the moon at his new abode and, even better, Deryn's girlfriend Kim had come along to support him.

We had one more night to make the most of our freedom so that evening, we ate out at a nearby pizzeria. We'd booked two tables – it was Valentine's Day and Deryn and Kim had a small table to themselves by the window, while Simon, Dylan and I sat at the other end of the restaurant trying not to catch his eye.

This was a precious bit of normality before the next stage in Deryn's treatment.

❖

The following morning, we set foot for the first time on the bone marrow transplant unit. Dylan stayed with Simon while Deryn, Kim and I went through a code-locked door to a changing area where we took off our shoes and coats and thoroughly washed our hands. The threat of bacteria was taken incredibly seriously and the safety of the fragile patients inside was paramount to staff.

In the middle of the ward sat the nurses' station and as we approached, they said a cheery hello. I immediately felt at ease – the ward didn't have a depressing air, it was serene, peaceful and full of positive energy.

Deryn was shown to room 6, which would be his home until the transplant engrafted and he was strong enough not to be in solitary confinement. It had its own TV and an ensuite bathroom, something he was thrilled about even though he wouldn't be using it much while every bodily function continued to be submitted for weighing.

We were introduced to the 'poo cupboard,' a genius design with doors on both sides so that the nurses could collect Deryn's waste without having to scrub up and enter his room each time. Then he spotted the menu: pizza, chips, lasagne, roast chicken, ice cream, Coke, crisps, chocolate… He couldn't hide his delight.

'I like it here,' he said happily. 'It's not half as bad as I thought it would be.'

I was dismayed by the menu but as I was under strict instructions not to bring in any food at all for him for fear of infection, I had to put my concerns to one side.

Deryn's first appointment was at the operating theatre to have a large amount of his own bone marrow removed via his hip ball joints and placed into cold storage, to come out only in the unlikely event that the transplant failed.

The staff at Bristol hadn't yet experienced Deryn's quirky rituals and bleak, dark humour. The anaesthetists were taken aback when he started telling them what was what but they quickly understood that this young lad knew exactly what he was talking about and followed his instructions to the letter on how he liked to be put to sleep.

'I can't believe you're bossing the doctors around already Deryn', I said with a laugh as his eyelids started to droop.

'If... you... don't... ask... you... don't... get...,' he faltered as he drifted off.

I gave him a kiss on the forehead and left feeling relaxed and not overly concerned. He emerged from theatre a short time later with his hips covered in bandages.

'My back is killing me,' he grimaced when he came round. 'I can't wait to get in the bath.'

He was given some drugs to head off any ulcers forming and we were allowed to go back to the apartment. It had been a very good first day in Bristol.

With transplant day as Day 0, the days leading up to it were referred to by the number of days remaining. From BMT -13, each day was pretty much a repeat of the previous one. Deryn would go into hospital in the morning for blood tests, after which the nurses would administer the optimum doses of medication.

It felt as if nothing was happening. Deryn was still incredibly well and didn't seem to be feeling the effects of the drugs that were slowly destroying his entire immune system. I was thankful but couldn't help feeling concerned that perhaps it wasn't working as well as it should have been. However, his blood tests confirmed that the conditioning was working very well, he was simply withstanding the side effects with amazing fortitude.

Knowing how interested I was in every step of his treatment, the staff kept me informed of every blood count, level and marker they were taking. Far from feeling overwhelmed at this deluge of information, I was thrilled to be involved in the process instead of being merely swept along by it.

Ever upbeat, Deryn was further buoyed by the arrival of a letter on House of Commons headed notepaper – wishing him all the best from the government and opposition parties.

'Wow!' he exclaimed, wide-eyed and grinning from ear to ear as he read it out to us. 'They even know who I am in Parliament! This is crazy!'

In addition to the press and MPs taking an interest, I was receiving emails and letters from people all over the country telling me about their personal journeys with cancer. Many offered advice or support while others told me that my blog about Deryn had given them hope and helped them through tough times.

I was truly humbled and realised that I had to continue writing about my son and sharing his story. It felt like there was some purpose to what we were going through.

On BMT -9, Deryn started direct radiotherapy. He was starting to feel some of the effects of the chemotherapy, particularly tiredness and loss of appetite, but it didn't stop him from having a laugh with Kim while he waited to don the dreaded mask and get zapped by green laser beams.

Just watching Deryn lie motionless on the table, clipped into the mask with no way of moving a single millimeter in any direction, I felt claustrophobic. I tried to imagine how he was feeling, remembering suddenly that he probably didn't mind nearly as much as I did.

Once everything was lined up and ready to go, I was asked to leave the room. I gave his hand a squeeze and told him I'd be just outside.

'It's okay, Mum, I'll probably just go to sleep,' he reassured me.

'Would you like some music to listen to, Deryn?' asked the nurse.

Deryn said he would and Michael Jackson started blaring out of the sound system.

Watching him on the monitor disturbed me more than other procedures I'd witnessed. The thickness of the door, the safe distance, the precision and the emphasis on getting each laser in just the right spot. Then the fact that this treatment was making him infertile, possibly causing cataracts and potentially giving him a brain tumour. This kill-or-cure felt very sinister to me.

Over the following five days, Deryn had further sessions as well as blood and platelet transfusions. Encouragingly, the treatment was doing its job and his numbers were falling at a rapid rate without ravaging him too much physically.

'I thought I'd feel a lot worse than I do by now,' Deryn admitted cheerfully as we ate lunch in his BMT room afterwards.

I did too, but I was incredibly grateful that he was dealing with it so well, unlike some of the other patients on the ward. I was meticulously washing my hands when a woman approached me and started asking questions. She explained that she was accompanying her son, who was due to have his transplant on the same day as Deryn.

She revealed tearfully that he was so terrified of having total body irradiation (TBI) that he had been crying all night. I felt awful for her. Deryn had coped so well and had never really got upset about any of it. It was sad to hear that her son wasn't coping as well.

I tried to reassure her and asked her how old her son was. I was shocked to hear he was 31, and there with his wife. Age was irrelevant – no matter how old children get, they are always our children and our protective instincts never go away.

❖

By BMT -4, Deryn had finished direct radiotherapy and was thrilled to be allowed to keep his creepy mask. He thought it was hilarious to leave it around the apartment for us to stumble on.

With just a few days to go until the transplant, TBI started as a last attempt to get everything out of his bones and enable the best chance of engraftment. This time I couldn't watch – I'd seen enough.

Meanwhile, now that Deryn's story had gone global, goodwill messages were continuing to flood in from all over the world. A group of British Royal Marines on the Indian Ocean isle of Diego Garcia sent a wonderful picture of them holding up a huge banner with an encouraging message for Deryn.

Photos also arrived from the beaches of Australia, the snow-covered mountains of New Zealand, from Singapore, South America and everywhere in between. People were sending pictures of themselves doing extreme sports while wearing Deryn's wristbands.

Birds of a Feather actress Linda Robson tweeted a picture of herself with her fellow cast members wishing Deryn well and she spread the word to her friends, asking them to show their support for him.

Deryn took all this in his stride. He was bemused by the attention and amazed that people were so inspired by him. The way he saw it, he had made a decision in 2010 to deal with everything that came his way in a positive, humorous fashion and he was just sticking to his word.

Chapter 28

Day Zero was upon us. Dylan and Simon would be heading back to Norfolk with Kim so that Dylan could continue attending school and have some semblance of normality. Simon and I planned a rota whereby he would return every two weeks to swap with me, bringing Dylan who could spend a weekend every fortnight with us all.

This plan would also enable me to catch up on my college work, which was suffering a little as a result of the upheaval.

Simon and I had washed, rolled and stuffed every single item of clothing that Deryn had into individual freezer bags. Once sealed, the bags were wiped with a sterile cloth and stacked neatly inside a large sterile plastic box. Deryn's PlayStation had to be cleaned, as did all of his games and each of the books he chose to bring.

His childhood teddy Bruno, which had always accompanied him on every hospital stay, was too old and fragile to be washed so he was placed in a plastic bag where he would remain during Deryn's stay in isolation, looking forlorn and a bit squashed.

Once everything was sterile and packed, it was time to leave the apartment and move Deryn's stuff into room 6 and try to make it feel a bit more like home for him. I covered the walls with laminated pictures of our photo-shoot in the woods and Simon set up his PlayStation.

While we were unpacking Deryn's things, a nurse told us that the precious bone marrow, which had been donated the day before, had arrived safely in Bristol having winged its way from

Germany in the care of a specialist handler. It was imperative that it reached its recipient as soon as possible and equally important that it didn't go through the airport scanners as they could potentially damage the fragile cells.

We were nervous as well as excited and even Deryn started getting a little exuberant, as did friends and family who were following his progress on Facebook and sending lots of good luck wishes.

As Deryn was whisked off to radiology for his final session of total body irradiation, there was a momentous feeling that the conditioning and chemotherapy was behind us at last.

'Are you ready, Deryn,' I asked.

'Yeah – let's do this,' he grinned.

I could see a large, square, yellow insulated bag and could barely contain my excitement.

'Look Deryn, that must be your new marrow!' I shrieked.

With the final checks finished, Simon arrived and we waited for nurse Vee to bring in the first of two bags of vibrant red bone marrow cells bound for Deryn. This was the moment we'd been waiting for. Vee was clutching the best gift anyone could possibly give us, marrow that would hopefully prevent both his previous cancers from wreaking havoc on Deryn's life ever again.

Vee attached the bag to the pump and pressed start. We watched with glee as the marrow made its way down the line towards Deryn's chest.

'Right, you're good to go Deryn, any problems just press your buzzer,' Vee said as she headed out of the door.

We had to mark the occasion. Simon and I had planned something to make this moment one we would all remember. As the marrow reached Deryn's chest, the room filled with the sound of Queen's smash hit *Don't Stop Me Now*.

'Tonight I'm gonna have myself a real good time, I feel alive and the world I'll turn it inside out...'

Deryn and I started singing along as we threw our hands in the air and gave the best karaoke performance of our lives. The energy in the room lifted and there was nothing but tremendously good feelings and a kind of karma. I'd never seen anyone have a bone marrow transplant before but this certainly wasn't how I'd imagined it to be.

Simon was filming the procedure – and our performance – as we wanted people to know that it wasn't scary or painful but something to be celebrated. I wanted to educate as many people as I could on the subject.

Deryn's bones were effectively hollow and once the marrow cells were infused into his veins, they knew exactly where to go and started naturally making their way into his bones where they would miraculously become his new blood-making factory.

After all the excitement and razzamatazz, it was strangely anti-climactic watching the process. It would take around three weeks to see any sign of engraftment and if the transplant was successful, Deryn would no longer be blood group A+. The donor was O+ and once the new bone marrow had replaced Deryn's own marrow, it would forever be O+. I was fascinated by the fact that it would produce blood cells that held the donor's DNA rather than Deryn's.

One of the nurses joked that Deryn could commit a crime and get away with it as the donor in Germany would get the blame.

'I really don't think that's any way to repay him!' Deryn sighed with mock indignation.

Midnight arrived and so did the second bag of marrow, a little smaller than the first. It was a hell of a lot of bone marrow. I couldn't stop thinking about the donor and what he might be doing. He was probably asleep, recovering from the procedure.

He knew as much about Deryn as we knew about him. He was our mystery saviour.

By 1:30am, both bags were finished and Deryn felt absolutely fine. He'd had reactions to blood transfusions in the past but this magnificent specimen was causing no issues at all.

It was an incredibly positive start and as both Deryn and I got ready for bed, I said a silent thanks to the universe and prayed that this was a sign of things to come.

The following days were like Groundhog Day, only broken by my leaving to go and get something to eat. There was no parents' area on the BMT unit and I couldn't bring food into the room for fear of contamination.

Each day, Deryn had to change his clothes and his bed would be stripped, sterilised and remade. The cleaners came in twice daily and I became quite OCD about manically cleaning everything before he touched it. Once I'd washed his clothes, I had to tumble dry them on the highest setting and bag them all up before taking them back into his room.

It was less fuss looking after a newborn but I enjoyed caring for Deryn; it made me feel useful. After spending the first night in his room, I told him that I wouldn't be sleeping there anymore unless I really had to. The walk back to the apartment on my own at night beat sleeping in a room with constant interruptions from nursing staff. Deryn could sleep during the day if he wanted but I had to be available to speak to staff and I couldn't do that if I was asleep or exhausted.

Deryn agreed. I think he was glad to get his space back after such a long time with me right there in his pocket. He had some wonderful nurses to keep him company and became very fond of Louise, one of the nursing assistants. She took the time to get to know Deryn and his likes and dislikes and as a result, she was able to care for him beautifully.

It was reassuring to know that while I wasn't there, someone who thought the world of him was keeping a close eye on him. The nurses didn't have time to sit with him during the night shifts, so Louise became like a protective big sister to him.

Deryn was getting frustrated just sitting in his room and three days after the transplant he asked for something to keep him physically fit. He didn't want to waste away. His Hickman line meant he couldn't do press-ups so the nursing staff agreed to have an exercise bike put in his room. He was over the moon and spent hours pedalling away while watching TV.

Amid all the good news, unfortunately there was soon a cloud, when Deryn's dietitian insisted he have a nose tube fitted. His appetite had dwindled, he was in pain when he swallowed and his mouth was so sore from the drugs that it seemed sensible to put one in before it became even more painful.

It had nothing to do with the transplant – it was more to do with the harsh conditioning that was catching up with him. A temperature spike led to IV antibiotics and my days became a repetitive cycle of washing and showering Deryn, applying cream to his skin to treat the dryness and sitting by his bed watching him drift in and out of consciousness.

I was still living by myself at the apartment and my plans to go back to Norfolk for two weeks at a time and catch up with my studies fell apart once I saw what Deryn was going through. I didn't want to leave him for a couple of days, let alone two weeks. Nevertheless, it was important that I spent time with Dylan and Simon spent time with Deryn so we agreed that Simon would do two weeks in Norfolk and one week in Bristol.

As the morphine doses increased, meaning Deryn struggled to stay awake, I spent lonely hours sitting around waiting for a few seconds of interaction with my son. So I turned to the very thing that had helped me so much during many difficult periods over the previous years. I went back to training.

I found a 24-hour gym in the centre of Bristol and signed up immediately. I'd head to the gym first thing in the morning and train for an hour before showering and making my way to the hospital to sit with Deryn for the day. It was a distraction and a way for me to meditate. Earphones in, music on, training programme in hand, I became Callie, the woman who loved to lift heavy things off the floor and put them down again. I felt alive.

The monotony of waiting for the marrow to engraft was broken up by a visit from Linda Robson, who had been such a support behind the scenes. Unfortunately, Deryn wasn't allowed out of his room and Linda wasn't allowed in so the pair of them were forced into a comical conversation – through the doors of the poo cupboard! We all had a photo taken together, and just as the camera shutter clicked, Deryn dramatically threw himself against the window with his arms in the air like a crazy person.

Linda and I were in hysterics and it made for a very good picture which soon spread across Twitter. Linda became Deryn's biggest fan, sharing his story with her many followers. We spoke in depth about her passion and involvement with the Anthony Nolan Register, which works to save the lives of people with blood cancer and which has been a part of her life for over 30 years.

The pain from the livid sores in Deryn's mouth was increasing and it crucified me to sit and watch him crying. The team was desperately trying to get in control of his discomfort and stem the constant nosebleeds he'd started having.

They had warned me that I might have to push Deryn when times got tough and he didn't want to shower or get out of bed. I had to show him some tough love but after seeing his mouth, there was no way in the world I was going to force him to brush his teeth. Despite the agony, Deryn tried his hardest to do just that and I helped him gently rinse his mouth with a salt solution. The stamina, tenacity and spiritual strength he displayed when he was at his lowest ebb was beyond belief.

Equally remarkable was the determination he showed to carry on with his education. A home tutor would come in most days and Deryn would work with him between naps. Before long, he was asking for quadratic equations. That was Deryn, not the teacher.

Although he was in a lot of pain it didn't stop him from playing the fool to raise a smile from me. On one occasion I came out of the bathroom to find that he had covered his face in surgical tape. I managed to capture almost everything that happened in videos and photographs. It seemed important to document Deryn's journey, not just for our future but also for the followers who were taking such a keen interest in what he was going through.

There were times when it felt odd sharing my son with the world but I enjoyed the support network that was growing around us as a family and derived so much strength from kind words from people I had never even met.

Simon arrived two weeks down the line – and the sight of him was a joy. A weekend spent with my family made a wonderful change from the daily grind of hospital life and as my two boys didn't see much of each other, family time together was very precious.

My subsequent week away consisted of catching up with studies, seeing friends and family and spending time with Dylan after he came home from school.

I found it quite bizarre standing outside the school gates with all the other mums, listening to them make small talk and playdate plans. It felt alien to me. My eldest son was five hours drive away going through God only knew what while I stood listening to people talk about what had happened on *EastEnders* the night before.

I didn't fit in anymore. I felt like a stranger in my hometown, completely out of the loop. I couldn't wait to get back to Bristol. I only wished that Dylan could stay in Bristol, too, but he was still at school and we had to try and maintain some normality for him.

Back at the hospital, Simon was keeping me up to date with each step of Deryn's progress, as his team anticipated he would be in Bristol for up to seven months. Thankfully, his mouth was healing and his team managed to lower the morphine dose so that he could stay awake for longer periods of time. And, most crucially, the signs we had been waiting for of early engraftment appeared in the form of some mild rashes on Deryn's body along with dry skin, a high temperature and raised blood pressure.

We were given a new, more convenient apartment to stay in at Charley's House, a beautiful four-storey Georgian house funded by the Rhys Daniels Trust, just 10 minutes from the hospital. It even had its own garden.

As the time approached for me to head back to Bristol, I was saddened at the prospect of leaving Dylan again so soon when I'd barely seen him during the school week. To make the parting slightly easier, I managed to balance the hardship of splitting our lives in two by concentrating on how relieved I was to be heading back to Deryn.

And there was some good news to focus on. As we approached the three-week mark after Deryn's transplant, his bloods started to change for the better. At the time of the transplant, his neutrophils were 0.02. Now they had risen to 0.08. A minute change but it was moving in the right direction. Three days later, it had risen again to a monumental 1.5.

CHAPTER 28

The donated marrow was showing positive signs of engrafting. One of the most positive signs, the return of his appetite, was heralded by the snaffling of a custard cream – Deryn's first solid food for two weeks – followed a couple of days later by a crumpet.

By BMT +24, Deryn had definitely engrafted, his neutrophils were up to 2.8 and platelets were being produced. This was incredibly exciting news and the team was really pleased with his progress. However, his temperature spikes started to become more regular. With the engraftment as the only real explanation, his team wanted to investigate further.

I placated myself with the thought that we couldn't really expect Deryn to go through all this with no problems at all. A CT scan was booked and Deryn donned a protective hospital mask to guard against infection as he was transported to the radiology department.

The scan came back clear but the team still wanted answers for the spikes so they arranged for an echocardiograph to get a clearer view of his heart and the line that went into it. To minimise any risks, the cumbersome machine was carefully wheeled into his room, crashing haphazardly into numerous robots that Deryn had around his bed.

'You got a licence to drive that?' I joked as the poor guy tried his hardest to steer it into the only available space.

A few days later the results came back clear and we were elated to hear that all the signs were positive although there was still a chance of the transplant failing as further symptoms arose that pointed to incompatibility between the donor marrow and Deryn's body. But the donated cells seemed to be doing their job: they were not attacking Deryn's body and the concoction of drugs was working well.

My next week at home soon came round and flew by and once again I felt guilty for hardly seeing Dylan. I didn't know how much longer we could go on with our family split in two and kept apart for weeks at a time.

Rather hearteningly, during Simon's week at hospital Deryn had been granted his first few days out of his isolation room. He was only allowed to go to our apartment at Charley's House, but he still saw this as a huge bonus and an opportunity to rebuild his strength. With Simon's help, he started to train with resistance bands, determined to leave Bristol in better shape than when he arrived.

So when Dylan and I arrived at Charley's House to find Deryn in residence, it was a wonderful surprise. Dylan threw his arms around his big brother and didn't let go until Deryn begged him to stop hugging him. What a wonderful sight! It was truly magical to have all of my boys together in one room again.

Simon soon had to make his way back to Norfolk, but this time nothing seemed too bad as we were told that, if Deryn carried on in the same vein, it would be just a matter of weeks before he could be transferred back to Addenbrooke's.

Even more reassuringly, Deryn's periods out of isolation grew more frequent and before long, he was only expected to go back in the late afternoon for his medication. He no longer had an NG tube, he was eating and the mild reactions were being kept under control.

Getting out of the BMT unit on a regular basis was wonderful progress. Things were looking so positive that it was hard to not get excited sometimes. Deryn certainly wasn't out of the woods yet but there seemed to be some light at the end of the tunnel.

This doesn't mean it was all sweetness and light. On BMT +46 Deryn was taken to the day ward to be given another hardcore new drug. Pentamidine was so toxic that it had to be administered in a sealed room. No-one could go in while Deryn was inhaling the drug via a nebuliser and the room had to remain empty for a few hours afterwards.

Nevertheless, eight weeks after his bone marrow transplant, Deryn was allowed to spend his first night out of the isolation room and we headed to Charley's House where he revelled in the first bath he'd had in many weeks – his face was a picture in amongst the myriad of bubbles he insisted on.

Having him home to spend the night was magical. Although we'd arrived at Charley's House with a bag full of drugs – I hadn't realised just how much medication Deryn was on until I had to administer it for the next 36 hours – being able to wake him up in the morning for this pharmacological concoction at least made me feel like his mum again instead of his roommate. I dared to allow myself to think that our ongoing nightmare might at last, please God, be almost over.

I continued with my routine, heading off each morning to the gym at 7am for an hour before coming back for breakfast with my son. My friends were bemused by my obsession with exercise but training was my peace, my challenge and my motivation. It was the only way to have some time to myself and still my mind.

Chapter 29

WITHIN A FEW DAYS, HOWEVER, IT WAS CLEAR THAT SOMETHING WAS most definitely up. Deryn's temperature was on the rise and he was experiencing severe stomach cramps, vomiting daily and feeling absolutely rotten.

My heart sank. Everything was pointing to GvHD (Graft versus Host Disease) in his gut and his team wanted to carry out a plethora of tests to establish exactly what was causing all this.

Deryn was mortified when the doctors told him what they were planning to do. An upper endoscopy and colonoscopy would be carried out under a general anaesthetic. What's more, not only would they be looking at his insides, they would also be taking 10 biopsies – small pieces of tissue would be cut away from his oesophagus to his rectum and everywhere in between.

'If you're using the same camera, I hope you go down my throat first,' Deryn managed to quip.

To add insult to injury, the adenovirus which he had already endured once was back with a vengeance. It felt like we were pedalling backwards and seemed unbearably cruel after the relatively smooth path leading up to and following the procedure.

Not surprisingly, Deryn was utterly miserable, his buoyant personality seeming to have temporarily deserted him. I had never seen him so deflated and dejected. But while he was down, he refused to be batted out. On the day of his tests, before he went down to theatre he was back with his maths teacher completing a mock GCSE paper – for the fun of it!

Throwing himself into his studies provided a welcome

distraction from how rotten he was feeling. The desire to climb out of his own body haunted Deryn during daylight hours while his constant bedwetting kept him awake at night. He endured everything: the ulcers, the vomiting, the nosebleeds, the stomach cramps, the headaches, the itchy skin... yet somehow he managed to conquer and control his mind and rarely allowed his emotions to get involved.

There was a tiny glimmer of hope when Deryn was given a higher dose of cyclosporine, the drug used to suppress his immune system in order to treat GvHD. This appeared to work and he started to improve each day, eating more and vomiting less frequently. So the team was baffled when his temperature started to spike once again. Tests showed that he was now virus free yet he had developed a terrible rash all over his body and his skin became dry and cracked overnight.

But Deryn's unwavering optimism was back and I tried to hold on to this. I was also grateful for the close bond that we shared. He never complained when I had to rub cream into places that no other teenage boy would ever want their mothers going. The situation he was in meant that our relationship certainly wasn't normal, but his acceptance that this was the way things had to be amazed me.

Day by day, I was spending as much time as possible at Deryn's bedside. Each evening, I would leave the hospital as late as I could. Something was going on inside his body and until the doctors could work out what it was and get on top of the suspected GvHD, we were at an impasse.

On BMT +63, Deryn had a chest x-ray, another bone marrow biopsy, a lumbar puncture and a skin core biopsy. This last procedure left him with a couple of small deep holes in the back of his neck that had to be stitched up and Deryn asked me to take a photo of his new wounds as he couldn't see them in the mirror.

'Cool, I look like I've been bitten by a vampire,' he laughed. 'Mind you, a considerate vampire that even stitches up his victim.' He laughed harder.

As I chuckled along with Deryn, I noticed that, while he was visibly thinner, finally – after many months of being bald – his hair seemed to be making a reappearance.

I was trying to manage my expectations but we were assured that the transplant had most definitely engrafted successfully despite the ever-mounting side-effects leaving their mark.

There was nothing else for it but to increase the dose of cyclosporine. This would treat the symptoms of GvHD, but as an immunosuppressant the risk was that too much could kill off Deryn's new bone marrow.

After an anxious wait, the test results came back. The news wasn't great. Deryn was diagnosed with grade 1 GvHD of the upper gut and grade 2 GvHD of the skin. Grade 2 is worse than grade 1 so we were pleased that his gut GvHD was less severe as it is much harder to treat.

So now Deryn's doctors found themselves in a catch-22 situation of which problem to treat first. If they treated the GvHD, this would suppress the immune system and any virus lurking in the background would have ample opportunity to wreak havoc. However, if they boosted his immune system to allow it to fight the underlying viruses, the GvHD would run riot as it was the immune system that was attacking Deryn's gut and skin, causing the disease. In addition, the team was worried that Deryn was harbouring something they just couldn't detect. I didn't envy them their choice.

At least there was also some good news. My plan to get Deryn to eat every two hours had managed to restart his metabolism. He hadn't used his stomach properly for such a long time that it had simply stopped working and gone to sleep. Deryn weighed just six stone, having lost over a stone in the previous four weeks. He was gaunt, bony and looking every bit like the cancer patient once again.

After much deliberation, the doctors decided to treat the GvHD and take the chance that the many viruses Deryn had been affected by didn't raise their ugly heads again.

Meanwhile, the results of the bone marrow aspirate and lumbar puncture were back and there was no sign of infection in the spinal fluid and no sign of cancer cells. The relief was immense; it was still the threat of cancer that haunted me the most.

After successfully treating the GvHD, Deryn enjoyed a wonderful weekend at Charley's House with the whole family. Some friends came to visit and we relished this little window of normality.

For a few days, he no longer had stomach aches and was eating like there was no tomorrow. Before long, though, the adenovirus was back. This time, the doctors chose not to treat it in order to give the immune system a chance to fight it by itself so we could see how well it was working. Deryn was also back on steroids but I had to remind myself how blessed I was: my eldest son was dealing with the most horrific situation and, for the most part, sporting a beaming great grin on his face.

As Deryn improved, his overnight stays at Charley's House became more frequent and I relished the chance to care for him, cook his meals and make sure that he had everything he needed. Simon and Dylan were still in Norfolk and as much as I missed them both terribly, I was enjoying having Deryn to myself under almost normal circumstances.

On the evening of BMT +67, Deryn and I settled in for the evening with a film and some popcorn. In the living room was a sofa bed which Deryn had claimed, mainly because it was a struggle for him to climb the four flights of stairs up to his bedroom, but also with the added bonus of being able to watch TV from the comfort of his bed.

Deryn told me he was having trouble seeing the screen. It was blurred and he couldn't focus properly. I went straight into nurse mode.

'Deryn, how many fingers am I holding up?' I asked.

'Four, but they're blurry,' he said.

On the table next to the sofa bed was a glass of water. I asked him to take the glass off the table. He reached out with his hand to grab the glass but overshot it by a hand span. Again he reached for the glass and again he missed it. Then he stood up to go to the loo and walked straight into the door frame.

I rang the BMT unit and explained what was happening. Within 20 minutes, we were back in Deryn's room on the ward with nurses rushing around carrying out observations and tests. His blood pressure was high due to the steroids and he quietly confided to one of the nurses that he was experiencing terrible pain behind his eyes.

After another battery of tests, the doctor diagnosed a migraine and gave him strong painkillers and instructions to sleep it off. Satisfied that the situation was in hand, I was about to head off back to the house for the night when Deryn stopped me.

'Please don't go, Mum, stay the night here,' he pleaded drowsily as I was about to leave.

Deryn had never asked me to stay with him before. Before I could even answer, he had fallen asleep.

I was torn. As much as I wanted to stay with him, I had nothing to sleep in. It seemed senseless to spend the night when the team was amazing and would look after him attentively. He knew they were brilliant, too, having performed a secret experiment whereby he pretended to be asleep each time a nurse came to do the obs. He wanted to see how they treated him when they thought he was asleep.

After being looked after by one nurse who happened to be pregnant, he waited until the morning to tell her about his experiment.

'You will be a really good mum when your baby is born,' he announced to the stunned woman.

I couldn't leave without telling him my plan so I gently woke him up.

'Deryn, I'm not going to stay tonight,' I whispered. 'You need some sleep and the nurses here will look after you. Louise is here, too. You'll be fine.'

He dozed off and I gave him a kiss on his forehead, said goodbye to the staff and headed back to the house to get some rest.

It was just past midnight and I was getting ready for bed. I plugged my phone in to charge but hadn't even put it down when it started to vibrate in my hand.

'Hello,' I answered it hesitantly.

'Callie, it's Louise. The crash team are with Deryn, he's had some sort of fit. Can you get here?'

I felt my heart in my mouth, adrenaline coursing through my veins.

'On my way, Lou,' I replied, grabbing the clothes I'd just taken off and hurriedly getting dressed again. I put my trainers on, knowing that the fastest way to get to Deryn would be to run.

I raced down the two flights of stairs to the front door and set off as fast as I could towards the hospital, sprinting down the steep hill. Each time my feet hit the floor, I thought I was going to fall. All I could think of was Deryn. I reached the bottom of the hill and started sprinting up towards the hospital which was now in sight.

Deryn was on the 7th floor but there was no way I could wait for the lift. I ran up the stairs, two at a time. It was almost as if my days at the gym had prepared me for this one moment. I didn't even pause to take my shoes off as I at last got to Deryn's floor, only stopping to quickly wash my hands.

When I opened the door to the ward I had no idea what to expect. I had already imagined a million different scenarios. I registered that both of Deryn's doors were wide open and, as so much onus had been placed on the fact that they needed to be kept shut at all times, seeing them open filled me with panic.

Inside the ward I couldn't see a soul. As I got closer to Deryn's room, I could see why. They were all in with him. Emerging from the panic inside the room, Louise came out to greet me.

'He's okay Callie,' she soothed, touching my shoulder gently. 'He's had a fit and the team are with him right now.'

I walked inside to see Deryn's bed laid flat. A nurse was cupping his head in her hands to hold him steady while the rest of the team carried out tests and observations. The small room was packed with people wearing different coloured tunics. I headed through the melee straight for Deryn. His eyes were half shut and his pupils pointing downwards.

'Deryn, are you okay?' I asked, stroking his arm.

'Uh huh,' he replied groggily.

Thank God. He could hear me.

'Deryn, tell me to shut up!' I thought that by giving him permission to be rude, he'd definitely take the chance if he was still compos mentis.

'Shuh hup,' Deryn replied.

One of the nurses explained that Deryn had had a seizure while he was alone in his room. He had bitten the inside of his mouth and when one of the team had came back to carry out observations, she'd noticed that his mouth was full of blood and he was totally unresponsive.

The crash team was called and that was when Louise contacted me.

I felt a massive pang of guilt. Deryn had been alone during that first seizure, absolutely terrified. And where was I? Back at Charley's House because I had no pyjamas. I felt wretched.

I noticed that Deryn's eyes were flickering to the right. Suddenly, his head started to nod and twitch. Then his right arm flew upwards, hitting the barriers on both sides of his bed. He was having another seizure. The fit gathered momentum and the crash team went into overdrive. The nurse held his head tightly as another nurse injected him with anticonvulsants.

Nothing was stopping the fit, in fact it was getting worse with every second. Deryn's entire body was violently thrashing about, his arms smashing against the barriers, making sickening thuds, his mouth still covered in blood. I had to leave the room.

A nurse approached me and squeezed me tightly as I crumpled and started to cry.

'You're not made of stone, you know, it's okay to cry,' she whispered in my ear and offered to make me a cup of tea.

For 12 minutes – an eternity to me – I listened to each thump on the barrier. It sounded as if there was an earthquake in Deryn's room, the heavy hospital bed being moved about by the sheer momentum of his seizure.

Then, over the banging and crashing, I heard Louise gently comforting him. My son may not have been conscious but I knew that hearing was the last sense to disappear and if there was any chance Deryn could still hear then he would be listening to the beautiful Louise speaking to him in her calm Bristol accent.

'It's okay Deryn, just try to relax. Mum is right outside… you're going to be just fine.'

❖

Deryn's violent thrashing stopped and he became totally unresponsive. There was nothing there at all, not even a flicker. I had to call Simon. It was almost 1am and while I knew that a phone call at this time of night would scare him, I couldn't deal with this by myself. I needed my rock.

Within minutes of my call, Simon had packed Dylan's overnight bag and was on the way to drop him at my mum's house. Then he made the five-hour drive to Bristol.

Back at the hospital, a CT scan had been booked and I followed as the crash team pushed Deryn's bed through corridors and into lifts. His blood pressure was still incredibly high and he was given more anticonvulsants to prevent further fitting. These controlled the physical effects but the seizures were still continuing in his brain.

Thankfully, the CT scan came back normal. But the team was not able to stabilise his blood pressure or stop the seizures so Deryn was transferred to the paediatric intensive care unit (PICU) for closer observation.

PICU was dark, with the only light coming from small dim spotlights illuminating the end of each bed. Tiny babies were hooked up to machines with wires protruding from their little bodies and toddlers were in slightly bigger beds, wearing only nappies and covered in more wires.

The nursing care was one on one, with observations carried out every few minutes. Deryn was wheeled into a glass-walled room at the end of the ward. Louise was also with us, an angel by my side, and she gave my hand a comforting squeeze as we made him comfortable in his new room.

Deryn was hooked up to machines to monitor his brain activity, heart rate and blood pressure. Still unconscious, he looked beautifully peaceful. Then, as I stood stroking his fuzzy, peach-coloured hair, he emptied his bladder. His onesie was saturated and obviously needed to come off.

The PICU nurse called over two young female trainees and asked them to strip and wash Deryn before putting him in a hospital gown.

As I stood at the end of his bed, his head in my hands, I couldn't help laughing. 'Deryn, here you are being stripped naked by two pretty young nurses and you aren't even conscious to enjoy it!' I chuckled, as Louise giggled next to me.

Louise stayed with me, keeping me company until Simon arrived at 5.30am. Her shift had ended hours earlier but there was no question of her leaving me by myself.

Deryn was taken for an MRI scan and we loitered nearby, fuelled by caffeine and adrenaline, waiting to hear the outcome. The scan showed significant changes and abnormalities symptomatic of cyclosporine – the drug they were using to halt the GvHD – so they switched to another immunosuppressant drug.

Deryn was also showing some physical changes to his brain due to his high blood pressure so antihypertensive drugs were added to Deryn's growing list of medication. His doctors decided to keep him on steroids, even though these were fuelling the flourishing adenovirus count and raising his blood pressure.

Deryn finally woke up while Simon and I were getting a few hours sleep back at Charley's House. Upon our return, the nurse who had been watching our son informed us that Deryn was none too pleased to find himself in PICU wearing nothing but a tiny gown and having to use a bedpan.

After just one night in PICU, Deryn was allowed back onto the BMT ward. He was elated to return to his room. Within a few days, he was more alert and his appetite returned with a vengeance. Not having eaten, coupled with having used up so much energy during his fits had clearly given him a healthy hunger.

As he eagerly tucked into his third plate of food, Simon and I looked at each other and laughed. Our Deryn was back.

❖

We had reached BMT +74. As Deryn had now spent more time in isolation than most patients, it was decided, as much for the state of his mental health as anything else, that he would be better off leaving the BMT unit.

Sadness, fear, relief, anxiety and excitement enveloped me. We had experienced some amazing and hilarious times in that room. It certainly wasn't all doom and gloom – once, I'd arrived to find Deryn prancing about with an adult nappy on his head. I'd seen him use the surgical tape to make his face like a monster and we'd entertained ourselves for hours by pranking each other.

We even had our very own prank caller. For days, we received phone calls from Bristol University asking for the head of IT and after a few days – much to Deryn's amusement – I started to play up to the role.

'Have you turned it off and on again?' I asked the caller as Deryn chuckled away in the background. 'Perhaps you should cut the plug off…'

The nurses were sad to see Deryn go. Many told me how much he brightened up their day with his deadpan sense of humour and wacky comedy skits. Every member of staff – from the cooks and cleaners through to the medical staff – had become like family to us and he occupied a special place in their hearts. Thank you didn't seem enough for the wonderful brigade whose care had got Deryn this far.

It was unnerving thinking about going it alone after such a long time. As we packed up Deryn's possessions and clothes, I started crying. Deryn was looking well and eating well so why couldn't I shake off the feeling that it was too good to be true?

I cast my mind back to September 2012, when Deryn had the rest of the cancer cut from his throat and Dr Mike had taken me to one side and told me confidentially that there was just a very small chance of the transplant working.

His team wasn't even sure if Deryn would make it through the preparation weeks leading up to the transplant because of the rarity and severity of his two cancers. His chances of recovery were very slim but while there was a tiny chance that he might pull through, it was worth going for.

Those odds made the choice to go to Bristol a decision that haunted us during the tougher times. I would have liked the hardest decision we had to make about our son to be which school to send him to.

While holding back on revealing the severity of his situation, I had been honest with Deryn about the fact that transplants were not always successful and had given him the chance to decide his own future. He chose to go to Bristol, knowing that if he didn't go, he would have no chance at all.

Deryn had to have one final blood transfusion before heading out into the world sporting his 'Who needs hair with a body like this?' T-shirt. As he sat patiently, he started getting upset at the austere look of his bare room as we packed everything up.

It was the first time I'd seen him nervous and frightened about the future. He had become institutionalised after so many months in hospital and was understandably scared about leaving his bubble and venturing out into the real world.

The transfusion finished and as Deryn waited for me outside room 6, my heart missed a beat. This was the first step towards the rest of his life. He posed for one last picture, the memory of

CHAPTER 29

leaving BMT sealed forever in our minds. All the other emotions I felt leading up to this moment vanished and I was left with just one.

Gratitude. My God, I was grateful.

Chapter 30

DERYN'S FIRST OUTPATIENT APPOINTMENT WAS APPROACHING AND I was looking forward to hearing about the progress his engrafting bone marrow was making. Following some blood tests, Dr Barbara came in to see him.

'Hello Deryn, I like your socks today,' she said in her usual jovial manner. Barbara was a breath of fresh air. She dressed in a crazy, colourful 'non doctor' kind of way, which I admired as I shared her love of eccentric clothing. Barbara was a big fan of Deryn's socks and controversial T shirts and always cheered him up with her compliments.

She told him that his neutrophil count needed boosting as it was hovering at just 0.5, rendering him neutropenic once again. This wasn't great news given that he was out in the big wide world of bugs, coughs and colds with no immune system to speak of. As for his bone marrow, there was good and bad news. The good news was that Deryn's own marrow had been totally replaced by the donor cells. However, the virus he had been harbouring for so long was complicating things, causing the new marrow to engraft incompletely.

By now, my heart no longer sank at bad news. I had developed a method of shutting off the emotional side of what I was hearing and was able to go straight into 'Okay, so what are we going to do about it' mode.

The best course of action was to go back to the donor in Germany and ask if he would be generous enough to donate another bag of bone marrow. The new cells would act like a top-up, kicking the virus into touch and helping the marrow produce far more blood cells than it was currently able to.

By his next outpatient visit, Deryn's blood counts had diminished further. A platelet transfusion was organised and Deryn was asked to spend the following day on the BMT unit having the anti-viral drug cidofovir administered as the virus markers were dangerously high. While this particular drug was detrimental to the already struggling bone marrow, the team had no choice.

Being in BMT for the day didn't bother Deryn at all. He was still on steroids, eating like a horse and his 'moonface' had returned. He was happy to go back for the day to a ward he knew so well and whose staff he trusted implicitly.

❖

Meanwhile, the Easter holidays were about to start. Simon had come back to Bristol with Dylan and we were planning some days out together. It was wonderful to have both boys and Simon at Charley's House. While I didn't mind living on my own, nothing compared to the joy of having my family around.

We wanted to give Dylan a break and had been contacted by the Over the Wall Camp, which funded Barretstown in Ireland, about their camps for siblings of children who were seriously ill. The camp gave them a chance to get away and be with other children who understood each other's plight.

Dylan jumped at the chance. He had been forced into his brother's shadow for a long time and although he was the quieter and more subdued of the two, I worried more about Dylan's mental health than Deryn's. Deryn was emotionally very strong, while Dylan was prone to bursts of anger, frustration and lashing out.

Simon and I had high hopes that the week-long camp would allow Dylan to express himself in front of people who were trained to help him. As we dropped him off at the incredibly grand Bryanston School in Dorset, any concerns I had that he might be nervous soon vanished. He couldn't wait to start playing with the other kids. I shed a few discreet but happy tears as I waved goodbye and made my way back to Bristol.

❖

The following week consisted of platelet transfusions and a plethora of drugs and blood count treatments as the doctors fought to control the virus and keep it at bay, boosting Deryn's immune system while waiting for the new donor cells to arrive.

With BMT +100 rapidly approaching and the virus destroying the cells quicker than Deryn could produce them, all our hopes were pinned on our anonymous German benefactor.

I threw myself back into my internet research. I had been reading up on material on and off since the day the radiologist first raised the topic of sugar and as much as I'd tried to implement a no-sugar diet for Deryn, while he was in hospital this had been impossible. The food was processed, the NG feeds were processed and the total parenteral nutrition was full of sugar, too.

But as soon as Deryn left the ward and I could control his food intake again, the no sugar diet – including artificial sweeteners – swung back into force. What I had found out about sugar and its effect on tumours was only the tip of the iceberg, but it was terrifying stuff and there was still so much more to learn.

During one of my late-night searches, I discovered an American doctor called Robert Morse. He had posted many videos online about how to treat cancer effectively without chemotherapy or other invasive methods that were standard practice. I watched videos made by people who'd been told they only had weeks to live who were now leading normal lives following the success of unconventional treatments.

I was shocked to discover Dr Morse's fervent belief that our lymphatic systems are incredibly important in our fight against any disease. His argument was that the lymphatic system processes cancer cells, causing them to become hard and calcified and instead of removing the affected lymph nodes, we should be cleansing them.

I felt sick. Deryn had lost his tonsils and his appendix while his spleen was rendered useless – all important parts of the lymphatic system. Deryn's tonsils had turned into hard, rock-like tumours. What if the reason the cancer hadn't spread was because Deryn's tonsils had done their job? Was the rock-like appearance actually dead and calcified cancer cells?

I was confused, angry, upset and frustrated. This newfound knowledge was a double edged sword. I didn't know what to believe. I was conscious that my digging and delving could easily lead me astray and leave me unsure about what was true and what was fiction but one thing I knew was that modern medicine didn't appear to treat the root cause of cancer, only the symptoms. Some of the treatment protocols could actually cause cancer, an unpalatable truth that many of Deryn's doctors had shared with me.

My gut instinct, which had served me well so far, had been screaming at me to not allow certain procedures to take place but I was frightened and couldn't be 100% sure that what I was feeling was right. The more I searched for answers, though, the more it became apparent to me that I was right to feel this way.

As the night wore on, I frantically searched for more information and alternatives to invasive treatments. If there were less harmful methods to treat cancer, then why were we not being told about them? My concern was no longer about getting rid of cancer – conventional medicine had done a great job there and I was grateful. The prospect of either cancer coming back was what kept me awake at night, as was preventing any long term damage to Deryn's body.

My son had been given a 'balance of probability' percentage survival rate of lasting beyond the next five years. If he was incredibly lucky, there was an 8% chance that he might make it to 18. I couldn't just sit back and accept such low odds. If there was anything at all that might help Deryn survive a little longer, or an effective and safe way to detox his body, I was willing to try, no matter what.

During another sleepless night spent researching online, I came across The Cancer Act of 1939 which, to my understanding, made it illegal for doctors to even discuss alternative treatments with a patient. As a result, I didn't feel at all comfortable about talking to Deryn's team about my findings, much as I trusted them.

I was contacted by an oncology friend who told me that I shared my views with a man she knew. Ken was a businessman and had treated his son a few years earlier using alternative remedies. His son had also had chemotherapy and despite low odds of survival, he somehow recovered from stage 4 neuroblastoma with virtually no side effects.

Ken had set up a charity helping other families access specialised equipment such as infrared saunas and macerating juicers.

'I think you should talk to Ken,' my friend urged.

I was willing to talk to anyone who could give Deryn the best chance of beating the virus, boosting his immune system and preventing a relapse of cancer. When BMT +100 dawned and Deryn's blood counts still looked dangerously low, I sent Ken a message on Facebook and he rang me straight back.

'First of all, do they still have that trolley outside the day ward covered in chocolate bars and sweets?' Ken asked.

'Yes they do,' I told him. He sighed.

'Sugar feeds cancer so please don't let Deryn eat from that

trolley.'

After a brief conversation, Ken asked us to visit him and his family in Devon. Before heading west, I spent hours reading up on the benefits of a good organic diet consisting mainly of fruit and vegetables.

Cutting out meat, cow's dairy, white flour and refined sugar from all of our diets was paramount. These were acid forming foods, an environment that cancer loves and thrives in, so there would be no more high-calorie processed junk food.

Ken very kindly gave us a juicer, a massive box of organic vegetables that he had grown himself under a poly tunnel, a water filter and a large range of high-powered super greens and other natural supplements.

My focus was on feeding Deryn as many cancer-fighting foods as possible while also eradicating foods that feed cancer from his diet. My rationale told me that if his body was the same terrain as it was before diagnosis, then there was every chance that cancer could return. Learning how much we could do for him through nutrition made me feel powerful, euphoric and in control of my family and our destiny once again. Simon and Dylan were keen to embrace the clean-eating regime too.

The so-called clean diet at hospital seemed anything but. It stated that Deryn was to have no fresh fruit and vegetables because of the risk from bacteria and pesticides. But I started soaking fresh produce in a small amount of food-grade hydrogen peroxide diluted in a sink full of water, which was sufficient to wash away any harmful residue. Even doing this one thing felt momentous, like we were making a dramatic U-turn in our lives.

Next, I devised a dietary plan, calculating exactly how many calories Deryn needed. I wrote down everything he ate to ensure he was getting the right amount of energy. The last thing I wanted was for him to lose weight and our new health kick to be blamed for it.

On BMT +103, the new cells arrived from Germany and Deryn's doctors decided to administer 50% of them, keeping half in reserve in case Deryn needed yet another helping hand. Only time would tell if this latest step in the transplant had worked. Meanwhile, he was going into hospital every other day to be transfused with drugs, blood, platelets and G-CSF in the hope that this would all hurry the new marrow along.

My mind was temporarily taken off the worry by an invitation to the York Theatre where Linda Robson was finishing the UK stage tour of *Birds of a Feather*. After Linda's first visit when she could only see him through the glass panel, she wanted to meet Deryn in person. So she invited us backstage into her dressing room after the show where she lavished gifts, hugs and kisses on him.

Just a few days later, on BMT +124, Deryn's neutrophils were 1.34 and his platelets were 66. For the first time in as long as I could remember, Deryn didn't need a transfusion. It looked like he finally had an immune system!

Reeling from the wonderful news that the second set of cells seemed to be working, Deryn was in high spirits. The virus was still on the rise but Deryn was feeling great for the first time in ages.

I got into the habit of spending hours juicing up fruits and veggies of various colours for the week ahead. Deryn wasn't a fan and I could understand why as some of them were quite earthy but he did his best to drink them without moaning or retching.

'Mum, I'm calling this one arse pop,' he quipped one morning as he showed off a vibrant orange, fruity moustache.

Simon was dancing around the kitchen, arse pop in hand, laughing. It was one of many beautiful moments that we shared in Charley's House, together as a family. This was a magical time. I felt like we were finally getting somewhere. We were all feeling more energised, clear-headed and healthy as a result of the new diet.

❖

Every day on our way to the gym, Simon and I used to walk through The Bear Pit. An open space underneath a large roundabout, it was home to a few ethical stalls, a tea shack and a lot of homeless people. One of the stallholders, Pete, chatted to us one day about what we were doing in Bristol and suggested that we look into the healing benefits of cannabis.

I had come across information about cannabis and how effectively it could help treat cancer before but I had always dismissed it. However, my curiosity was awakened and as I researched further, the anecdotal evidence from normal people who had used it to 'cure' themselves was overwhelming.

Many of these people had been given just a few months to live yet against all the odds, they were still here and shouting about their recovery. I couldn't help feeling horrified that these poor people had had to break the law just to give themselves a better chance at staying alive.

While I was intrigued, I didn't want to risk a hefty prison sentence. I felt that my efforts to detox Deryn and change his diet were a better way forward.

❖

By July, after five months in Bristol, Deryn was not only holding on to transfused platelets but producing his own. To ensure that the marrow had definitely engrafted, another biopsy was carried out to have a good look at the cells.

The results came back, revealing that the marrow was indeed producing cells, albeit very slowly. Hallelujah. Deryn was taken off immunosuppressants and the doctors' hope was that once the marrow was allowed to produce fully, the virus would disappear.

With GvHD also on the wane, we had good reason to be cheerful. Now that Deryn's immune system was showing positive signs, we took every opportunity to enjoy our newfound freedom – visiting the newest addition to our family, baby Isla, a cousin for the boys, and Longleat safari park. Dylan excelled as Deryn's carer, pushing him around purposefully in his wheelchair as Deryn held one wheel so that he and his brother could perform donut turns in the gravel.

Since Deryn had become ill, we had grown closer as a family. The distances between us had not broken us like they did with many families. Our constant separations only made the times we were all together that much more special.

Being bullied, being bald, being a bouncer, being obese; there wasn't much I hadn't had thrown at me over the years so seeing people talking about my son didn't upset me at all. But I was utterly impressed with the boys, who had also developed a blasé attitude to the stares without becoming hard-hearted.

It was always strange to see other people's reactions to Deryn. Many would simply stare at the bald boy with the swollen face. Others became visibly upset. None of us minded – I'd had bright pink hair for most of my adult life so I was no stranger to staring onlookers and had developed a very thick skin.

Other children had tried to bully Deryn when he was younger but it never amounted to anything because he genuinely did not care if he had no friends or a hundred friends. He was happy with who he was and that was all that mattered. My, how I envied that.

❖

Meanwhile, Deryn's good progress continued. He was enjoying our new healthy lifestyle, avidly consuming the tomato and garlic pasta sauces we made together along with wholewheat pasta. One afternoon, he decided to walk into town and back. It took him three hours but he managed it despite the brutal hills.

During the school holidays Deryn's girlfriend Kim had become a regular visitor to Bristol, staying for a week at a time and helping to cheer Deryn up with a little window on the outside world. Unfortunately, their budding relationship wasn't destined to last and Kim informed Deryn she no longer felt the same way about him and just wanted to be friends.

It was sad but not entirely unexpected. I was concerned that their break-up might be detrimental to Deryn's recovery but I needn't have worried. Kim texted Deryn to say she was worried that he was angry with her, and he responded immediately.

'I don't have the right to be angry just because you don't have the same feelings for me anymore,' he told her. 'Please promise me that you won't just get a boyfriend because you don't want to be alone. Only go for someone who deserves you and treats you like a princess because that's all I ever wanted for you.'

I was so proud of him when he showed me his message – once I'd managed to stop crying.

The following day, Deryn was due back at hospital for a long antiviral drug infusion and for the first time he was put on the teenage ward where the decor was bright and exuberant and the views across the city to the Mendip Hills were mind-blowing.

Deryn was elated. 'I love it in here mum,' he enthused.

It was now BMT +138 and the pesky virus was still refusing to shift. The arrival of his three doctors together did nothing to alleviate my concerns. Being in front of a trio of doctors never meant good news.

Dr Doom – so-called because he always drew the short straw when bad news had to be delivered – revealed that, due to the virus, Deryn's bone marrow wasn't working as well as it should have been. The team felt there was no point in transplanting more donor cells as the first batch and the top-up hadn't worked.

Then Dr Glam chipped in with talk of chemotherapy and a mini transplant as further options for the future. But first, they needed to get rid of the damn virus.

Finally, Dr Barbara explained that the antiviral drug was not only destroying the new marrow, it was also causing significant damage to Deryn's kidneys and liver. It wasn't working against the virus so the team had decided to put him on a less harmful drug which might be more effective.

I was distraught but reminded myself that there would always be options, which is reassuring until more problems arise and the list of options gets shorter. Yet again, it felt like our light at the end of the tunnel was being cruelly blown out.

As I sat by the window overlooking the city, I closed my eyes and listened to my breath to try and calm my mind for a few seconds.

'I'm still not going to die from this you know,' Deryn said matter of factly.

I needed to believe that.

✥

For weeks we watched as Deryn underwent a multitude of blood transfusions and drug treatments while I tried to bolster him daily with juicing and various supplements.

Simon and I talked long and hard before deciding that if Deryn was still in treatment after the summer holidays, we would move Dylan and our dog Ozzy to Bristol until he was well enough to leave. Being parted so often had taken a toll on all of us and we'd had enough. Dylan's education as an eight-year old was less important than being with his family.

BMT +150 arrived, also marking the third anniversary of Deryn's leukaemia diagnosis. There was no way we weren't going to celebrate the anniversary of the worst day of our lives, for one very good reason – it marked another year that Deryn was still with us. One more year that cancer didn't get him.

When we were first told that Deryn would need treatment for three years, we were overwhelmed. It felt like forever. Today we should have been counting down the final few treatments and planning his future. Instead, we were in Bristol with no end in sight and no idea of what the future held.

Yet we were so grateful. It wasn't where we had planned to be three years later, but Deryn was alive and fighting on.

A new drug combination was rolled out and, encouragingly, Deryn's virus count had diminished from six million to a mere 84,000 – proof that the new regime was working. However, it was taking a heavy toll on his body, something I noticed when I saw him in his underwear one morning.

His knees were almost twice as big as his thighs and were incredibly swollen and painful. His underwear was baggy and his body looked pitifully frail. His legs were covered in stretch marks, with thin, dry parchment patches of skin across his ankles, shins and thighs. The lower part of his legs were covered in petechiae – tiny red spots caused by bleeding under the skin. While I understood that this was a symptom of low platelets, it didn't make looking at his legs any less harrowing.

Deryn spent most of his time in a wheelchair. The prolonged periods in bed had atrophied his muscles, his ankles were twisted and although he tried his hardest to exercise back at Charley's House, he was always too weak. The only saving grace was that he was feeling okay mentally. I held on to that.

Our healthy-eating regime was in full swing and I found I was enjoying cooking from scratch while all three boys were enjoying eating my creations. Deryn was eating like a horse but just couldn't maintain his weight so I decided to increase his daily intake to 3,000 calories a day.

CHAPTER 30

BMT +161 arrived and, following discussions by many different doctors all over the world who were taking an active interest in Deryn's case, heralded a new plan of action.

The options were a mini transplant and further chemotherapy – which saddened me now that he had a full head of soft, downy baby hair – or a top-up of T-cells, also known as police cells because of their success in tracking down and killing any residual cancer cells.

Deryn's team studied both ideas and decided on the T-cell top-up, which would be requested from the mystery German donor. We would have so much to thank him for if we ever got the chance to meet him.

Before they could transfuse the T-cells, another endoscopy was imperative to confirm that there was no sign of GvHD in Deryn's gut. Any dreaded sign of this would result in the top-up being cancelled, leaving only the option of another transplant and more chemotherapy.

Getting ready for surgery, Deryn's arms were too weak for him to tie up his hospital gown himself. Dylan didn't hesitate and stepped forward to assist. Watching him carefully tend to his big brother and seeing Deryn graciously accept help was very poignant.

It was nearing the August bank holiday weekend and once the endoscopy was complete, Deryn's doctors announced that we could take him home for the weekend. We didn't need telling twice and – in record time – we packed up the car and headed up to Norfolk to see the family.

It would be a few days before the results were back so I wondered why they were letting us go home out of the blue. Had they found something terrifying in theatre? If that was the case, I didn't want to know. I wanted to go home and see my mum and let Deryn see his friends.

That evening, just before we went to bed, I asked Deryn how he felt about the planned top-up.

'It'll be alright in the end,' he sighed with a wink.

'Yeah because if it's not alright... it's not the end,' I smiled.

❖

Our local newspaper, the Eastern Daily Press, had been following Deryn's story and they asked if he would like to write an open letter about what he was going through. We didn't know it would end up on the front page alongside a huge photograph of him.

'Hi, I'm Deryn,' he began. 'I'm 13 and since last September, I have been in hospital preparing, having and recovering from a bone marrow transplant. It is very boring a lot of the time because of how long it has taken. I feel like I'm going crazy.

'I know it might sound bad but I really don't mind not seeing my friends because I like to spend time on my own. I haven't seen them for so long. It's kind of "out of sight, out of mind." I'm sure it's the same the other way round as well.

'I feel very upset sometimes because I haven't been "normal" since I was 10. I have missed a lot of trips and going out with my friends because I have been ill.

'I don't really feel anything regarding my future, I live in the moment. I always have but the last three years I have had to do that so much more because you can't plan when you're in my position.

'I feel very lucky to still be here and that there are still a few options left to treat me. I have met a lot of children over the last three years who have died. It is always on my mind that I might be next. I can't think like that or I will go mad.

'My family drive me crazy sometimes but I know they are just trying to help me. I am very lucky to have a family who want me to get better and are willing to change so much of their own lives so that I don't feel like the odd one out.

CHAPTER 30

'All I want to do now is put on weight, get home, get fit, see my friends and ride my BMX again.'

Chapter 31

We were approaching the first anniversary of Deryn's diagnosis of Langerhans cell sarcoma in August 2012. Hearing cancer for the second time was much harder than the first. Especially when accompanied by the words 'extremely rare' and 'we don't know what to do'.

To celebrate the second worst day of our lives and the fact that Deryn was still with us, we headed down to Devon to visit Ken and his family. Out of the blue, I received a phone call from Dr, Ponni who gave me some wonderful news: there was no GvHD present anywhere in Deryn's gut.

'Fantastic, so this means we can go ahead with the T-cells as planned?' I asked enthusiastically. 'No more chemo!'

Dr Ponni took a deep breath.

'You can cope with whatever she says next,' I told myself, feeling devoid of any emotions as I prepared myself for the worst.

'Because of the results of the bone marrow sample that Deryn also had taken on Friday, I'm afraid the T-cell top up is no longer an option for us,' she said solemnly. 'However, there is some good news, which we can talk about when you get here.'

I stood stock-still, suddenly mesmerised by the floral pattern on Ken's dining room tablecloth while Dr Ponni did her best to explain exactly what they had found, or rather, what they couldn't find: Deryn's bone marrow was non-existent. The antiviral drugs had completely wiped out his bone marrow and there was absolutely nothing left. Zilch. The bone marrow transplant had officially failed.

'Okay, thank you,' I heard myself replying. 'This makes sense.'

So that explained why, after three bags of platelets, Deryn's count shot up into the 80s but, after four days, dipped back down to zero. There was absolutely nothing there to make any blood cells. Deryn was living on transfusions, just as he had been before the first transplant 180 days ago,

I didn't get upset. I should have felt more devastated but my defence mechanism kicked in once again. I felt cold-hearted that I wasn't more distressed but I knew we still had options. There was still hope. We were not giving up.

I felt dazed as I stared out of the window across the beautiful, hilly South-West countryside. Fleetingly, I imagined getting into the car and disappearing into those hills, never to be seen again. Away from it all.

'Callie, you okay?' Simon said, squeezing my shoulders and snapping me out of my daydream before I could grab my car keys and run.

❖

Many months earlier, they had taken bone marrow from Deryn to use just in case all else failed. All else had failed so Deryn would now be getting his own bone marrow back.

The hope was that with his own cells going back in, there would be functioning bone marrow, T-cells, lymphocytes and all the other good stuff needed to dispatch the virus for good. On the downside, the cells being transplanted back could well contain the two cancers that Deryn had fought so hard against. In fact, it was quite likely.

I felt utterly desperate and deflated.

If this third bone marrow transplant was successful, Deryn would merely be back to exactly where he was seven months ago and it would be just as if the donor transplant had never happened. The suffering Deryn had gone through, everything we had all gone through as a family… it had all been pointless.

Questions swirled around in my mind. Surely there had to be another way to get rid of this virus without giving Deryn his own cells back? Why couldn't they just do another stem-cell top-up from the donor as well as the T-cell top up?

Dr Ponni had answers. There was no point giving T-cells again as there was absolutely nothing there for them to work with. It would be like pouring water through a sieve.

Another donated bone marrow transplant was an option but Deryn would need conditioning all over again and there was a very high chance that, this time, the toxicity of that process could kill him. The risk was too great.

Dr Ponni went on to explain that a transplant using the patient's own cells is virtually guaranteed to work. She had never known anyone not to engraft with their own cells as the cells recognise the body, rendering the risk of GvHD non-existent. Once his own cells had grafted and the virus had finally gone, Dr Ponni explained that Deryn would go back to Addenbrooke's to be monitored for signs of cancer. If either cancer came back, then he'd need another bone marrow transplant.

All through this meeting, Deryn sat by my side as he usually did, listening to every word and soaking it all up. Usually, he said very little but this time he made his feelings quite clear. All he wanted was to go home, pick up the pieces of his fractured life and start enjoying it as soon as possible. He was tired and fed up with fighting and feeling like death. He had just one overwhelming desire – to start living again.

I could feel myself spiralling into negativity, into the dark place that beckoned in times of desperation and despair. I reminded myself that we had to try everything and that everything possible was being done. The risk of the transplant failing had always been there. Deryn's team had said from day one that they had no idea if a bone marrow transplant would work against Langerhans cell sarcoma.

We decided to focus on getting Deryn's own cells back into him as soon as possible, giving him the best chance of eradicating the virus. We had learned so much and, although we would be leaving Bristol with our mission incomplete, we'd given it our best shot and Deryn was still with us. We would carry on with our extremely healthy new way of life to try and ensure that Deryn's cancers didn't return.

The following day, Deryn received a bag of his own bone marrow. His own cells were now racing around his body and all we could do was hope that once they started to engraft, the virus wouldn't stand a chance.

Back at Charley's House, Deryn watched patiently as I filled a bath for him, adding copious amounts of relaxing bubble bath. As I watched my weak teenage son gingerly step in and try to swish the water around him, I felt a huge wave of sadness wash over me.

'What's the matter, Mum?' Deryn asked.

'Don't you ever feel just a little bit angry with your life?' I asked him. 'Don't you ever get mad that this is the hand you were dealt? Doesn't it seem unfair to you?'

'No,' he replied without hesitation. 'I don't get angry or annoyed because I chose this.'

I gasped inwardly as goosebumps covered my skin.

Deryn and I had always been 'spiritual' people, deeply connected to our senses and psychic abilities. When Deryn was three years old, I'd found him standing in the hallway one day, looking as if someone had their arm around his shoulder. When I'd asked him what he was doing, he told me that a man was with him.

He then described my grandfather Pawel down to a tee. Deryn was born four months after my grandad died. Deryn had never seen a picture of him before so I dug one out and he recognised him as the man with him, before giving an eerily accurate description of the man my grandfather had been.

Back in the present, Deryn took a deep breath and continued.

'I chose this and I chose you as my mum. I chose you because you needed to learn some lessons. And I chose Dad because he needed to learn quite a few more,' Deryn quipped with a cheeky grin.

'I chose everyone around me and I chose to go through all of this before I was even born,' he added. 'I don't feel cheated because I know that this is what my soul needs to grow. Without this, my soul wouldn't evolve.'

I felt tears well up in my eyes.

'Our souls need to experience all there is throughout our many lives. Only when our souls are strong enough can they go on to face their biggest challenge. This is my biggest challenge.'

I was lost for words.

'Is that what you really believe Deryn?' I asked him.

'It's not what I believe. I just know it – like I know that I'm not going to die because of this. Everything happens for a reason. Now, can I have a bath please?' he asked, ushering me out of the bathroom.

I reflected on Deryn's words of wisdom. Perhaps this inner knowledge was how he was able to deal with everything he faced so calmly and graciously. I felt like I understood him a little better.

❖

The next morning, for the first time in three months, Deryn spiked a temperature and was in considerable pain. We headed to hospital where he was put on a morphine drip for the pain in his knees and his liver. Once he was comfortably set up in his room, four of his medical team came in to see us. But with the morphine, he was barely conscious for longer than 20 minutes at a time so as the doctors came in, he dozed off.

A week had passed since Deryn's own cells had been transfused back in but the virus was going nowhere. In fact, the viral markers were on the increase daily and the antiviral drugs they had been giving him were not working. Deryn's own bone marrow hadn't started to engraft yet and he was still aplastic anaemic – meaning he was deficient in all types of blood cell – with no immune system.

Dr Doom started to tell me how concerned the team was for Deryn.

'We'd really hoped to see the virus eliminated by now, although there is still time for it to work,' he added.

I heard the anguish in his voice and saw the fear on the faces of his fellow medics. The virus that Deryn had wasn't as deadly as some, meaning they could afford to spend a little more time waiting for the marrow to engraft.

The extensive use of antiviral drugs had caused the failure of the last two transplants. Naturally, the team didn't want that to happen again. The same drugs had also caused significant damage to Deryn's liver, which was now extremely enlarged and painful.

Nevertheless, Deryn wasn't nearly as ill as he should have been, given his bleak symptoms and diminishing blood results.

'How Deryn isn't experiencing liver failure is beyond us,' Dr Doom added. 'So we are no longer going to treat the virus. We are going to leave Deryn to fight this himself. Only Deryn and his bone marrow can get rid of this virus. Either the marrow engrafts and kills the virus or the virus will kill Deryn. If the marrow cannot engraft and kill the virus very soon, there is nothing more we can do.' He paused then added gently: 'I suggest you start praying.'

The real reason for the team's visit became crystal clear. Although Deryn was tired and ready to give up, they wanted him to give this all he had and fight desperately to survive. I wanted him to fight with every fibre of his soul. After everything else my son had faced and conquered, a pathetic little virus was not going to see him off. He was a warrior, I was a warrior and we were going to war.

As they left the room, the team expressed how sorry they were. Deryn was still sleeping soundly, blissfully unaware of the bleak prognosis. Apart from the endless beeps of the machinery, the room was eerily quiet.

❖

'I suggest you start praying!' I repeated to myself. 'I don't do praying, I do proactive things. Nothing more can be done? My arse,' I muttered to myself, frantically searching for my iPad.

Falling back into the armchair, recovered tablet in hand, I opened up Google. This was just another obstacle, failure was not an option and I was going to do whatever it took to help save Deryn's life.

I tapped in 'natural remedies for adenovirus' and clicked return.

❖

Just a couple of hours searching for alternative remedies yielded a list as long as my arm of natural treatments that had been proven to have great results with many different viruses.

The doctors might have given up treating the virus but I certainly hadn't. Clutching my list, I headed into the city to buy the ingredients that I truly believed would give Deryn a fighting chance.

First stop was a herbal shop across the road from the hospital. I'd spoken to the owner when I was looking for something to ease Deryn's mucositis – which had led to painful ulcers in the lining of his digestive tract – and he'd recommended camomile tea. Today, after I explained Deryn's situation, he mixed up some lemon balm and olive leaf extract to add to tea.

Next stop was a health-food shop where I bought copious amounts of unaltered Manuka honey, garlic capsules, elderberry extract, olive-leaf extract, Pau D'arco dried bark tea, vitamin C powder and bicarbonate of soda.

I walked back to the hospital carrying the huge plastic bag that had left me a couple of hundred pounds lighter but with a spring in my step and an optimistic heart. I felt full of purpose and like I could take on the world – which was just as well as it certainly felt like I was about to declare war on the powers that be in the cancer club.

Deryn was awake when I got back and although I was dubious about telling him the brutal prognosis as he was already feeling so low, I knew that I couldn't not tell him. I had to be honest, as I had always been with him.

Thankfully, Deryn was feeling far more positive than he had in a long while. I unloaded my purchases, explaining what each one could do for him and he too was enthusiastic about the regime he was about to embark on, which would put him in control once again.

'We can do this, buddy!' I cheered as I made him his first cup of herbal infused tea. With two teaspoons of Manuka honey stirred in, Deryn was quite happy to drink it.

A friend sent me some Lypo Spheric Vitamin C, a potent natural source of vitamin C in a form the body can easily absorb and which wouldn't get destroyed in the stomach – the fatty layer protected the vitamin C, allowing it to reach the liver intact.

Morning, noon and night, I dosed Deryn up with various remedies, my mind at rest because nothing I was giving him could possibly cause him any harm. I had researched every ingredient to make sure of that. Some of Deryn's doctors did not agree, however. One in particular took umbrage at the supplements I was giving him and she took samples of everything to send off to the lab for testing. To my great relief – and her chagrin – the results came back with all the ingredients deemed totally harmless.

Five days earlier, the doctors had suggested that I start praying. Deryn's virus count was 3.8million, he had no immune system, his blood cells were non-existent and he was surviving on blood transfusions and Total Parenteral Nutrition.

I wondered what the issue was with me giving Deryn natural remedies when it was the toxic antiviral drugs he had been prescribed that were responsible for causing two transplants to fail.

Dr Ponni came to see us that afternoon. She discovered that Deryn's weight was increasing, his bloods were stabilising and the virus count was down to 200,000. She couldn't disguise her joy and punched the air with delight.

Whatever we were doing seemed to be working. I was also over the moon. His count was still dangerously high but it was a marked improvement. Even Deryn's liver function tests were better than expected, considering the sheer size of his liver.

Once again, Deryn had defied the medical odds – and he continued to improve on a daily basis. The team stopped the G-CSF, which was helping to bolster the neutrophils, as he had started to produce his own, indicating that the last bone marrow transplant was grafting successfully.

The virus count dropped further to 47,000 – down from 3.8million in the space of a week – and even the usually serious doctors couldn't hide their excitement at the results they were recording. Even more impressive was how many T-cells Deryn was producing, far in excess of what was expected so soon after the transplant. Just 17 days after Deryn's last transplant, his marrow was starting to work effectively.

Finally, it felt like we were making progress. BMT +200 was approaching and while Deryn would remain in hospital for a while, things were moving in the right direction. Simon, Dylan and I also started taking many of the natural remedies ourselves and noticed positive results very rapidly.

All the while, the atmosphere on the teenage ward was amazing. Dylan came in every morning with us and Simon and I would sit and watch our two sons playing board games or building Lego.

❖

In the midst of all the excitement, Dr Doom paid us an unscheduled visit – and he had some dispiriting news. Deryn's virus count had shot back up to 3.8million overnight.

My whole body felt like slumping to the floor. I wanted to give up. I was utterly confused. Deryn didn't look as ill as they were telling me he was. With numbers so high, according to science Deryn should have been spiking temperatures and suffering immensely. He wasn't. Apart from his liver issues, his painful knees and a rather strange occurrence of bright blue veins all over his torso, he was doing really well despite the infection markers rising slowly over the previous few days. This indicated that, as well as adenovirus, there was a bacterial infection.

Deryn's blood results didn't ever match up with how he looked or felt, stumping his team time and again. But as much as I loved having a unique child, I sometimes wished he could have been a brilliant artist or a dancer who stunned the world, instead of a medical anomaly who was doing nothing for my nervous system.

Dr Doom was also perplexed. I asked him if there might have been a mistake in the lab. The answer was no.

'Are you sure?' I pleaded. 'It seems odd that the count is exactly 3.8million again. Could they be old results?'

Deryn had been suffering with extremely painful knees, to the point where he couldn't sleep at night or walk with ease. Dr Doom reckoned this symptom, coupled with Deryn's increasing bilirubin and rising infection levels, pointed to septicaemia. Brilliant! If that was their considered opinion, at least we could get on and start treating it.

A blood clot on the end of his line was the likely cause of infection, so an ultrasound was booked and a CT scan for his legs also planned. Deryn's pain had started to radiate down from his knees to his feet and he was in agony, so an on-demand morphine machine was also mooted. This filled me with concern as morphine is highly addictive and would mean no more home visits for Deryn.

Dr Doom paused and turned to the table at the end of Deryn's bed, which was laden with teas, tinctures, potions and foods that I had brought in to help him.

'What are all these for, then?' he asked with interest.

I cheerfully showed him each item and, in great detail, explained how it worked.

'Well, clearly they don't work because Deryn's count has gone back up to 3.8million.' He laughed.

I felt like someone had punched me hard in the stomach. I was seething. This medic was laughing because I had tried to help my son and failed. I didn't get the joke.

'It's okay, Mum, I feel better since taking this stuff,' said Deryn, trying his best to console me as the doctor left. 'I think it's helping.'

I couldn't stay downhearted. I had to hold on to the fact that Deryn's immune system seemed to be flourishing and that maybe, with a tiny bit of help from the supplements, it could take over and kill the virus by itself.

❖

Deryn, meanwhile, didn't buy the septicaemia story at all. He was convinced he had a line infection. I promised to speak to the doctor about getting the line removed and an echocardiograph was booked to take a closer look.

An X-ray also revealed that Deryn's legs had not grown as much as they should have. Unfortunately, this is common in young people who have been exposed to prolonged steroid use.

As Deryn lay on the couch, I could see the growth lines in his bone from his X-ray as well as other lines that coincided with the intensive chemotherapy regime. It was like some sort of macabre timeline etched on his body that he would never be able to forget.

That evening, after making him one last cup of Manuka honey tea, I tucked him in for the night. Just then, another doctor arrived. He had a huge grin on his face and announced that he had some good news.

'Deryn's virus levels are actually 3,000 – they made a mistake in the lab,' he told me cheerfully.

A clinical error – I bloody knew it! I felt totally vindicated. The natural remedies were not rubbish, they were working. Clearly it helped that there was also some engraftment of Deryn's own cells, but the virus was starting to surrender and I was going to take some credit for it.

Deryn's infection markers were also lowering so, coupled with his increasing immune system, the antibiotics seemed to be working. He had even managed to put on 6kg. I wanted to believe that, after so many false starts, finally we were turning a corner.

❖

CHAPTER 31

Not long after this, I was contacted by ITN news via Twitter with a request for an interview with Deryn, to run in their evening bulletin. Deryn readily agreed. For a few hours, we all sat around in Charley's House while the journalist posed questions and asked Deryn to build his Lego for the cameras. That evening, we all had a bit of a giggle at how we looked on screen, ribbing each other about our performances.

In fact, as time went on, Deryn's story was gathering more and more momentum. More parcels were arriving for him every week. He'd already received so many gifts from well-wishers, everything from books to martial-arts fighting gear. His followers were a mixed bunch… young girls, fighter pilots, royal marines and cage fighters were all fascinated by his story.

His list of celebrity followers was also climbing and, within a short time, I was in contact with some of the most famous faces in the UK: TV personalities Amanda Holden, Davina McCall and Caroline Flack (actually an old school friend of mine), Corrie star Helen Flanagan, Only Fools and Horses' Boycie, John Challis, hard-man actor Danny Dyer and Hot Fuzz stars Simon Pegg and Nick Frost were all hugely supportive and very interested in Deryn's progress.

It was wonderfully exciting, if surreal, to see that he was touching so many people – I found it quite weird being recognised in the street by complete strangers. People would approach me in shops across Bristol and ask: 'Are you Deryn's mum?'

I always made an effort to talk to everyone as without the support from our community and beyond, life would have been much harder to cope with.

❖

Deryn soon got into a routine whereby he was allowed out by day but had to go back into the teenage ward every evening. The virus had been virtually eliminated and his immune system was now strong enough to cope with close interaction with others.

We decided to take advantage of this and, using the wheelchair lent to us by the hospital, took the boys to see the sights in Bristol. It was magical to roam the streets with all of my boys. Dylan enjoyed pushing his brother along and Simon and I could actually walk together, holding hands like a normal couple.

On Dylan's ninth birthday, just as we were all heading off together to spend the day on the SS Great Britain museum ship, we were stopped in the corridor by Dr Glam. She announced good-naturedly that Deryn was yet again baffling the professionals.

'What's he up to this time?' I asked, trying to keep my tone lighthearted as I put my hand on Deryn's shoulder.

Dr Glam explained that the team had carried out a chimerism test on Deryn's recent bone marrow aspirate. When he received the donor's bone marrow, his blood group changed to that of the donor's and he became a chimera – someone with two genetically distinct types of cells and two types of DNA.

Having been given his own cells back, Deryn was no longer a different blood type and there shouldn't have been any more of the donor's cells present. However, suspicious of the high levels of T-cells in his blood, they had decided to test his new bone marrow again. The results showed that while Deryn's T-cells were his own, his myeloid cells were the donors – this shouldn't even have been possible.

'Surely Deryn's T-cells should be attacking the myeloid cells because the donor cells are imposters and the T-cells should be destroying them?' I asked.

'We don't understand it either,' she told me with a puzzled shake of the head.

Deryn's donor wasn't even a 10/10 match yet now his body was producing myeloid cells and T-cells from two different sources! Still not fully understanding what was going on, we decided not to let Deryn's unique, mischievous and unpredictable body system stress us out, but to make the most of Dylan's birthday. The outing passed by in a happy blur.

But that day was also a turning point in Deryn's pain threshold. He was now in such unbearable agony with his knees that he decided he no longer wanted to come to Charley's House during the day. He wanted to stay in hospital where he could be given much stronger painkillers.

The MRI results came back with an explanation for his extreme pain. Lack of blood flow to the area, caused by long periods of steroid use during a crucial period of growth, had caused avascular necrosis behind his knee, so the end of the bone had simply rotted away and died. At some point, he would need a knee replacement.

Dr Ponni ordered a bone density scan and further tests to determine whether this necrosis was spreading elsewhere in Deryn's frail body. His left ankle was swollen and immensely painful, as were his shoulders, hips and ribs, which didn't bode well.

Bad news always seemed to affect his appetite and for weeks he ate barely anything, sipping feebly at water and cups of herbal tea. He was being sustained purely by the TPN supplement. The longer he went without eating, the less inclined he felt to try and his increasing frailty and muscle wastage meant that we were completely dependent on a wheelchair to move him around.

Depressing as this was, we all accepted an invitation to a cancer charity ball in Bedfordshire which happened to coincide with my birthday.

It was a manic rush to get Deryn's drugs sorted before we made the three-hour car journey to the event but the thought of seeing friends we hadn't seen for almost a year made all the upheaval and effort worthwhile. Being in a room with others who had travelled a similar journey to us was wonderful; there were no quizzical looks about Deryn's strange appearance and no expectations.

Penny, Marcie and Joss also attended the ball and Deryn was overjoyed to see his best friend again. I could not have wished for a better birthday celebration. For the first time in four years, I wasn't celebrating it in a hospital room. After a couple of hours, Deryn was exhausted so we all headed back to the hotel.

The following morning, Simon had to go home to deal with important family issues so I was left holding the fort with Deryn and Dylan until he could get back. I'd learned to deal with all sorts of challenging situations on my own so I wasn't concerned.

But we arrived back at the ward to discover that Deryn had spiked a temperature the previous day. He would now have no choice but to stay in hospital until the cause was identified.

One trauma after another. When was it going to end?

With Deryn's blood counts dropping dangerously fast, the doctors decided that a further transfusion using the donor's stem cells might be necessary.

Dr Barbara explained that some of the donor cells had reappeared and seemed to be taking over Deryn's entire bone marrow. He had only been given his own cells back because the donor cells had seemingly disappeared and the marrow was empty.

This bizarre set of circumstances meant that the donor cells and Deryn's own cells were fighting for dominance. So, in the midst of all this, his other symptoms could be a result of graft versus host disease – GvHD. It felt like we were going round in circles. Deryn was in a critical situation, that much I understood.

I thought back to the off-the-cuff remark three years earlier, from one of Deryn's team, that he would rewrite medical history... it seemed to be a prophecy.

Dr Doom arrived clutching a large bundle of notes. He pushed some sheets towards me, printed with numbers, charts and graphs, and asked me to take a look. To my great surprise, I understood every single reading.

Deryn was facing a number of issues. His temperature hovered at the 38.5°C mark but antibiotics were no longer bringing it down. His platelets stood at a mere 4, even after a very recent transfusion. His liver was no longer inflamed but was producing a lot of protein and he was retaining fluid, which was making him swell up like a balloon.

In addition, his permanent feelings of nausea made it impossible for him to eat and even the morphine was failing to take the edge off the pain in his legs.

Dr Doom admitted he had no idea what was at the root of all these problems and asked me: 'What do you think is causing these symptoms?'

He wanted my advice? After laughing at my natural remedies, it seemed he'd had a change of heart and now valued what I had to say. I read back through the notes and suggested that Deryn's bloods might be dropping due to a line infection, which could also explain his raging temperature. Dr Doom nodded respectfully in agreement.

For the first time, I felt like his equal, valued and empowered as Deryn's mother, with an instinct and understanding of my son that should be listened to. Hell, by now, I knew exactly what I was talking about.

I also shared my theory that the fight between Deryn's own cells and the donor cells was coming to an end and these symptoms could be a result of all the cells literally fighting to the death.

'That is also a strong possibility,' he concurred amiably.

I forgave him for having laughed at me. Dr Doom had more than made up for his unfortunate attempt at a joke by treating me with newfound respect.

As we were finishing our conversation, though, he cleared his throat.

'I need to tell you that we have been discussing how much further we can go with Deryn,' he said gravely. 'That is, how much more we should and can do before we say enough is enough. We will leave no stone unturned but we are running out of options.'

He placed his hand on mine in a show of empathy but I didn't need it. I'd been told many times that Deryn's survival was far from certain but I was comforted by the fact that he and I passionately and fervently believed he wasn't going to die from this.

Blind faith? Maybe. Denial? Perhaps. But while Deryn was still alive and something could be done, I wasn't about to give up hope.

'It's okay, Doctor, Deryn tells me that he's not going to die from this and I believe him,' I said, as I made my way back to Deryn's bedside.

❖

In removing the Hickman line as a possible source of infection, they had to replace it with something long term. A peripherally inserted central catheter (PICC line) was inserted into Deryn's left forearm. A cannula, which wasn't suitable long term, was also mysteriously inserted into his right hand but by the end of the first evening, it had blown the vein and Deryn was screaming out in agony.

A young female doctor came to prod around and find a new vein to insert it into. Her bedside manner was sadly lacking and

CHAPTER 31

Deryn was wincing with each prod into his swollen and inflamed hand.

'It doesn't hurt that much, stop making a fuss,' she admonished sternly. My ears pricked up. Deryn's face was screwed up, it was obvious he was suffering.

'FUCK OFF, you're hurting me,' he suddenly yelled at her. Deryn had never sworn at a doctor before. She hurried out of the room and Deryn burst into tears of relief when he saw Dr Barbara at his door.

He was hooked up to two machines via both arms, making it awfully difficult for him to move around. Going to the toilet, getting out of bed, even sipping a glass of water became extremely painful and uncomfortable.

I wasn't surprised that he had reached a point where he didn't want to do anything anymore. If I were in my son's shoes, I would have given up long ago.

The doctors feared Deryn's painful joints, high fevers and constant sickness were all signs of Langerhans cell sarcoma returning. Also giving them cause for concern was an ulcer on the side of his tongue. It didn't help that the ulcer looked suspiciously like those that had been excised from the back of his throat over a year before.

I sent out requests online for prayers and positive thoughts. Deryn was being followed by numerous prayer groups. Prayer trees with Deryn's name on were also popping up all over the world and Native American Indian Tribes were sending Deryn healing wishes.

We were absolutely blown away by the worldwide support and even after the very worst of days, the positive messages and comments on the Facebook page were a real tonic. I had no particular religious faith but I passionately believe in the power of prayer and healing and it was heartening to know that people from many different creeds and faiths were praying for him.

❖

With the line removed, Deryn started having fewer temperature spikes and his feverish shivering fits also stopped. But he was still in tremendous pain so was constantly on morphine. Over the course of the next few days, as a result of the high levels of morphine, he slept day and night.

When he was awake, his pain was so intense that he felt physically sick all the time so he was placed on a powerful anti-sickness drug, cyclizine, which made him high. Deryn liked the feeling it gave him and before long, he was addicted to it.

The sparkle in my son's eyes had disappeared. They were flat and dull. It was like a light had gone out in his soul. More than anything else, it was this that broke my heart.

Chapter 32

I SAT IN SILENCE AS THE FOUR DOCTORS IN FRONT OF ME REVEALED
the latest test results. Deryn's bone marrow was empty. Again.
The two sets of cells had fought to the death and eradicated each
other.

'So what are we going to do about it?' I asked, my voice
trembling.

The first option was to give Deryn another full transplant from
the donor, however, considering his past history with the donor's
cells, the chances of this working were very slim.

The second option was to start further chemotherapy to kill
any other cells lurking in his marrow before infusing his own cells
once again. His team had learnt the hard way that even if his
marrow looked empty, like it had the last time, it was best not to
take any chances. When Deryn had donated his cells a year
earlier, there had been enough to split them into two bags. How
timely that decision now felt. Deryn's last chance remained with
that single remaining bag of his own cells.

The third and final option was to stop all treatment and
transfer Deryn to a hospice for palliative care.

Dr Glam asked me if I needed time to think about the options
or talk things over with Simon, who was still away. I didn't need
to think about anything. As far as I could see, there was only one
option. Either I let him have more chemo and try the last bag of
cells in the hope they would engraft or I give up on him and take
him away to die.

Giving up was not an option. We decided there and then that

chemotherapy should start immediately. The aim, Dr Glam told me, was to get Deryn to a point where he could come home and have some quality of life for however long he had left. It sounded to me like they had already given up on him.

Dr Glam was now glassy eyed and she hugged me hard as I left the room.

'Please don't cry,' I said.

She told me that the entire team was in awe of me and the way I was dealing with everything. I wondered why. I was just a mum doing what any other mum would do. I got my strength from Deryn, who had told me a few days earlier that he wasn't scared of dying. If this was his time to go, as far as he was concerned, it was the way it was supposed to be. I didn't want to believe that, though. While he had one more chance, he could fight back and keep on living.

The one piece of good news was that the results ruled out any further signs of cancer – although this could still change once they transplanted his own cells back.

I had a plan. As soon as I could get Deryn out of there, I was going to take him away and get him on as many holistic and alternative treatments as possible to make damn sure that neither cancer could come back. Unrealistic? Maybe, but I could live with that. What I couldn't live with was not trying everything in my power to help him.

On autopilot, I sat beside Deryn's bed, repeating the three options I had only heard myself an hour earlier. Perhaps the most bizarre thing of all was that I wasn't scared. I felt the same way I had when Dr Doom had told me to pray: empowered and full of fight.

❖

I had made the decision to start chemotherapy again but I also needed Deryn's agreement. From the start, we had always discussed everything and made decisions together.

After I explained the three options to Deryn, he told me he didn't want to live any longer. He wanted to be left in peace to die. My heart started pounding furiously. Whatever I expected to hear, it wasn't this.

I repeated the options just in case he hadn't heard them correctly. But he had. And he made his feelings abundantly clear to me.

'I'm tired mum, I don't want to live like this anymore,' he said quietly, his lip quivering. 'I'm sick of being sick.'

Even though I'd tried to kid myself that he was still up for getting through whatever came next, I could see his flame had gone out and his lust for life had disappeared along with his bone marrow.

As I hugged him, I could feel his spine and shoulder blades digging sharply into my flesh. His poor, pitiful body was wracked but there was no way I could let him give up like this and admit defeat.

I let him go and stood at the end of his bed. He was going to have to listen to what I had to say before he could make that decision.

All the while, Dylan was sitting underneath the desk in Deryn's room, a spot he had made his own for the last few months, where he would spend hours playing with Lego while silently witnessing all that went on.

'I want you to listen to me Deryn,' I said firmly. 'I want you to remember what it was that you told me not that long ago.'

'I told you that I chose this,' Deryn answered reluctantly.

'Yes and you said that this was your biggest challenge. You're not coming back.'

'Yes,' Deryn agreed. He knew I was going to use his own words against him.

'So if I let you give up now and THIS is your biggest challenge, then I will have let you fail. You want to come back again and have to learn these lessons again?'

Deryn thought about it. I could see that he was annoyed with me for using his own wisdom as a weapon against him but I had to use everything in my armoury.

'No,' Deryn sighed under his breath.

When Deryn was younger, it had been easier to be tough on him when he needed it. But disciplining a teenager in his unique situation, with nothing left to lose, was incredibly difficult. Before Deryn was ill, we would ground him or restrict his privileges, but after diagnosis our tactics had to change dramatically. We were still trying to bring up a child with good ethics and decent behaviour, regardless of his illness or surroundings. I knew only too well the damage that allowing him to do whatever he liked because he was sick could do. In my eyes, he still needed guidance and boundaries.

'So if I let you do whatever it is you want to do, even though it's not what is best for you, won't I have messed up as your mum?' I continued.

'Yes,' Deryn muttered, looking increasingly anguished and annoyed at my line of questioning.

'You told me that you chose me because I needed to learn lessons. I think you also chose me because you knew I would never, ever give up on you. You knew this would be hard and you knew that I would never let YOU give up, either,' I said.

'You learned how to be stubborn from me and my job now is to push you when you want to give up,' I added, this time with a smile.

Deryn's mouth, which was incredibly sore, his lips blackened and cracked, turned up slightly at the edges. A smile, the first for many days.

The autumn nights were beginning to draw in as Deryn started chemotherapy once again. He was in a ridiculous amount of pain, controllable only by high doses of morphine, having contracted klebsiella, a flesh-eating bacteria, in his tongue.

Consciously cherishing every single moment with him, I wanted to give him little things to enjoy, memories of the fun we had together. On day two of chemo, he felt well enough to come out for a couple of hours in the evening so I brought him back to Charley's House to spend some time with his beloved Ozzy.

The team decided to give Deryn a couple of days to recover before transplanting the final bag of cells. If the chemotherapy had destroyed everything in Deryn's bone marrow, we would have a chance of success at least.

As I watched Deryn lie in his bed, unconscious throughout most of the day and night, it felt like we were fighting a losing battle. I could see my son slipping away before my eyes. We had to think of something to pull him out of this downward spiral.

Then, out of the blue, I received a call from Great British Bake Off star Paul Hollywood, who had been keeping up with Deryn's progress via Twitter. Paul asked if I would be able to get Deryn to Ston Easton Park, a luxury hotel a half-hour drive away, at the end of October for a day to remember. Intrigued, I said that we would make it happen.

During one of Deryn's rare conscious spells, Dylan decided to help his big brother compile a list of experiences he would like to try before he died. A glimmer appeared in Deryn's eyes as he started thinking about all the wonderful things he'd like to do. If he could get through this, there was a chance that at least some of those dreams would come true. And it was good to have another focus while we waited for Deryn's last bag of cells to arrive.

A few hours later, Deryn's bucket list had been shared on social media by his amazing army of supporters.

There were a few people he wanted to meet: comedians Russell Howard and Jimmy Carr, Simon Pegg and Nick Frost, the cast of TV sitcom The Big Bang Theory and Top Gear star Richard Hammond. He loved fast cars and also wanted to ride in a host of supercars and had on his list – in no particular order: a Lamborghini Quattroporte, Pagani Zonda, Ferrari Enzo, Aston Martin DB9, Aston Martin Vanquish, Bugatti Veyron Super Sport, Lamborghini Aventador and Audi R8.

Flying in a hot-air balloon and a fighter jet and swimming with turtles and dolphins also made the list. He'd also always dreamed of going on an African safari and being drawn as a character in the TV comedy Family Guy.

I didn't think any of these things would come to fruition but the smile and enthusiasm I saw on Deryn's face that day was enough to make me believe that the dream alone was doing him some good. Deryn had to believe he had a future.

If I had been able to add one wish to his list, it would have been for Deryn to be out of pain but not out of his mind. While he was so heavily sedated on morphine there was very little sense or conversation coming from him.

I started to research online for alternative forms of pain relief and once again, cannabis came up in the search engine as the top result for natural pain relief. Intrigued, I read on about its effectiveness as a painkiller. There were endless posts and threads from people who had swapped high-dose tablets for a spliff – with remarkable results.

A friend told me he knew someone who could send me some cannabis oil to get us started. I thought about it, wrestling with my fears over what might happen if I got caught by the authorities administering illegal cannabis oil. From what I'd read, I could face a long prison term. On top of everything else, I really didn't need that.

I was taken aback when, the very next morning, a package arrived from a wellwisher, with a small syringe inside. As I held it up to the light, I realised that this thick, dark green, tar-like substance was indeed cannabis oil. I sent it on to a friend whose child was losing their battle with cancer and who had expressed an interest in trying it out. There had to be some other way to help Deryn, I just needed to find it.

The cells for Deryn's transplant arrived the following day and Deryn was transferred to the Bone Marrow Transplant unit. Once again, the bright yellow refrigerated bag was placed outside his room, waiting to save his life. My stomach was full of butterflies and I could only think of one thing – what if they hadn't managed to get rid of all the cells? They thought his marrow was empty the last time. I told myself to snap out if it. I had to be positive.

The bag of beautiful red bone marrow cells went up on the stand, the pump started but a few seconds later, it stopped abruptly. The nurse restarted the machine then a few seconds later, it stopped again.

This stop-start cycle went on for a good five minutes before a nurse realised that the thickness of the bone marrow and the thin diameter of Deryn's single PICC line meant that the cells couldn't fit through it. The marrow was blocking the line, causing the machine to stop every few seconds.

These new cells had to be inside Deryn within 20 minutes. We were rapidly running out of time. We came up with a clever solution: I would sit on the floor in front of the pump and, the second it stopped, I would cancel then restart it.

'I'm sitting here literally saving your life, Deryn – you owe me!' I joked as he looked down from his bed smiling.

After what seemed like an eternity, the 30-minute transfusion finished. Now we just had to wait an interminable three weeks for news and pray that nothing else happened to throw a spanner in the works.

Chapter 33

TWO DAYS AFTER DERYN'S FOURTH TRANSPLANT, SOME SPECIAL allowances were made so that Dylan could come and visit the ward. Simon had also made it back after three weeks away and it was wonderful to be all together again.

The following day, Deryn was unexpectedly allowed to go out for a few hours. Even more surprisingly, he decided not to use his wheelchair. I was so proud to see him actively working towards his recovery, choosing life. I didn't know whether it was my mini lecture or something else that had given Deryn a push, but I was thankful.

The end of October was drawing near and our special day out with Paul Hollywood was approaching. Louise knew what we were up to and was keen to accompany us and keep an eye on Deryn. I couldn't think of anyone I'd rather spend the day with. Louise deserved a treat.

After two bags of blood, a bag of platelets, G-CSF and a multitude of antibiotics, Deryn was ready for his big surprise. We loaded the car with everything he might possibly need and headed off to Ston Easton Park. Deryn was hugely impressed as we swept up the long-sweeping gravel driveway of the beautiful Palladian mansion set in 36 acres of Somerset parkland. When he spotted the four sports cars Paul had organised for the day, he almost passed out.

A pale-blue classic Aston Martin DB5 that used to belong to Princess Margaret had been loaned to us by TV and radio personality Chris Evans. A dark-blue Ferrari F12 owned by ex-Liverpool Football Club owner David Moores, who had driven it down specially, was parked next to it. Paul's own Aston Martin DB9 and a bright orange McLaren MP4-12C completed the line up.

We spent the day being driven around the rolling countryside in each of these amazing cars. Even Louise got to have a ride with Paul. Dylan and Simon couldn't stop smiling. When my turn came in the McLaren, with Paul in the driving seat, I was terrified. Within seconds of speeding off, I grabbed his leg and was pleading with him not to kill me. Paul laughed as we raced around the narrow, twisty roads.

Reluctantly, we had to leave to get Deryn back for some important drugs. We hadn't even reached the end of that long driveway when Deryn was sprawled across the back seat of the car, fast asleep.

There was more excitement the next day, when a wonderful man called Mark Thomas arrived in a brand new Audi R8. He had seen Deryn's story on the internet and, having survived a rare and aggressive cancer himself many years earlier, he had been so touched by Deryn's plight that he'd driven from Cambridge to Bristol to give him a spin.

Deryn loved every moment of this special time. Two days of fast cars took their toll and Deryn slept for the entire weekend.

❖

Perhaps it was exhaustion from all the excitement but while trying to get out of bed a few days later, Deryn slipped and trapped his hand between the mattress and the guard rail, causing the tip of his middle finger on his right hand to turn bright red.

An infection started to track down Deryn's finger and he was placed back on antibiotics. Within 24 hours, the redness had spread to two other fingers and into his hand. Cracks and scabs were also appearing and weeping.

The pain in Deryn's fingers surpassed even the agony he was experiencing from the ulcers and klebsiella in his mouth. Even morphine wasn't helping. I was desperate to get Deryn pain free without him being comatose, particularly as another of his wishes was about to become a reality.

Simon Pegg and Nick Frost had agreed to come and visit. Deryn had no idea and while I was excited about seeing his face when he clapped eyes on his two favourite actors, I was concerned that he was in so much pain that he may not fully appreciate their visit.

As I guided Simon through the BMT washroom, Dylan was acting out his favourite scene from Simon and Nick's movie *Paul*. Just as he reached the peak of his performance as Nick's character, in walked the man himself! Dylan screeched in surprise and immediately blushed with embarrassment.

'Pretty good impression, Dylan,' Nick said with a smirk. Dylan beamed from ear to ear.

Simon followed him into the room, arriving with a mountain of signed T-shirts, DVDs and CDs.

Both men were lovely, everything I'd hoped they would be. I had warned them that Deryn wasn't doing too well but the next few hours passed very pleasantly as Deryn shared stories with the pair, despite being in excruciating pain. They had us in stitches with their stories. Deryn's right hand had just been set in plaster in an attempt to reduce the pain. Fortunately, it had dried by the time Simon left so he signed the cast 'Punch that shit,' which tickled Deryn.

They both promised to return when Deryn felt better and Nick thoughtfully sent Deryn an ancient bead that he'd bought in Boston, to add to his beads of courage.

❖

Fatigued and heavily reliant on blood transfusions, Deryn now had at least two serious infections and was no closer to engrafting. I was extremely worried that his struggling new marrow would be beaten back by the infections.

I remembered Cheryl telling me that Dawson had been given granulocytes – white blood cells – during his transplant to help boost his neutrophil count. I mentioned this to Dr Ponni and she immediately agreed it was a good idea.

Simon and I would be tested to see if we were suitable donors and we were asked to nominate 10 people who were also willing to help. I appealed to Deryn's followers on social media and within 24 hours, had been inundated with over 5,000 responses.

Simon and I were blown away by this gesture, the hospital, not so much. I was told off for putting out a direct appeal for help. Privately, though, Deryn's team told me they understood why I did it.

Two long weeks later, we finally heard the news we'd been hoping for. The chemotherapy had worked and Deryn's bone marrow was 0% donor and 100% his own. The news perked Deryn up although he was still in immense pain. His tongue was healing slowly but his fingers were getting worse as a result of herpetic whitlow – an abscess caused by infection – and cellulitis.

Simon had suffered from recurring bouts of cellulitis – an unpleasant bacterial skin infection – since childhood and knew only too well how painful it was. On the plus side, though, he was able to empathise with what Deryn was going through.

'I'll never laugh at your big red legs again, Dad!' Deryn joked after they compared notes on who'd had the worst bout.

Deryn was going to start on granulocytes from the hospital's blood-donor store. They would cause some pretty nasty side effects – excessive shivering, a drop in oxygen levels, sickness and fevers. If they weren't effective, his team planned to approach the 10 nominees I had put forward for their cells.

By now, Deryn's body was no longer holding on to any platelets and he had also lost the ability to clot blood effectively. It felt like we were taking one step forward and three steps back.

We had been in Bristol for 10 months. Almost a year away from close friends and family and we were feeling it. I was mentally exhausted and struggling to concentrate on what the doctors were telling me. Simon and I had made some new friends at the gym who were wonderful and we had become very close to a few of the nurses, sometimes meeting up with them outside the hospital. Their unwavering support was paramount to my mental wellbeing.

I didn't have time to focus on what was going wrong. I had to try and remain positive and with Simon's help, I did a fairly good job of at least pretending to be upbeat.

A meeting was called to discuss the latest transplant with Dr Doom, Dr Ponni and Dr Barbara. We all knew that we should have been seeing some engrafting around day 21. However, three weeks had passed and there was absolutely no sign of engraftment.

In addition to his existing infections, Deryn had also developed the fungal condition aspergillosis in his right lung. The combined efforts of these infections were stealing anything and everything that our boy's brand new marrow was trying so hard to produce. But before writing off this last treatment as a failure, the doctors wanted to give it a decent chance and urged patience.

I was pleased to hear that they weren't about to give up on Deryn just yet. The infection had reduced in Deryn's fingers while his mouth wasn't as sore. Plus, the pooled granulocytes had been effective. Great news – but he still needed concentrated granulocytes from our nominated loved ones as the pooled ones weren't effective enough on their own.

I wasn't a match and neither was Simon, unfortunately. But, while Simon's sister Gemma couldn't donate as she'd recently had a baby, her partner Ben and my brother Ian were both a match. I allowed myself to feel hopeful that close members of our family might be able to help Deryn even though Simon and I couldn't.

❖

Around this time, Deryn's medical team came to us with a grave announcement. Dr Doom told us that they wanted to discuss Deryn's long-term care.

'Do you want Deryn to be resuscitated if needs be?' The question dropped like a bomb in my lap. Of course we did.

'Well, you need to be aware that the chances of Deryn recovering from this in the long term are minimal,' he added gravely. 'If the most recent transplant has failed, we need to talk about palliative care.'

My eyes started to well up. Even if Deryn were to pull through this, Dr Doom was telling us that he wouldn't live for much longer afterwards. They feared that he was relapsing with cancer and that the sarcoma might already be spreading around Deryn's body, hence the pain in his knees.

Dr Ponni and Dr Barbara were both crying. They had become incredibly close to Deryn and I knew that this was almost as hard for them as it was for me and Simon.

I turned to look at the man who had been by my side through thick and thin for so many years, the man who always reassured me when it got too much. A solitary tear ran down his cheek as he squeezed my hand. Neither of us could speak as the doctors told us that they'd had a meeting with a local hospice which was happy to offer Deryn a bed. A place to die.

I started to doubt the survival instinct that Deryn and I had held on to so doggedly. If his medical team was to be believed, it wasn't going to play out that way after all.

But I had to be proactive. I reminded myself that I'd always known there were no guarantees the treatment would work. From the second our child was diagnosed with cancer, there was always a chance that we would end up saying goodbye to him.

We had hoped things wouldn't get this far but perhaps we weren't meant to be the lucky ones. For now, though, Deryn was still with us and while he was, there was still a chance that he could recover.

We were bucked up the following day by a call from comedian Russell Howard's assistant who asked if Russell could come and visit. I headed to reception to find a nervous-looking Russell sitting in the corner with his bag on his lap. He jumped up to follow me back up to the ward.

Russell stayed for hours and was brilliantly warm and friendly, chatting about comedy sketches with Deryn and Dylan and posing with the boys for photos. It was magical to see Deryn laughing and joking. He was more animated than he had been in a long time and was tickled when the nurses kept 'popping in' to check on him, rather more often than usual. When a nurse asked Russell to say hello to another patient, he didn't hesitate.

Making such wonderful memories with our boys was a tonic for Simon and me. If Deryn was to die in the near future, at least Dylan's lasting memories of his brother's final days wouldn't be full of sadness. Before the evening was out, Russell had texted to say that he'd like to come back and visit Deryn again soon.

Meanwhile, the plaster cast on Deryn's hand had been replaced by bandages across his infected fingers and he was moved back onto the teenage ward, where the vibrancy, colour and upbeat atmosphere cheered him up a little, despite the intense pain he was in.

Soon it was so bad that he began pleading with the doctors to cut his fingers off.

'Take my whole hand, I don't care anymore,' he screamed at Dr Barbara one afternoon after crying for hours on end.

The pain team couldn't get on top of it. All they could offer was more opiates. His fingers looked necrotic and frostbitten and the tips were dying from a lack of blood flow. I was devastated to see his hand deteriorating so frighteningly rapidly. The granulocytes from our family members couldn't arrive quickly enough – but I feared that maybe it wouldn't be enough to repair the dying tissue.

I just couldn't believe that there were no other options than opiates for treating Deryn's painful fingers. I resumed my research and cannabis appeared in front of me yet again on the web page. I couldn't ignore it any longer. We had exhausted every other avenue as far as pain relief was concerned and I was willing to try anything to help Deryn.

I'd read a story about a young guy who travelled to Amsterdam to collect Bedrocan, a cannabis-based medicine that could be prescribed by a doctor but wasn't available in the UK.

I discussed things with Simon and he told me he was more than happy to travel to Amsterdam and pick up anything that might help Deryn. Morphine had taken away any quality of life from this brave kid and had robbed us of our son and Dylan of his big brother. Bedrocan had to be a better option.

Now all I had to do was convince a doctor to prescribe it.

Chapter 34

I steeled myself to talk to Dr Barbara about Bedrocan. But before I got a chance to bring it up, she told us that Deryn's neutrophils were 0.11, an improvement on his last readings. Even more promising was that Deryn's platelets were a whopping 124 – the highest they'd been for more than three years.

Of course, his neutrophils could have been granulocytes and Dr Barbara also explained that granulocytes contain platelets so, again, it could be a false reading rather than a sign of engraftment. But it was promising nevertheless at a time when even holding onto blood cells was nigh on impossible for Deryn.

We continued to wait for the granulocytes from Deryn's uncles. The pooled cells had done such a good job that we could only hope the concentrated family cells would perform even better.

I took a deep breath and broached the subject of Bedrocan, citing the evidence I had uncovered online. Dr Barbara patiently heard me out before telling me that she wasn't allowed to prescribe it because, although it was an effective painkiller with very few side effects, it hadn't been tested rigorously enough to be used on children.

I was absolutely gutted. Our only other option was to watch Deryn's morphine intake increase until he was out of it all the time. What kind of life was that? If he only had a short time left, he would be unconscious for most of it. I wasn't going to leave it there. I couldn't take no for an answer.

Simon and I spoke in great detail about our options and agreed that we couldn't watch him suffer like this any longer. In our minds, there was nothing else for it. We had to find another way to get some cannabis into Deryn.

Days passed and Deryn hadn't had any granulocytes for a while. His blood cells dropped back down to nothing, confirming the doctor's fears that his count was made up of those alone. And still there was no sign of engraftment. The small improvements we'd seen on his fingers ground to a halt and overnight, they deteriorated dramatically.

As more of Deryn's flesh turned necrotic, the pain was getting worse. The tips of his fingers were now hard and black, his nails were peeling away and any remaining live flesh was covered in weeping sores.

'Please tell them to cut my hand off, Mum, I can't take this any more,' Deryn begged every day.

He was nauseous all the time and had become addicted to his anti-sickness drugs. He was allowed a dose every seven to eight hours but within hour of being given some, he'd press the buzzer to call the nurses back in.

'When can I have my cyclizine?' he would ask. 'It's the only thing that helps with the pain. It makes me feel safe. It doesn't hurt for a little while, just long enough to forget about it. Then it all comes back again.'

When he was told he would have to wait a few hours longer, akin to someone on heroin Deryn would get angry and aggressive and start kicking off. In the past I had known drug addicts and, just a couple of weeks off his 14th birthday, my son was ticking all the same boxes.

Enough was enough. I went into the city and purchased a vaporiser pen for inhaling cannabis liquid. Now we just had to find some cannabis and work out how to make the liquid ourselves. Simon agreed to take responsibility for the whole operation. If either of us was to get into trouble over this, he wanted it to be him. He wasn't going to allow anyone to take me away from my children just for alleviating our son's suffering.

After speaking to one of our friends at the gym who had connections, it was agreed that Simon would go to a nearby service station and collect some cannabis.

I was very frightened. Simon was driving to meet a man we'd only known for a few months, to collect a donated Class B drug, which carried a sentence of up to five years' imprisonment for possession and up to 14 years for supplying the drug to another person.

While we didn't relish having to accept drugs from anyone, we had to believe that our friend wouldn't allow any harm to come to us or Deryn. He knew our story and we trusted him. As scared as we were about getting caught, we had no choice. We couldn't watch Deryn suffer any more.

Our decision was hastened by Deryn's worsening condition. He was developing bed sores and his right lung had slightly collapsed. The team brought in a large inflatable mattress to prevent further sores developing and enable him to sit up so that fluid couldn't sit at the bottom of his lung.

As Christmas approached, we reached a crossroads. By then, Deryn would either have engrafted and be on the road to recovery or he would be in palliative care. My nerves were fraying and dark thoughts of losing my son started to take over every waking moment.

I spent hours searching the internet for recipes and instructions on how to make something that could go into this new vaporiser pen. I discovered I needed to buy a rice cooker and vegetable glycerine to make the tincture.

This would take a couple of days to make. We were both excited to see the outcome of this last-ditch attempt to get Deryn pain free. If it didn't work then so be it, we'd have to revert back to copious amounts of morphine. But if it was a success, we would have Deryn compos mentis for however long he had left.

Back at hospital, Simon and I were called into a meeting with the team. They were unanimously agreed that Deryn's last bag of cells was very unlikely to graft following more than 30 days with absolutely no blood count whatsoever. Even if the infections cleared up immediately, their experience told them that the cells had gone past the point of no return.

I started to cry. Simon was also welling up. They were giving up on him. The conversation turned to making Deryn as comfortable and in as little pain as possible. That was all we could hope for now.

The granulocytes would be continued in the hope that they might keep the side effects of his infections to a minimal level, 'so that he can pass peacefully, not in pain and full of infection,' Dr Doom told us.

It seemed Deryn's death was a done deal and now all we could do was wait until he drew his final breath.

The team still had some questions for us. If Deryn was overcome by one of the infections, did we want him to be kept alive artificially on tubes and drips? I hated the thought of seeing tubes hanging out of him. I didn't want that for him and I didn't want Dylan's abiding memories of his big brother to be tubes, wires and machines.

Dr Barbara gave us the other option. We could let Deryn go without a fight. This was also not an option for me. I wanted to try everything possible while there was still even the tiniest chance that Deryn might be the first person in 35 years to engraft after 30 days.

The doctors told us they were willing to carry on treatment for another two weeks. If there were no further improvements or progress and no producing of his own blood cells, Deryn would be placed in palliative care.

Simon and I sat down to have the most honest, brutal and frank conversation of our lives. Most couples we knew were worrying about money or where they might go on holiday. We could only dream of going back to the day where our concerns were that simple.

We agreed that Deryn had fought longer and harder, enduring far more than anyone should ever have to. It would not be fair to keep him alive through artificial means.

Simon and I went back into Deryn's room and looked at our son as he lay there sleeping. My little baby boy who would soon be 14. My firstborn who would be forever 14. I cried and cried until I had no more tears left.

I cried because of the lost potential. I cried because Deryn could have been something wonderful. He was already something wonderful. Meanwhile, Dylan sat in his 'safe place' underneath the desk, playing with his Lego, trying to pretend he couldn't hear his mother's heart breaking.

The physical pain wracked my whole body.

Suddenly, Dylan leapt up, ran into the bathroom and locked the door. Hearing the door slam, Deryn woke up and saw me.

'Please don't cry, Mum, just tell me what they said,' he whispered.

I told Deryn everything. He smiled serenely and simply said: 'Okay.' He was at peace with this and had already accepted his fate. He seemed not to be scared. It wasn't an act. He'd had a long time to mull things over and if anyone could teach me that everything was as it should be, it was my brave boy.

I gave Deryn a hug and kissed his forehead while Simon tried to coax Dylan out of the bathroom.

Eventually our youngest son emerged, standing in the doorway with tears streaming down his face. His fists were clenched into tight balls. Neither of us really knew what to say to Dylan and, in a fit of rage, he snarled angrily and punched the mirror, damaging nothing but his little hand.

I grabbed him and held onto him tightly while he thrashed about furiously in my arms. After a minute or so, he went limp and started to sob uncontrollably. When he had calmed down, we all sat down together to discuss Deryn's final days.

The privacy on the ward was zero and whenever we left Deryn's room, we were greeted by the smiling faces of many of the other parents. Most of the teenagers on the ward were in for routine operations that were not life threatening so no-one could even remotely understand what was going on in Deryn's room.

None of us wanted to have to say goodbye to Deryn on a busy hospital ward. To my relief, Deryn agreed to come and visit the hospice with us and consider a move there when the time came.

To say the least, this was a surreal conversation to be having with your children.

As the day wore on, I'd burst into tears only to be told by Deryn that crying wasn't going to help.

This brave, bright boy had taken us all on such a wonderful, yet truly terrible, journey. I'd had almost 14 years with him. I wanted more. I wanted him to prove the doctors and the medical books wrong. I would have given my own life to give Deryn back his.

And yet, in a bizarre way, I envied him too. I envied his peace. He would be forever innocent, he was never going to be tainted or hurt or have his heart broken. He had suffered so much but never complained. I was in immense awe of his courage.

I sat with him by myself for an hour or two longer and as it got dark, I gave him a goodnight kiss and popped my headphones in for the walk back to Charley's House. I pressed shuffle and the opening bars of *I Won't Give Up* by Jason Mraz started playing in my ears.

I listened to the lyrics as tears streamed down my face. My knees buckled and I almost fell to the ground. I'd heard this song many times before and it had always felt as though it was written for Deryn and me.

If ever I needed a sign to get a grip on myself, this was it. I had to remain positive no matter what the doctors were telling me. I'd heard it all before and had to steel myself to believe that the outcome would not be what they expected. My instincts overruled everything.

I got back to the house to find Simon in the kitchen. The house stank to the heavens as he experimented with infusing vegetable glycerine with the cannabis. While I had been having my wake-up call, Simon had been having one of his own. Standing outside on the terrace looking at the stars, he told me he'd tried to make a deal with the powers that be.

'I pleaded with the universe, Callie,' he explained through his tears. 'I asked for my son to be allowed to live and I made a promise that if Deryn was allowed to live, I would dedicate the rest of my life to helping others. I felt something change. We mustn't give up now.'

We truly believed we'd both been given a sign – and it was this that drove Simon to start making cannabis tincture at midnight.

The following day, we arrived at the hospital feeling more positive. My brother Ian had arrived from Norfolk to donate his granulocytes. Within a few hours, they would be making their way into Deryn's veins. It was lovely to see my brother after such a long time. We weren't close but this proved that whenever I needed him, he was there.

Deryn was a little more upbeat, too and after his infusion with the granulocytes, we managed to have a few giggles with Dylan and the nurses. It was lovely to see our sons laughing again.

The following morning Deryn was due to have his infected fingers cleaned up in theatre. A specialist surgeon had arrived from another hospital with some bold ideas about how to make Deryn pain free. The most favourable option was to amputate his three dead fingers but Deryn told me he'd rather have his entire hand amputated.

'If I do engraft miraculously, I am not going around looking like a lobster!' he said with a laugh.

'Deryn probably isn't going to be alive by Christmas, so I don't think such drastic measures are necessary,' I explained to the surgeon, who looked mortified and clearly had no idea just how sick Deryn was.

Our main aim was to get Deryn pain free and comfortable for however long we had left with him.

'You're in good HANDS, Deryn,' I quipped with a wink as Deryn shook his head and groaned loudly at my terrible joke.

I was going to do exactly what he had advised me to do all along: live in the moment and not worry about the future. All worry did was take away that day's happiness.

Next to visit Deryn was Simon's sister Gemma, with her baby daughter Isla, while her partner Ben donated his bag of granulocytes.

Simon, meanwhile, was back at the house trying out the vaporiser pen with his first batch of tincture.

Deryn was really excited to be trying cannabis with the blessing of his mum and dad, while I felt incredibly nervous and anxious at the prospect of my son's underage and illegal drug use, especially as we were in hospital. It wouldn't even have been a consideration just a few months earlier.

After drawing the curtains so that no-one could see through

the window, Simon handed the filled pen over to Deryn. We felt like naughty school kids who were having a sneaky cigarette around the back of the bike sheds.

Deryn sucked on the pen, breathed in and blew out a massive cloud of vapour. Simon and I had a fit of nervous giggles as we frantically waved our hands around trying to disperse the distinctive smelling cloud of vapour. Amazingly, there was no smell of cannabis, it was more like a popcorn aroma.

After taking a few more draws on the pen, Deryn tucked it away discreetly down the side of his bed. After 10 minutes, he said that the pain had decreased a little and he felt more relaxed – music to my ears. We agreed to help Deryn continue using the pen but warned him he should only use it when we were there to supervise him.

I had smoked cannabis occasionally when I was much younger, but hadn't been aware of its medicinal benefits. My only experience had been seeing people getting so high they couldn't leave the couch. I'd never seen anything positive come of smoking it and in my days as a bouncer, illegal drugs had been my enemy.

However, after reading anecdotal evidence and seeing the tremendous damage legal prescription drugs could cause, I reached the conclusion that there might be less danger in cannabis. Anyway, if Deryn was already dying, where was the harm? And what if it actually helped him?

The day of the operation on Deryn's hand came and as he was wheeled down to theatre, I glanced one last time at his fingers and wondered how they would look once the dead tissue had been stripped away.

While he was being treated, I headed into Bristol to buy both boys an Advent calendar. It hadn't occurred to me how difficult it would be to buy one for Deryn this year and as I stood in Marks & Spencer trying to decide which one to go for, I broke down. I wondered how many of the tiny doors would remain shut; I didn't want a half-open Advent calendar to remind me that my son wasn't around any longer. Still, I forced myself to choose a couple and went to pay as tears coursed down my face.

I got back to the hospital just as Deryn got back from his surgery. For the first time in months, his hand didn't hurt. The surgeons had placed a blocker on it to keep him pain free for a few hours and morphine was on standby for when it wore off. Then there was our secret stash of cannabis tincture.

He took the opportunity to use his PlayStation for the first time in many weeks, the bulky dressings not seeming to bother him.

Shortly after this, Uncle Ben's granulocytes went in without a hitch. Now we waited. Deryn experienced severe shivering, sweating and fever so his team decided that further granulocyte transfusions were not worth the risk.

The team was willing to give Deryn 10 more days to improve drastically. Whatever way we looked at it, he was running out of time.

In the interim, however, I had a birthday party to organise.

Chapter 35

DERYN'S 14TH BIRTHDAY WAS FAST APPROACHING AND GIFTS WERE arriving by the dozen from wellwishers while his celebrity friends were also tweeting and sending their best wishes. Deryn read every single card and I spent hours sticking each one around his room until every inch of every wall was covered.

We had been given the games area on the teenage ward, with a jukebox and an air hockey table to use for a birthday celebration. The night before, Simon and I spent hours hanging up banners and blowing up balloons. The hockey table was laden with brightly wrapped presents and piles of cards. Our nearest and dearest had been invited. A friend made a cake and Simon had arranged for some party food. The room looked amazing.

As Deryn's special day dawned, I was overwhelmed by the messages of love and support. Our social media feeds were buzzing with notifications from hundreds of people across the globe. It was truly uplifting and reminded me just what I was fighting for. Deryn meant so much to so many people. I had a responsibility to not give up on him for them as well as for myself and our family.

I helped Deryn out of bed. It had been several weeks since he'd walked further than the bathroom, his knees were painful and he was incredibly weak. He was unsteady on his feet and his right hand was still sore from the clean-up operation. He had a few puffs on his vaporiser pen and felt ready to face the crowd.

I pushed his robot as he slowly shuffled his way across the hallway. He was greeted by the smiling faces of his guests singing

Happy Birthday. I found myself wondering if this was the last birthday I would share with my son. Would this be the last time most of these people saw Deryn?

Many found it difficult to hide their anguish as they watched this frail, fragile shadow of a boy tentatively open his presents. The exertion made him vomit violently but he wasn't embarrassed in the slightest, only miffed that he had ruined his favourite pyjamas.

He got changed just as a video call from Simon Pegg came in, wishing him a lovely day. Deryn introduced Simon to his guests and they had an animated chat. Then the birthday boy even managed to eat a small piece of birthday cake.

As a special treat, one of the local cinemas opened a screen especially for Deryn and we all trooped down there, Deryn in his wheelchair. We watched *Cloudy with a Chance of Meatballs 2*, munching on popcorn with our feet up on the seats. For a couple of hours, life really couldn't have been any better. Once the film was over, we went to visit the hospice. Deryn was again in so much pain that we didn't stay for long but it was enough for him to know that he liked it.

Back at the hospital two days after his birthday, the head nurse told Simon to go and fetch Ozzy and bring him to the ward for a visit. While they were elated to see each other and enjoyed a precious hour together on Deryn's bed, anything that went against usual hospital policy gave me the shivers. They didn't break the rules for no reason.

Sure enough, after Simon took Ozzy back to the house, a nurse arrived to say Deryn's team wanted to talk to me urgently. Simon couldn't get back in time and although I was feeling sick, my stomach in knots and my heart pounding, I knew I would have to deal with whatever was coming. Some of the nurses who knew us well turned away as I approached, their faces sad, their eyes avoiding mine.

Through the small window in the door, I saw our four-strong team already seated and waiting for me. For a moment, I couldn't bring myself to open the door. I wanted to freeze time and not ever hear what they had to tell me.

Dr Barbara opened the door and beckoned me in. It had been 41 days since Deryn had been given back his own cells. The 10 days' grace for the engraftment to take place had passed so it really shouldn't have been a shock when I heard the words I had hoped and prayed never to hear.

'Deryn has failed to engraft,' she said softly. 'He is not going to recover. I'm sorry.'

All four sat looking at me, glassy-eyed. They had given Deryn all the time they could but it was to no avail. Suddenly, Simon appeared, completely oblivious to what he had walked into. He sat down next to me as I wept quietly. I looked at him and shook my head sadly.

We sat listening to the various ways in which Deryn could die. Medical assistance would be geared towards letting him go peacefully rather than prolonging his life. Regular platelet transfusions would prevent Deryn from 'bleeding to death from every orifice' as one doctor unceremoniously put it.

I had seen Deryn go though many horrendous experiences but to be given such vivid and horrific descriptions of what could occur during the final chapter of his life made me want to curl up and die. He was a patient to them, but he was our child. I thought back to the euphoria I'd felt when he was born 14 years and two days earlier. I remembered witnessing the miracle of his first breath and here was someone talking coolly about his last. It was surreal.

The meeting came to an end and the female doctors, trying

their hardest not to cry, hugged us and told us they had done everything in their power to save Deryn. We made our way back to Deryn's room and, as we had done for the previous three years, resolved to tell him exactly what was going on.

'So when am I moving to the hospice, then?' he asked, as if he was asking what time supper was. His voice didn't even tremble. He was dealing with this as he had done with every other blow. Like a warrior.

The four of us spoke at length but I deliberately omitted to share with him the grim details of what would happen as each organ in his body shut down. Deryn was tired but in good spirits. He didn't seem at all scared and confided that he had felt for some time that he was probably going to die. He had made his peace with that possibility and didn't want to fight it, or live in constant pain, any longer.

The vaporiser pen hadn't solved the issues we'd hoped it would but it did give Deryn some much needed relaxation, which was a good enough reason to continue using it.

I hugged Deryn and told him that I understood how tired he was. I reassured him that it was okay to feel the way he did and that whatever happened, he was not alone.

Inside, though, I felt useless. I had failed in my primary duty as a mother to protect my son. But I also realised how fortunate I was. How many mothers get to plan everything they want to happen in the lead up to their child's death?

With so many children snatched away through accident, murder or on missing lists, we were lucky that nothing would be left unsaid. Nothing would happen that Deryn didn't want to happen and he would be allowed to move on to the next stage of his journey peacefully, with love, pain free and surrounded by his family.

I could only wish for my own death to be as pleasant.

As I held him close that evening, I told him he had done everything he needed to do. I wanted to reassure him that he had nothing left to prove. He had fought as hard as he could and he hadn't let anyone down. I was so proud of him.

Deryn wasn't giving up. He had done all he could and now it was out of his hands. Over the previous few months I'd talked him out of giving up several times. This time was different. I had to recognise that he needed my blessing to make his choice.

He was the bravest, most courageous person I had ever met. I was in awe of his inner strength. From the day he was born he had taught me so much and for that, I was eternally grateful. I had been blessed with an incredible 14 years with my beautiful young man.

I couldn't be anything but thankful for that.

I had no idea how I was going to break the devastating news to our families. Many of them hadn't known half of what we'd experienced as Simon and I had tried to protect them from the worst.

I felt especially sad for my mum, who had doted on Deryn from birth. After trying to comfort her on the phone for half an hour, I felt helpless. My brother promised to go and see her but I couldn't do any more. I had to hope she understood that.

I told Deryn we would try and give him everything he wanted now – within reason, of course, so no nightclubs or strippers! His first request was very easy to fulfil.

'Now I actually have some hair, I want my pink mohawk back!'

I had been given strict instructions not to go anywhere near Deryn's head with bleach as it could damage his sensitive scalp. We didn't care about that any more. Simon brought the clippers in and I shaved Deryn a nice new mohawk, to the surprise and joy of his regular nursing team. Deryn felt like himself again. It was amazing to see how much a new haircut could change his mood.

'So will you have an NG tube put in now, Mum?' Deryn demanded, ever one to push his luck.

Previously, I had used every excuse under the sun to avoid it but now I could hardly say no. So Deryn's wonderful nurse came in and fitted me with my very own feeding tube. I couldn't believe how vile it was. Now that I had experienced a tiny proportion of what he had endured, Deryn was a complete hero in my eyes.

He thought it was hilarious and derived great joy from the second I started to gag as it was inserted, to the moment he took pity on me and mercifully pulled it out three hours later. But I couldn't deny him that.

❖

Over the course of the next few days, Deryn started to plan his funeral.

'I want it to be fancy dress,' he announced. Of course he did. I was game, as were Simon and Dylan. Even the nurses were up for it and Deryn took great pleasure in revealing who was to wear which costume.

Mine was pretty predictable; he wanted me dressed as a Victorian nurse. Dylan could choose to come as any *Star Wars* character while Simon was under strict instructions to wear something rather more controversial.

Years previously, Simon and Deryn had made a secret pact. Whichever one of them died first, the remaining one had to arrive at the funeral dressed as the Grim Reaper.

'Well, Dad, are you going to come as Death?' Deryn quipped.

Simon nodded. Deryn couldn't stop laughing as he instructed Simon to carry a scythe, telling him that if anyone coughed during the funeral, Simon had to point at them, lift up his scythe and aim it at them. I wasn't at all surprised to hear the two of them giggling as they planned this one last prank together. A dark sense of humour had got us this far and it would carry me through the worst of what was still to come.

Simon ordered his outfit, which was delivered to the hospital the next day, much to the receptionist's utter horror. He thought someone was playing a sick joke on us – but soon saw the funny side when Simon explained.

Walking down to theatre with Deryn for his final anaesthetic to sever the nerves in his fingers was just as hard as it had been the very first time in Addenbrooke's, three years earlier. The surgeons were happy to alleviate the pain he'd been living with for over a month and when Deryn came round after the operation, he was beaming from ear to ear.

'I can't feel my hand at all,' he sighed happily.

I was staying every night at the hospital with my son and as I lay there watching him sleep that night, I couldn't stop thinking about how our lives were going to change.

Our top priority now was to make the most of the time we had left with him.

Deryn told me he wanted to set up a charity to help other teenagers, giving them a place they could go to to heal themselves physically and spiritually. I promised that we would do that for him.

Late one night, I wrote a message to his supporters on social media. As much as we were hurting as a family, lots of people had also invested their energy in Deryn, praying for a miracle and sending him messages. I thanked everyone and reassured them that this wasn't the end.

It was just the beginning. In Deryn's own words: 'All is as it's supposed to be.'

❖

We knew that no-one had ever engrafted after 50 days and as each day brought us closer to that marker, the reality of what was happening started to hit home. The 280 days since Deryn's first transplant seemed to have whizzed by.

Preparations continued to steer us towards the inevitable and we were asked to fill in a form about Deryn's last wishes for before and after he died.

Underneath the heading 'Plans for care during an acute life threatening illness,' there were simple yes or no boxes to tick:

'Oxygen via facemask?'

'Airways management?'

'Bag and mask ventilation?'

'Endotracheal tube & ventilation?'

'External cardiac compressions?'

'Defibrillation and adrenalin?'

'Advanced life support requiring PICU?'

I read through the form with tears pricking my eyes, ticking 'No' to each question.

There would be no more intervention to prevent his death, only to minimise his suffering. His team urged us to set a date for his transfer to the hospice. They wanted us to have as much quality time away from the hubbub of the ward as possible.

We'd managed to spend a few hours at the hospice earlier that day. The atmosphere was never depressing even though it was full of very sick children. The staff were truly amazing and the whole place was alive with joy and love.

We watched as more than 200 motorbikes arrived, ridden by bikers in festive fancy dress. Deryn found a comfortable armchair and didn't budge for the entire visit. We stayed for lunch and ate more mince pies than was strictly necessary.

Dylan was not forgotten and he spent an hour on a festive

CHAPTER 35

Ryanair flight over Bristol, specially arranged by the hospital, helping Santa hand-deliver presents to lots of children onboard.

As we got up to leave, Deryn asked if he could see his room. A large bedroom called Wren, it offered spectacular views across the valley towards a waterfall. Deryn had his own large shower room, a sofa and armchairs. There was a TV at the end of his bed and the staff had even put in a separate Wifi after they found out how much he loved watching films and playing on his PlayStation.

I looked out of the window to see eagles circling above. It was very easy to pretend that we were somewhere else.

Opposite Deryn's room was another large room called The Sanctuary, filled with oversized, comfortable sofas. In the corner was a tree dressed with stars, each holding the photograph of a child who had died there. I thought about which one of Deryn's pictures I would use for his star.

There was one other room Deryn wanted to visit. Starborn was where children who had died were taken to be laid out and visited by their families. It was a beautiful, serene bedroom with a single bed in the middle, surrounded by large sofas. The bed had no mattress, it was refrigerated and the room had to be kept cold for obvious reasons. The shelves were lit up with beautiful lights and statues of angels.

I was blown away by the sheer innocence and beauty of that room. The energy was overwhelming. It felt like every part of it had been created from pure love. I asked Deryn if he knew what the room was for. He said that he did. Dylan also wanted to come in.

We spent a few minutes in there before Deryn asked to leave. He wasn't disturbed or upset by it, he told me he loved the peace and tranquility and he too could feel the energy.

In the days leading up to the hospice visit, Deryn had started waking up in the night, very distressed by what was happening to him. He told me that he'd never envisaged he would die in a hospital bed, wearing a nappy and so off his face on opiates that he had no idea what was going on.

I tried to comfort him, assuring him I would do everything in my power to make sure his every wish was respected. He spoke about his wants and needs in great detail during the day but increasingly, the nights held fear and terror for him.

After visiting the hospice, however, his night terrors became less frequent. The visit seemed to help him come to terms with what was happening and he felt peaceful and calm about spending his final days there.

He made a list of his final wishes. He fervently did not want to be doped up to the eyeballs on morphine. The cyclizine however, was a different story. He wasn't willing to let that go. I knew he was addicted to it but to try and stop it now seemed utterly pointless.

Other things he wanted were to have a pint with his dad, handle an owl, have Ozzy to stay over at the hospice and enjoy one last Christmas Day.

He had received more than £200 worth of Amazon vouchers for his birthday and he spent them now on a beanbag, a chew toy and some dog biscuits for Ozzy, two DVDs and two games for Dylan and some guitar picks for his dad (he already knew that Simon had his eye on his electric guitar.)

Later that evening I found him tapping away furiously on his phone.

'I'm writing a will,' he told me solemnly.

He didn't have a lot to give away but he made sure that everyone who had been there for him got something relevant to remember him by. I only discovered later that Deryn hadn't bought anything for himself with his vouchers.

CHAPTER 35

After thinking that I couldn't be any prouder of my boy, he had surpassed himself. I was going to miss him.

Chapter 36

DERYN WAS ON A FORM OF LIFE SUPPORT, BEING KEPT ALIVE BY A cocktail of antibiotics. Would it be easier if he was covered in wires and unconscious? I doubted that. There is no easy way to say goodbye to your child.

Our dilemma was exactly when we should start the process which would inevitably lead to his death.

'How long after we take Deryn off medication is he likely to die?' I asked one of his team.

'Three days, maybe a week. But no longer,' came the answer.

I hadn't expected it to be so quick. A few weeks, maybe, but three days? How could I possibly decide when those three days would start?

After a long discussion with Deryn, we decided that we would all move to Charlton Farm Hospice on December 11th 2013. I told everyone that if they wanted to see Deryn, now was the time and the days leading up to our move were filled with visits from our dearest friends and family.

Many refused to believe that this was the last time they'd see Deryn. Jovan was adamant that Deryn would be at her wedding the following February. She'd asked me to be a bridesmaid and told Deryn that no-one else would have his space, she was going to save it for him.

Before Jovan left, Deryn told her that she would have to wear a gingerbread man costume to his funeral. It was a standing joke that Jovan drank way too many gingerbread lattes! Penny also came with Marcie and Joss. It was like old times, Deryn was showing off to Joss with his vaporiser, blowing out huge impressive clouds of smoke.

The nurses often came in while Deryn was vaping and we would all rush around laughing as we tried to disperse the thick cloud. Deryn's regular nurses, the ones closest to us, knew exactly what was going on.

We confided in them and told them the truth. Not one of them thought it was wrong of us, they all agreed and off the record, they condoned what we were doing. Thankfully, Deryn had the same nurses on a rotation so there was very little chance of any other staff finding out.

Deryn derived great comfort from the cannabis tincture. It couldn't alleviate his pain completely but it helped to ease his anxiety during the night, which the morphine seemed unable to help.

My brother brought my mum to visit from Norfolk. She hadn't seen Deryn for such a long time and tried her hardest to hold it together. It never occurred to me that the people who came to see Deryn were trying to be strong for us. We were so consumed by what was happening, we didn't grasp how difficult it must have been for those visiting Deryn for the last time.

For three years, we'd faced one dire situation after another and as we dealt with each problem, our ability to cope with what came next grew stronger. We were prepared, as much as we could be, for the 'end of life' care to start.

Day 48 saw Deryn and me spend our last night in Bristol Children's Hospital. For almost 10 months, this place had been Deryn's home. As I sat in his room surrounded by bags and boxes, waiting for the ambulance to take us onto his final stage of life, I thought about all the people who had helped us.

Tiegan's mum Emma was my source of strength when I felt alone. Another lady called Rosie Barker contacted me via

Deryn's Facebook page. She had lost her son in similar circumstances and in the midst of her own pain, she reached out to me and took away some of mine.

Out of the window, I could see the Christmas preparations taking place. Fairy lights and spruce trees seemed to be everywhere, taunting me. We would be very lucky indeed if Deryn was still with us by Christmas Day. He hadn't grafted after 49 days. No-one ever had after 50 days. And he had been in so much pain, plagued by sickness, digestion issues and weight loss. His tongue had been eaten away by klebsiella, he had serious mobility problems and he was now in nappies. The spark had gone from his beautiful eyes.

But some things had changed for the better.

Deryn's pain had decreased, he'd started to eat a little and was very slowly putting on weight. He was also starting to hold onto his platelets, a development none of the doctors could understand as tests had shown that there was definitely no active bone marrow.

Even his tongue was slowly healing and the infections in his fingers had stopped spreading. With no immune system and no bone marrow, this was nothing short of miraculous as cells are unable to repair without neutrophils.

It made me doubt whether we were making the right choice in invoking the end-of-life plan. I actually begged Dr Barbara to tell me that Deryn would never recover. I needed to hear it again, to be 100% sure.

She took my hand and told me that no-one had ever engrafted after 50 days. She couldn't be absolutely sure that Deryn wouldn't live if he was given the right support but it was highly unlikely. What she didn't want was for Deryn to come down with a nasty infection that killed him painfully. The kindest thing to do was to let him go while he was still feeling well enough to enjoy life.

So realistically, Deryn could be kept alive for some time but he would need to live in a sterile bubble to prevent any further infections. There would be no quality of life. I knew that the team hadn't taken the decision lightly – but I still couldn't help wondering if I was giving up on him too soon.

The ambulance arrived and many of the nurses popped in to say their goodbyes. We felt so indebted to the staff for everything they had done for us. I pushed my son out of the hospital in his wheelchair, a ghost of a boy, a shadow of his former self. I didn't feel sad or angry, I was just grateful that we could take Deryn somewhere wonderful to see out his final days.

Simon had taken Deryn's belongings to the hospice and was waiting there with Dylan. I'd taken less with me when I left home at the age of 18.

As soon as we walked in, I felt a huge weight lift from my shoulders. For years, we hadn't fully been able to be Deryn's parents. We had taken on many different roles: pharmacist, nurse, psychologist and oncology specialist, to name just a few. I was thankful that we could now just be mum and dad again.

The staff were amazing. Deryn often took some time to get used to new people but he felt instantly at home there. We felt like we had known them all for years.

Dylan would have a sibling worker at his beck and call. Someone to play with him whenever he wanted. He was overjoyed. There was nothing left for us to do but be with our children. The feeling of freedom was immense. None of us was daunted by what the future would bring.

Deryn checked out his room before heading off to explore the hospice facilities. Fairy lights and Christmas decorations were hung across the corridors, community spaces and around the doors. A sparkle started to return to Deryn's eyes.

He couldn't wait to leave the confines of his new four walls.

CHAPTER 36

After so many months of virtual immobility, he was desperate to venture further afield. It was wonderful to see him using his legs again.

Unhampered by any restrictions – simply a plastic bag on his hand and a waterproof dressing on his chest – Deryn headed off to the hydrotherapy pool with Dylan. I watched the lads larking about in the pool, dunking each other, throwing beach balls and floating amongst the bubbles. It was divine.

We had been allocated a room upstairs from Deryn's room Wren. It was palatial, with a separate bathroom, king-size bed and a balcony that overlooked the valley.

Dylan had his own room, too, and he and Simon slept upstairs on the first night. I couldn't bring myself to leave Deryn's side. If he was going to die in his sleep, I wanted to be there with him. I was there when he came into the world and I wanted to be there when he left.

I made up a bed on a large padded window seat and we snuggled in for the night. Deryn didn't sleep particularly well, he was tossing and turning, sometimes crying in his sleep. I was glad to be there to console him.

The following morning, I woke up to find the bedroom empty, with Deryn nowhere to be seen. Panic-stricken, I threw on some clothes and rushed out to look for him. They wouldn't have let me continue sleeping if Deryn had died in the night, surely?

I found him in the kitchen, devouring some breakfast for the first time in over five months.

'Why are you crying, Mum?' Deryn asked, looking puzzled.

I was totally overwhelmed. Charlton Farm was working its magic on Deryn. If he only had a short time left, there was nowhere in the world we would rather be.

❖

Deryn was devouring breakfast, lunch and dinner each day. He seemed to be getting stronger, not weaker, which was baffling the team as well as reducing me to tears of joy on a daily basis.

Every morning we got up early and filled our time making memories, always mindful that each day could be our last as a complete family.

Russell Howard popped by to see Deryn again. He had visited a number of times and had been affectionately dubbed Uncle Russ by both boys. Russ loved the hospice food and was overjoyed to be fed what he referred to as school dinners.

As Russ and Dylan took it in turns to thrash Deryn on the PlayStation, Deryn turned to his friend.

'Russ, will you come to my funeral?' he asked.

The comedian looked uncomfortable. Deryn's forthright attitude to dying was something that confounded many of his visitors.

'Umm, yeah, of course I will, mate,' he mumbled.

Russ already knew that it was fancy dress and was willing to come as anything Deryn wished for.

'What do you want me to wear?'

'Oh I think you know…' Deryn answered with a cheeky glint in his eye.

On a previous visit, Deryn had revealed that his favourite Russell Howard sketch was Russ dressed up as a six-foot dildo.

'You have to come as Mr Dildo,' Deryn cheerfully insisted.

Russ looked mortified but graciously agreed. When the time came for him to leave, I walked him to the exit and he turned to me as we reached the door with an unusually serious look on his face.

'I will do that for Deryn BUT I need a letter from you saying that this was Deryn's idea,' he pleaded. 'If everyone else is dressed in black and I walk in dressed as Mr Dildo…' he tailed off.

Trying to control my laughter, I agreed to make sure that he had a letter.

All talk of Deryn's impending funeral felt heartily premature. He didn't look as if he was going anywhere soon and while his night terrors persisted despite regular use of the vaporiser, his days passed by in a blur of activity and jolliness.

Ozzy arrived the following morning with my dad. Dad had moved to Bristol so that he could bring him in every day, which made Deryn – and the other children and staff – incredibly happy. Two beautiful owls were also brought in from a local sanctuary for a few hours for Deryn to handle – another wish crossed off his bucket list.

Meanwhile, I had been in touch with Jamie McCarthy, a sculptor who specialised in making casts of body parts. We'd talked about him making a bust of Deryn which I could treasure forever.

'Isn't that a bit weird, Mum?' Deryn asked me.

I didn't think so. Photographs felt very two-dimensional and never fully captured the essence of Deryn. I couldn't touch or feel the contours of his face from a picture. The one thing I knew I would miss most was the touch of him, so a bust would be a wonderful permanent reminder.

Jamie came to the hospice to work. He applied a thick layer of barrier cream to Deryn's face, neck and chest before covering him in blue gloop. This gloop sank into every crevice and all that was left of Deryn was two little nostril holes. He didn't panic or feel claustrophobic, though, joking that eight sessions pinned to a radiotherapy table in a tight mask had been good preparation for the sitting.

After another layer of blue gloop was applied, along with some plaster-cast bandages and wet bandages, Deryn looked uncannily like a mummy from a low-budget horror film. I knew

Jamie would do Deryn justice and I couldn't wait to see the finished piece.

There was another visitor when our dear friend James arrived from Norfolk to stay for a few days. He had spent a lot of time in India and Thailand and brought with him a copy of the Bardo Thodol, the Tibetan book of the dead.

Buddhism had always resonated with Deryn and he asked me to read to him from the book. It advocated not moving the body for three days after death in order to allow the spirit to move peacefully on to its next stage.

James and Deryn spoke privately in great detail about death and Deryn's spiritual journey on to the next realm and Deryn took great comfort in their time together. Before he left, James blessed Deryn and gave him some Tibetan prayer flags to hang in his room.

It was just two days since Deryn had left the hospital but instead of teetering on the brink of death, he was improving as each day went by. We had been warned that many children had spurts of energy after leaving hospital but it never lasted long. Instead of getting excited about this turnaround, we focused on enjoying every minute and planning an early Christmas Day for Deryn to enjoy.

All the presents were wrapped and Deryn's room had its very own Christmas tree. The stockings were hung and the festivities were in full swing. Penny, Marcie and Joss had arrived and the conservatory had been decorated by the staff, ready for our own private Christmas breakfast. Dylan even put out carrots and mince pies for Santa and his reindeer.

I decided I wasn't going to be sad anymore. I had deep spiritual beliefs that guided me and it was an enormous comfort that Deryn felt the same way. I had an unshakable feeling that

CHAPTER 36

Deryn would be having two Christmases this year.

And so, when we awoke on the morning of December 14th, it was Christmas! The hospice made it one of the most memorable celebrations ever. The boys spent the whole day lounging around in bear onesies while wonderful chef Michael put on an amazing spread – Deryn finally ate more than just one pig in a blanket!

The boys opened their presents in delight. Then Tracey, one of the hospice staff, presented us with a sack filled with more gifts for the boys. She had paid special attention to Deryn's favourite things, including a bottle of eggnog and some mini bottles of Babycham with his goodies. We were spoilt rotten – there were also gifts for me and Simon and even a bone wrapped up for Ozzy!

We couldn't have wished for a more special day. I never wanted it to end. How bittersweet that our best Christmas yet would also be our last.

The days that followed were peaceful but still full of joy. Dylan went out most days with his sibling worker, returning with amazing stories about his adventures in the woods.

By now Deryn's stomach had started to produce a lot of bile, which meant that it had to be aspirated every couple of hours. Our hopes that Deryn was getting better were dashed when his team told us that his stomach shutting down was the beginning of the end.

The hospice had a strict protocol to follow if Deryn suddenly deteriorated, whereby a special drug could be administered to 'speed things up' if necessary. I couldn't help feeling that this was tantamount to euthanasia but I was assured that it was simply the kindest thing to do rather than let Deryn suffer needlessly.

Two days after our special Christmas Day, Deryn took a turn for the worse. He started spending most of his days sleeping. He'd been violently sick numerous times and was so cold that we had to put a heater up close to him to try and keep him warm. His temperature had spiked at 38.5 but this time, there were no antibiotics to control the spike, as had been normal practice for the previous three and a half years.

Deryn was feverish all that night so I took his pyjamas off and positioned the fan directly on him. He was sweating profusely and we all sat in his room, frightened to leave in case something happened. I started to feel very nervous and could see that Simon was equally anxious.

A few of Deryn's school friends were due to visit the following morning. I knew they'd be leaving at dawn to make the journey and I had no idea whether I should ring and tell them not to come. The last thing I wanted was for his lifelong buddies to turn up only to find Deryn drawing his last breath. I decided not to cancel. If they arrived and Deryn was too ill, we would have to deal with it. I couldn't deny his friends their chance to say goodbye.

Too terrified to sleep, I stayed awake for most of the night, wiping Deryn's forehead with a damp cloth and watching his chest rise with each breath. As dawn broke, the sun beamed in through the window and woke me up. I had nodded off. Immediately I panicked and jumped off the mattress to check that he was still breathing.

Deryn woke up around 10.30am, just before his friends arrived. Within seconds of them entering his room, he was cracking jokes and chatting away like he'd never been apart from them. They had lunch together and he took them to the ball pit where they all larked about, laughing and giggling like typical teenagers.

Suddenly, the resident hospice doctor appeared on the other side of the glass to the play area. She knocked on the window to attract my attention.

I smiled at her as she turned up her hands and mouthed the words: 'What the fuck?'

'I know!' I mouthed back.

She explained that she had been called during the night to prescribe Deryn the 'special' drug as he'd started to deteriorate. She was flabbergasted to see him in the ball pit playing with his friends, his temperature back to normal again.

'It's Deryn, what can I say?' I shrugged with a smile.

Because of Deryn's unusual energy levels, I couldn't help but ask for another bone marrow aspirate. I had to have definitive proof for my own sanity that there was still nothing doing with the bone marrow.

The team from the children's hospital arrived and took Simon and I away for another meeting. They had heard Deryn wasn't well and wanted to discuss whether or not he would be able to make it to hospital for the aspirate. They clearly hadn't spotted Deryn on their way in.

I explained that as he'd just spent an hour chucking himself about in the ball pit, I didn't think there'd be any trouble getting him there. Deryn's bloods showed no activity but if there was any tiny glimmer of hope in those bones, we needed to know about it.

The team left after saying a quick hello to Deryn. Even the most pessimistic doctor in the group seemed shocked to see him looking so well.

That evening it felt decidedly odd to be looking at funeral directors and crematoriums, but that's what we needed to do. Deryn announced that he wanted the same hearse that Winston Churchill had been driven in. He also finished off his will.

I read it and felt enormous pride at what a thoughtful young man he had become. It was such a shame that the world would no longer have him in it.

But tomorrow was another day and hopefully, once again, he would defy the laws of science and medicine.

Chapter 37

Deryn left the hospice briefly to undergo the final bone marrow aspirate and have more damaged tissue removed from his fingers which were still bandaged up.

The little finger on his left hand also appeared to be infected and he turned to his vaporiser pen to relieve the pain. The tincture we had made was concealed under Deryn's bed. The few staff who knew about it had no issues with him using it as they could see it was doing him no harm.

During surgery the thumb on Deryn's partially paralysed hand and the little finger on his good hand bled quite a bit, suggesting that there was a good blood supply. His middle and index fingers, though, didn't bleed at all. The surgeon was apologetic that he couldn't do more to save Deryn's fingers but I was only concerned about keeping him comfortable and pain free.

After surgery, Deryn struggled to get out of bed. The high doses of morphine he'd been given during the night had totally wiped him out and took away any motivation to move.

However, with another treat looming – a driving lesson under the guidance of a local instructor – I managed to persuade him to get up. And so, with his heavily bandaged fingers on the wheel, he joyfully drove around a disused car park for over an hour as the instructor complimented him on his road skills.

It was wonderful to see Deryn living life to the full and making the most of every day. I tried not to feel sad at the knowledge that he was living on borrowed time. We all wanted Deryn's last few weeks to be full of laughter and good times instead of being stuck in bed.

The next day, he had another visit, this time from Donna the donkey, delighting both the staff and other kids in equal measure. Local zoo farm Noah's Ark had gifted her to Deryn so she now belonged to him! When Donna left, we took Deryn to the cinema where he nodded off in the middle of *Anchorman 2*. We arrived back at the hospice to be greeted by Linda Robson and her granddaughter, and Russell Howard.

The next few days saw Deryn drifting in and out of consciousness, sometimes waking in the middle of a conversation only to doze off again. He tried so hard to stay awake and had been very specific that he did not want to die while out of his mind on morphine.

We tried to savour every moment, taking one photo after another of the most mundane moments that I could never get back. It was comforting to plan so much in advance but heartbreaking at the same time, particularly since it was only two more days until Christmas arrived for real.

We tried to make light of it, joking that Deryn was probably pretending to be ill just so he could enjoy two Christmas dinners and two helpings of presents.

I would have bought him everything he wanted if I was in the position to do so but I wasn't and Deryn didn't mind. He told me he didn't want any more stuff cluttering up his already overflowing room. Huge completed Lego kits lined the shelves, many of them so huge we had no idea what we'd do with them once all of this was over. Deryn had a plan, however, and had already told the staff that the hospice could keep them for other children to enjoy.

We were still waiting patiently for the results of the bone marrow aspirate when Deryn confided to me privately one evening that he hoped his marrow was empty. He'd had enough and just wanted to be left alone. I wasn't surprised because I secretly hoped the same.

There was a time when I would have given anything to keep Deryn with me but I no longer wished for that. I just wanted what was best for my son and if letting him go was best for him, then I had to wish for that. I had watched him suffer long enough.

❖

Later that evening, Deryn showed me a news article he had found online about a new law in Belgium where children as young as 12 could be given an assisted suicide.

'Will you take me to Belgium?' Deryn pleaded.

At that moment, I realised just how much Deryn wanted to die. I told him I couldn't take him to Belgium and he wouldn't want to go there anyway as it always rained. Deryn didn't push it, he merely smiled and we carried on looking for crematoriums.

The following morning, a nurse knocked on the door with the results from the bone marrow aspirate. The boys were watching a film although Deryn was half asleep. I closed the door behind me and glanced at the piece of paper in her hand. I opened it to find a handwritten note from Dr Ponni.

'So very sorry, the marrow is empty,' it said.

I wasn't surprised or upset. I was utterly relieved. Finally, we had the closure that we were looking for. I went back into Deryn's room to tell him the news and he simply replied: 'Good.'

❖

We knew that no stone had been left unturned. There was definitely nothing more to be done now. We had to admit defeat. If there was anything to point to hope, we would have had to make a difficult decision about whether to opt for further treatment or let him go. He didn't want to leave his life thinking that he'd given up or that there could have been another ending. This way, there was no other ending available.

Being at the hospice made it very easy to be at peace with what was happening. It was a wonderful place and while everyone who visited us initially arrived with a feeling of dread, they all left looking lighter, with a sense of acceptance.

After everyone had settled for the evening, I slipped away to sit alone in the Starborn room. I wanted to take some photographs before Deryn's body was placed there. It was so beautiful, I wanted to share it with family and friends without showing them potentially distressing pictures.

The first thing I noticed as I stepped inside was the temperature drop. I was overwhelmed with sadness looking at the bed that so many children had slept soundly in. One day soon, my own child would also sleep there.

This thought was made easier by the fact that Deryn felt very peaceful there. After visiting Starborn the first time, he said he could feel souls all around him.

'They were welcoming me into their group,' he explained. 'I'm going to like it.'

As I sat there taking pictures, I felt incredibly lucky. We were in a privileged position. How many people got to know exactly how and when their child was going to die? To know for certain that he wouldn't be alone, in pain or scared?

There would be no regrets. We'd tried to give him everything he wanted, we'd said all we needed to say to him and he'd had the time to prepare for the next step of his journey. Deryn also realised how lucky he was and had chosen to write some final letters to certain people.

I'd spoken to many people about how fortunate I felt during those days and the universal response was always that there was absolutely nothing lucky about what we were going through. I had to disagree. Being able to make choices on how to let someone go was a wonderful gift.

Chapter 38

D AY AFTER DAY I RECEIVED MESSAGES FROM PEOPLE WHO TOLD ME they were praying for a miracle. Many believed that the power of prayer would make Deryn better but it was hard not to believe that a miracle had already happened. Deryn was still alive almost three weeks after we had been told to expect just a couple of days.

I was confused. We'd been told that his days were numbered but he had spiked two temperatures in recent weeks only to make a complete recovery within 24 hours.

I hurried out to buy a present for everybody to open on Christmas morning. I couldn't let the day go by without the boys having at least one thing to open. But Santa hadn't forgotten about us and I awoke to find two massive sacks full of presents for the boys in Deryn's bedroom, along with another box of goodies for Simon and me. We couldn't believe it.

Outside Deryn's door were snowy footprints left by Santa. The stockings had also been filled… it really was Christmas! It was amazing not to be the one trying to create the magic, instead the hospice was making it happen for all of us.

I had told the team that I didn't want them to prolong Deryn's life just so that we could have him here for this but deep down, I was so thankful that he was holding on to spend one last Christmas Day with us. He had defied the odds yet again and I loved him for that. Forever the rebel, just like me.

It was so nice to see him being a regular teenage boy, having a drink with his dad and sharing a stein of cider with Russ. He was living a normal life, eating food that hadn't been prepared in a clinical environment, drinking cider, driving cars, handling animals, even going in a jacuzzi.

Normality was wonderful, although eventually normality would kill him, we had to remember. No-one could tell us when and the only way to cope with not knowing was to live each day like it was his last and cram in as much as possible.

Deryn was looking forward to dying, he considered it his next adventure. Most of all, he was looking forward to his suffering coming to an end. Imagine walking down Death Row only to find the electric chair isn't working that day. Most people would be pleased with a reprieve but when your life is filled with pain and suffering, it's pure torture to be kept waiting.

I could understand his frustration and I knew it was time. I had to trust Deryn and believe him when he said enough was enough.

I explained to my friends that we wouldn't be going home once Deryn had died. I didn't want anyone to feel sorry for us, but they understood. It would tear me up to see Deryn's friends growing up and enjoying their lives. I didn't begrudge them but I thought staying away would be easier.

I felt guilty for even mentioning the future but Deryn told me we should all be looking forward to the day when our lives could revert to normal again.

That night, he woke up in the early hours, sobbing. After staying so strong for so long, he was begging for me to end it all.

'I don't want any more morphine mum, it makes me feel like I'm not here,' Deryn cried.

I sat next to him and held his hand. My eyes alighted on the jar of golden cannabis tincture that I'd hidden under his bed.

I wondered what would happen if I gave Deryn a small amount under his tongue. The vaporiser brought him some relief but not enough and a higher dose could have better results.

It was 69 days since Deryn had been given his last bag of cells. There was no chance that he would engraft now. I had promised Deryn I would try everything within my power to help him. I couldn't sit and watch him suffer any longer.

I took a small syringe from the medicine cupboard and quickly checked that there was no-one outside. It was the early hours of New Year's Eve so staffing was minimal. I unscrewed the lid and drew up 5ml of the honey-like tincture. I'd already tasted it and knew that Deryn would enjoy the sweet, floral cannabis flavour.

Still sobbing uncontrollably, Deryn opened his mouth and I popped the syringe underneath his tongue. Deryn held it for a minute before swallowing. Half an hour passed. He was no longer having a panic attack. He looked peaceful. I asked him how he was feeling.

'I feel relaxed,' he told me. 'I'm aware of everything. I just feel at peace mum, it's beautiful.'

Moments later the nurse came back in with his dose of cyclizine. I panicked. There was no way he would turn that drug away and I was worried about the effect the cannabis tincture could have on it. Then I heard Deryn tell the nurse he didn't want it. She was flabbergasted. Everyone knew how much he relied on this particular drug.

'I don't feel like I need it anymore, thanks,' he said before rolling over and going to sleep.

New Year's Eve 2014 was the first in four years that we hadn't been confined to a small hospital room with Deryn. He was very chilled and sat in his bedroom munching on peanuts, sipping a glass of cider and watching movies. He was free to come and go with no tubes or wires. It was heavenly.

Earlier, he'd been topped up with platelets and a bag of red cells but he had decided that this would be his final top-up. If it bought him a couple more weeks to finish watching Breaking Bad, his favourite TV series, he would be very content.

As a family, we made a promise to each other. Even though Deryn's loss would leave a massive gap in our lives, this would be our year.

No more looking over our shoulders, waiting for cancer to return or dreading the results of the next test. No more worrying about blood results, hospital appointments, transfusions or nasty medications. No more night feeds, checks that he was still breathing and most important of all, no more suffering for Deryn.

The very thought of peace was wonderful. It was something I'd dreamed of for a long time but it came at a very heavy price: a life without Deryn.

As we watched Big Ben strike midnight on TV and marvelled at the firework display, it was lovely and cosy. We raised our glasses to celebrate and shortly after midnight, went to bed.

Deryn slept soundly until 4am when he awoke abruptly to be sick. Once his stomach was full of bile, it would empty itself, regardless of the time of day but this time I was surprised to see that instead of the usual 500ml, there was barely enough to fill a teacup.

I feared that his pain might become unbearable without morphine but for now, thanks to the cannabis tincture, he was totally pain free. Allowing him to die with his faculties intact was my priority. Whenever Deryn felt a twinge somewhere, I would put another 5ml of the tincture underneath his tongue and within a few minutes, he felt good again.

Deryn hadn't been pain-free for as long as I could remember. His mouth, fingers, stomach, gums, tongue, hips, knees, legs and back had been constantly painful so this was nothing short of fantastic.

After stuffing our faces with a mountain of leftovers, we carried on planning Deryn's funeral. The crematorium had been chosen and we were just deciding where to hold the service. Deryn had chosen some music and decided exactly when he wanted the tracks to be played.

It was going to be an upbeat affair, with Move your Feet by Junior Senior probably the most unusual choice for a funeral but Deryn had fond memories of dancing around to it as a toddler. He wanted people to arrive at the service to this song and once everyone was seated, Deryn wanted his coffin to be brought in to the sounds of Hall of Fame by The Script.

The final song on Deryn's list was Somewhere Over the Rainbow by Israel Kamakawiwo'ole. I'd heard it a few times and it was a beautiful rendition of the Judy Garland favourite but I wasn't sure why Deryn had chosen this version. The reason broke my heart.

'When I used to stay at Barretstown, they played this song every night as we got into bed,' he told me. 'It was the last song I heard before I fell asleep. I had the happiest times of my life there and I want to be cremated to that song so that it's the last thing I hear before I go to sleep for ever.'

Once the boys had gone to sleep, I updated Deryn's Facebook page. One thing I never mentioned was the cannabis tincture I was giving him. I was too terrified to even write or say the word cannabis, let alone share it with the world – the fear of having Deryn taken away from me was too real. But after seeing the relief it brought him with no obvious detrimental side effects, I didn't want to stop it, either.

Suddenly, my whole body started shaking. Standing in the dimly lit bedroom looking over the body of my sleeping eldest son, I couldn't hold back the words, or emotion, any longer. As tears rolled down my face, my thoughts came tumbling out loud even though it was the early hours of the morning and I was the only one awake.

'This isn't fair, this isn't right. You're only 14 years old, you haven't even had the chance to live yet.'

I immediately felt a pang of guilt as I realised I'd woken Deryn up. He wasn't annoyed, he just looked up at me through half-open eyes and took my hand.

'It doesn't matter how old we are when we die, it's about what we did while we were here,' he whispered. 'We all have to die at some point, whether it's 14 or 94, it doesn't matter. Please don't be upset, you will be okay.

'Life will go on.'

I collapsed on the floor and Deryn reached out to me. I stood up and he put his thin arms around me. I told him that I was not ready to let him go. I breathed in his smell, the touch of his soft skin and the way he hugged me, trying to hold on to as much as I could because I never, ever wanted to forget what he was to me.

Deryn told me that I needed to accept it, that we both knew some time ago that this was how it would end. I didn't want to hear that he was ready to go. It felt so wrong. It wasn't the order of things. No-one should die after their children.

Deryn was so wise.

'Why is that the order?' he asked. 'Who says? This is life and everything is as it should be.'

He went on to tell me that I'd be okay once he'd gone and so would his dad. Deryn promised me that Dylan would have a wonderful life. He reassured me that he would always be with us, no matter what. He had accepted that it was time to start the next step of his journey.

'You were so young when you had me yet you only made a few

mistakes,' he told me. 'You have been the best mum so please don't ever think you haven't.'

For my entire parenting life, I had held on to guilt from Deryn's early years but he had just forgiven me for everything.

Deryn asked if I wanted to sleep in his bed and I spent that night with him holding my hand and checking that I was okay. I could feel every little squeeze and movement as he fell asleep.

It was then that I accepted it. He could go at any time he needed to go. I fell asleep feeling at complete peace.

Chapter 39

D<small>ERYN'S HAND WAS STILL HEAVILY BANDAGED BUT HE DIDN'T LET IT</small> stop him having fun. Each evening, he spent an hour in the jacuzzi before heading back to his room to watch films and graze on snacks and treats from the pantry.

One evening, Deryn was sitting in the lounge with Louise watching a film. The lounge had a cosy, Christmassy warmth to it, and Deryn soon drifted off to sleep with his bandaged hand resting between his knees.

Unconsciously, he tugged his hand from between his knees and woke himself up. From the other side of the room, I heard him yell. He held up his right hand with a surprised look on his face.

'Mum – LOOK!' he shouted.

The bandage on Deryn's middle finger had worked its way loose and completely come off. It was one of the bandages we were told must never be removed because his fingernails had been removed and the ends of his fingers had come off with them and were blackened. We didn't want to see what was underneath.

Only the ring finger and little finger had been unaffected so how on earth was I now seeing a third perfectly normal finger?

I had seen them before he went down to surgery. They were red and the ends were black, swollen and necrotic. I'd even taken pictures of them. I took a closer look at his hand now and was amazed. Deryn's middle finger looked like mine but wrinkled, like he'd been in the bath for too long. From the second knuckle up, his finger was a little thinner where the skin had been removed but to all intents and purposes, it was a normal finger.

I ran down to find Simon as questions raced through my mind. How on earth had a child with NO immune system, NO white count, NO platelets and NO way of fighting infection managed to heal himself after being off medication for over three weeks?

I called Deryn's team to tell them what had happened. Not one of them could understand it or give me any answers.

Deryn removed the dressings from his index finger and thumb, revealing both looking just as healthy as the middle finger, with blood flow clearly circulating. They were a healthy pink and there was no sign of any open wounds.

None of us knew what to do. It was absolutely amazing but also difficult to comprehend. If the doctors were wrong about this, could they be wrong about Deryn dying too?

We knew that his bone marrow wasn't functioning and he wasn't able to make his own blood products but it was not scientifically possible for wounds to heal with no neutrophils. Deryn had spent so many months being isolated because a common cold could be fatal yet somehow, he had overcome three catastrophic infections.

Once again, we were thrown into turmoil. Surely it couldn't end like this? How could he defeat the odds so many times and just sit there waiting to die?

Dr Barbara insisted on taking some blood samples back to the hospital with her. Deryn's bloods had only been taken five days previously and were the most accurate indicator as to what was going on. I emailed her a photo of his fingers for her meeting and waited with bated breath.

The following day, a nurse came to find me in the lounge. He was carrying a piece of paper in his hand. He placed it face down and slid it towards me, smiling. With shaking hands, I picked it up. I couldn't believe what I was seeing.

Deryn's platelets were 7, which was fantastic. He had managed to hold onto platelets for four days since his last transfusion, something he'd not been able to do for many months. Even more surprising was Deryn's neutrophil count, which had increased from 0.05 to 0.25.

Hundreds of people had been praying for Deryn, sending him distance healing and blessing him in their own ways. Was this a miracle?

❖

Later that evening, the hospice doctor arrived.

'We're no longer sure that Deryn is dying,' she admitted, then asked: 'If he were to spike a temperature, would you like us to help him?'

Deryn immediately piped up.

'I want you all to leave me alone!' he shouted angrily.

I insisted that if Deryn wanted no further intervention, that's how it would be. I wasn't going to force him. Unbeknown to me, Simon was down the corridor with the staff shredding the Do Not Resuscitate forms we had signed.

Deryn's doctors were not sure whether or not the hospice was now the best place for us. When we'd arrived four weeks earlier, he'd been given three days to live, now here he was a month later, in far better health than when he'd left his hospital room. They had no idea how this was possible.

In just one week, Deryn had experienced a huge leap in his recovery. The infections had cleared up, the pints of bile that had been building up in his stomach were virtually non-existent and instead of continuing to lose weight at a rapid rate, Deryn had only lost 1lb in the previous seven days.

What on earth had caused this dramatic turnaround?

According to his team it wasn't the steroids. Then it dawned on me. Only one thing had changed since Deryn started to recover. The cannabis tincture.

I couldn't tell the doctors what we'd done. I was sure the authorities wouldn't see it the same way we did but if there was even a minuscule chance that the cannabis tincture was responsible for my son still being alive, I wasn't willing to risk stopping it.

The team suggested that we play it by ear and wait for the results of his blood tests so we tried to carry on as normal. Deryn was now free to lark about in the jacuzzi as much as he wanted and he and Dylan spent most of their time in the ball pit or lounging around watching films.

I was astonished when he burst into tears as he confided in me one evening that he was disappointed at not being able to die as he had planned.

'Mum, there was a door and behind that door was everything I've ever wanted,' he explained tearfully. 'Peace, no pain or suffering and no more hospitals. It was all promised to me and all I had to do was walk through the door.

'And then, just as I was about to walk through the door, it was slammed shut,' he sobbed. 'I don't want to be alive any more if it's going to carry on like this. I want to be well or be dead – I'm tired of being ill.'

I could only assure him that we would do everything in our power to get him well again. There were no assurances from his doctors, who were as bemused as we were by these developments.

The following morning, we were called to an emergency meeting to discuss Deryn's blood results. Deryn's neutrophil count was now 0.5 – double the previous reading!

Having seen his new fingers, Deryn had changed his mind

about no more transfusions and agreed to have another bag of red cells before joining us with the doctors. The words rare and miracle were being bandied around the room. As we sat there, his latest blood results arrived, revealing that his neutrophils had risen yet again.

Simon and I caught each other's eye and shared a discreet smile. We had an inkling of how this was happening but, while we were overjoyed about Deryn's miraculous recovery, we were also frustrated at having to keep such important information to ourselves. I wanted to tell the world, share it with everyone including the doctors so that they could help others, but I knew it was too dangerous to breathe a word to anyone in a position of authority.

We had seen news reports on TV about parents who'd had their children taken away from them after trying alternatives such as cannabis. I hadn't forgotten one doctor's words to me about my child being made a ward of court if we went against traditional treatment methods.

The team checked that Deryn's blood products were all his own and not some crafty donor cells that had resurfaced. Every blood test showed a higher neutrophil count than before and indicated that he was holding the transfused platelets well. Could he be engrafting after all this time?

The irony was that the better Deryn seemed to be faring, the more depressed he became. He wasn't dealing well with the loss of the exit strategy he had laid out so meticulously. He hadn't planned for a future because he was told that he wouldn't have one. He now felt he was in some weird kind of limbo where not even death was a certainty any more.

While Deryn was experiencing depression, my elation turned to anger that had we not hung in there and taken the law into our own hands at a time when we had nothing to lose, he might no longer be with us.

A visit from Isla helped to perk Deryn up, as did the news that we might be making a permanent move to North Somerset, a place we all felt very much was home. Our recent application for housing had been accepted and we were allowed to put in a bid on any houses we felt suitable.

We had found an amazing gym that Deryn could join when he felt strong enough. Simon and I had stopped training when we moved to the hospice and while I had lost weight as well as muscle tone from not eating much, Simon had ballooned through comfort eating. We desperately wanted to get back into control again and do something nice for ourselves.

It had been 95 days since Deryn's last bone marrow transplant and 46 days since we'd brought him to the hospice to die. It looked as if we might be able to celebrate day 100 with a child who was healthy enough to enjoy it.

Deryn no longer needed transfusions. His red cells were holding tight and his platelets had been hanging on for dear life for some time. He was creating neutrophils like they were going out of fashion and in a further extraordinary discovery, he was starting to produce new red blood cells by himself. Not bad for someone with no bone marrow.

Chapter 40

THE HOSPICE STAFF TOLD US THAT WE NEEDED TO MOVE OUT OF OUR rooms and into a separate farmhouse in the grounds as they were having a refit. The following night, Simon and I slept in the same bed for the first time in many months.

Deryn had his own room next door with a lovely big bed, Dylan had a bedroom, too, and we had a lounge all to ourselves. There was even a little kitchen with a dining table. Finally, we were living a normal life in a beautiful environment and we celebrated with Russ, who joined us for our first Chinese takeaway since Deryn had been placed on the clean diet more than 300 days earlier.

We had been put in sole charge of Deryn's medications. All two of them. It was hard to believe he was on just two when not so long ago, he was ingesting a cocktail of dozens of different drugs.

The leveller was that Deryn's team wanted to give his marrow time to prove itself before they got too excited. I also wanted to see a more progressive improvement before cracking open the Champagne.

There were other things to be dealing with too, chiefly leaving the hospice after 48 days there. We had to be out within a week, which was a shock as we had nowhere obvious to go. The hospital told us they wanted us to stay near as they weren't ready to hand care back to Addenbrooke's.

While we waited for a house to come up in North Somerset, we were offered rooms at Sam's House, a purpose-built three-storey 'home from home' built and run by cancer charity CLIC Sargent, close to the hospital, where we had stayed in the lead up to Deryn's first transplant. Having spent four years packing and unpacking our lives, I was looking forward to settling somewhere more permanent.

While Simon and I packed our belongings, the boys went to school at the hospital. Dylan was pleased to be back among kids his own age, while Deryn was still a bit subdued.

According to the latest blood test, he had doubled his platelet count in a week. His haemoglobin levels had only dropped slightly after having no transfusions for a couple of weeks, which meant Deryn was definitely holding on to red cells. However, the team wanted to see his red blood count increase by itself before they were certain he had engrafted.

Dr Barbara pointed out that after each of Deryn's transplants, he had shown high numbers, yet they had all failed. I hoped that by continuing to give Deryn 5ml of tincture twice a day, we could keep any nasties away until Deryn had engrafted completely.

Deryn's miraculous recovery was making headlines and he was being interviewed by journalists and appearing in TV news interviews and internet snippets worldwide. Everyone was dubbing what had happened some kind of miracle and much as I believed that, I wondered if it wasn't largely to do with the tincture. There was no way of knowing for sure unless I stopped giving it to him for a while, a risk I wasn't prepared to take until he had engrafted.

On BMT 104, Deryn's blood test indicated that, with absolutely no medical intervention, his red cell count had increased.

'You have officially engrafted, Deryn,' one of his doctors gleefully announced.

Deryn just stared at her.

'Does this mean you're not going to give up so quickly on people from now on?' he deadpanned.

❖

If someone had told me at the beginning of December that I would be watching Deryn idly thumb through Facebook posts on his phone at the end of the first week of February, I would have smiled and told them they were in denial. I was trying hard to get my head around it.

I had to admit to myself that I was struggling a little, as was Deryn. We all were.

At Sam's House, we met a lovely couple who we'd seen in the teenage ward. It was really nice to spend evenings relaxing with other parents who understood us. We helped them through the early stages of their son's leukaemia diagnosis, although he had been paralysed as a result of his treatment. They were tough cookies too and we felt we had found some kindred spirits.

But we were finding it hard living in such close quarters. After having our own space, the prospect of sharing a house with 16 other families hadn't filled me with glee and we were finding it tough. The boys had two single beds side by side and a foot away was our double bed. We had a small bathroom and the kitchen was across the hallway, where we had one shelf in a shared fridge. Often we'd find meat on our shelf or sugary cereals and sweets in our cupboard space. I didn't want to upset anyone by pointing out that their choice of food wasn't doing their children any good so I kept my opinions to myself.

In the hospice, I'd allowed Deryn to eat whatever he'd wanted and he had grown sick of crisps and sweets. I didn't see the point in restricting his intake while he was dying. Now that he wasn't dying any more, I was back on the case.

While we were there, I was being approached by many of the

parents after they found out about my miracle child. They all wanted to know how they could 'cure' their children. I told a couple of the more understanding parents about the tincture that we'd made and also shared everything I could about our dietary changes. Most of them were intrigued but I was also targeted in some vicious online attacks by people I had considered friends. They accused me of giving my son an eating disorder by spouting nonsense with my healthy-eating cancer-fighting ideas.

While it didn't upset me enough to let it to stop me from continuing on our healthy nutrition path, the eating disorder comment cut deeply; it was torture dealing with Deryn's refusal to eat anything on a daily basis. I had to ask myself whether I was indeed responsible for Deryn's lack of interest in food.

He was struggling to eat anything at all. No matter how hard we tried to encourage him, he point-blank refused. I asked to speak to someone who knew about eating disorders only to be warned that if Deryn didn't start eating soon, he would be forced to have another NG feeding tube.

Jovan's wedding in Norfolk was a welcome distraction and we all enjoyed an amazing weekend of celebrations. The people of Watton welcomed Deryn back with open arms and it was fantastic to be around our friends again after such a long time.

I was a bridesmaid and for once, I thoroughly enjoyed being in a dress and having my make-up done with a glass of Champagne in my hand. The ceremony was beautiful and as the bride and groom turned to walk out of the church, their walking down the aisle song came on.

Incredibly, they had chosen Somewhere Over the Rainbow, the same song Deryn had picked for his funeral. I burst into tears the second it started playing and felt my legs giving way beneath me. The whole congregation was staring at me. I somehow pulled myself together, gave Jovan a wink – she had refused to move until she knew I was okay – and we walked back down the aisle.

Arriving back in Bristol, we were given the news that Deryn had doubled his neutrophil and white cell count despite four whole weeks without any blood products. If this continued, he might never need a transfusion again.

I reached a point when I was confident that Deryn's blood count was high enough to stop giving him the tincture. I needed to know for sure whether or not it had a direct effect. I wasn't expecting to see any difference but his blood results showed that during the week he didn't have the tincture, his neutrophils had dropped.

Over the following weeks, I continued the experiment and watched as his neutrophil count went through peaks and troughs. There was a direct correlation between Deryn having the cannabis tincture and his blood counts. Whenever he didn't have it, they dropped.

It was enough hard evidence to suggest that cannabis tincture was playing a vital role in his recovery. I hadn't imagined in my wildest dreams that it could have saved Deryn's life. I only started giving it to him to alleviate his anxiety. The fact that it also helped with his pain, taking him off morphine and cyclizine, was an added bonus.

None of the anecdotal stories I'd read mentioned the positive effect cannabis could have on neutrophils. I wondered if cannabis had ever been used in transplant patients before. How many pharmaceutical drugs could be replaced with this one plant? I had so many questions and no-one to turn to for answers.

Meanwhile, we were offered a little mid-terrace house just outside Bristol. It was scruffy and in dire need of some TLC, but we decided to take it.

Worryingly, Deryn's mental health was continuing to deteriorate. Food was his nemesis and the sheer amount of work that the new house needed only added to the pressure Deryn was feeling. Every obstacle felt overwhelming and he was struggling to get through each day.

Simon and I packed up our old house in Norfolk and transported everything to the new place, which Deryn said reminded him of a crack den. Fortunately, our lovely new friends from the gym offered to help us decorate. Talk in our family had turned from crematoriums to which colour to paint Deryn's bedroom.

No wonder he was struggling – it was a monumental change for all of us to get our heads round. Thankfully, Russ was on hand to try and cheer his friend up. He arrived at the hospital to pick the boys up from their classes as a surprise. They were thrilled to see him...how many children get picked up from school by Russell Howard?

He also had a proposition for Deryn.

'I'd really like to tell your amazing story on my upcoming world tour,' Russ told him. 'Is that okay?'

Deryn was taken aback but immediately agreed – although he couldn't understand why his story would be funny enough to feature on a comedian's world tour. Then came the bombshell.

'I would really love it if you would do me the honour of appearing on stage with me,' Russ added.

'Ummm yeah, of course,' Deryn gasped. 'I'd love to do that. What do you want me to wear?'

A mischievous grin spread across Russ's face.

'Oh I think you know', he said as he led us into the hallway to look at the costume he'd brought with him.

We were greeted by a six-foot replica of a penis. It had been especially made for Deryn and had a hole cut out for his face to fit in. We couldn't believe our eyes. It was hilarious but I wasn't sure Deryn would go for it. Although he had a wicked sense of humour, he'd never been very good at laughing at himself. This would certainly test him.

Deryn cracked up with laughter and immediately agreed. The first gig, in just a few weeks' time, was taking place in Cardiff. We were all incredibly excited.

❖

The following day, Deryn was back in for blood tests. I was incredibly nervous. We had the promise of a new house, a new mobility car, we were about to get our beloved pooch back and we might even be able to go on holiday, too. We were trying not live our lives in fear but each blood test hovered over us like a threatening dark cloud.

It was February 13th, almost a year to the day that we'd first arrived in Bristol. For the first time in almost a year, the results showed that Deryn was not neutropenic. He had a fully functioning immune system and was duly booked in to have his Hickman line removed.

Treatment was over!

However, an even bigger challenge was now presenting itself. Deryn was literally starving himself to death and there seemed to be nothing we could do about it. Every evening, he pushed his food around his plate listlessly. He'd lost the will to live and within a week, Deryn had lost another two kilos.

He weighed 32kg, 4kg less than when he was diagnosed at 10, almost four years earlier. I explained to Deryn that if he tried to eat, I would help him. I would try my hardest to stop the team from putting another tube in but if he was going to refuse to eat, I had very little choice but to allow them to intervene.

Reluctantly, he agreed to try but after a few days of eating pizza for breakfast, lunch and dinner, he had lost yet more weight. He was totally disheartened but we both knew it would take a few days for the food to show up on the scales. One day wasn't going to cut it.

I begged and pleaded with him, only to be met by a blank stare. The light in his eyes had gone out again and I had no idea how I could get it back. We feared that Deryn was going to die in front of us if he didn't start wanting to live. The hospital team didn't seem to have any answers that weren't tantamount to force feeding.

If Deryn didn't put weight on soon, he would end up back in hospital on Total Parenteral Nutrition and any possibility of touring with Russ would disappear. They also wouldn't be able to remove his line because he would be at risk of a heart attack under general anaesthetic.

We knew it was a psychological issue as Deryn had admitted that he wasn't eating because he wanted to die. He wanted an end to feeling ill and he thought he was a burden to us. Simon, Dylan and I cried with Deryn over some of the things he said. How could he ever think that he was a burden?

He told us that he felt the move and all the to-ing and fro-ing was all his fault. If it hadn't been for him, we'd still be living in Norfolk leading a normal life. We did our best to convince him that we would go to the ends of the earth for him and nothing was too much for us to cope with. We would rather have had him with us and go through hell than have a 'normal' life without him in it.

Deryn had taught us so much more than we could ever have learned by ourselves. Now it was frustrating for Simon and me not to be able to help Deryn any more and lift him out of this terrible depression.

We asked the doctors for help. Deryn sat in the hospital room with his arms tightly wrapped around his skinny, bent knees, refusing to lift his head up or make eye contact as three of his team tried to talk to him.

One of them adopted a harsh tone in a bid to shock him into action.

'If you don't eat soon, we will treat you like an anorexic,' she announced sternly. 'We will section you, sedate you and force-feed you if we have to. Is that what you want, Deryn?' she demanded as I looked on aghast.

There was no mention of mental health care, no-one to talk to, just straight in with the force feeding. I asked if he could speak to someone before we resorted to such drastic measures but because Deryn wasn't a haematology and oncology patient any longer, he didn't qualify for help. I thought it was disgusting that there wasn't help for anyone who needed it.

Deryn's state of mind had clearly affected Dr Barbara, who had always been able to lift his spirits and commanded his utmost respect. I'm not sure what strings she pulled but, a couple of days after the meeting, she gave us the news that they would be able to offer Deryn mental health support after all.

Chapter 41

D<small>ESPERATE TO TAKE PART IN</small> R<small>USS'S TOUR</small>, D<small>ERYN HAD BEEN MAKING</small> a real effort to eat more. In the space of a week, he'd managed to put on 600g. The following few days saw him put on another 600g. Line-removal surgery was looking more likely as each gram went on.

As an oncology parent, you look forward to the line coming out because it means the end of treatment. Deryn was finally getting what he wished for, an end to the prodding and poking, something he'd thought only death could grant him.

He had been left with no life threatening side effects from his treatment. His joints were sore, the severed nerves in his hand meant that it wouldn't work again, puberty was stunted and he was infertile but there were no issues with his internal organs, liver or heart. He had walked away from it all a very lucky young man.

On February 25th 2014, he went down to theatre for what we hoped would be the final time. He was given a couple of bags of platelets to ensure he wouldn't bleed too much. He came out of theatre and I couldn't help but stare at his beautiful bare chest. No line, no cannula, no PICC. Deryn was finally free although his chest bore some pretty impressive scars which told his story more powerfully than words ever could.

Just two days later, Deryn was in Cardiff for Russ's first gig. We arrived at a swanky hotel to meet Russ and his crew and after being shown to our rooms, we joined them in the bar. At the arena, we were shown backstage and given VIP status. The boys and I had dinner with the crew and Dylan was allowed to test the microphone before helping Russ run through the opening minutes of the show.

We felt like royalty. After watching Russ run through what Deryn had to do one last time, we took our seats in the front row for the show. Deryn beamed from ear to ear throughout and when Russ's performance was reaching the end, the security guy came to collect Deryn for his turn on stage.

Russ came back on for his encore and started telling the story of how he met Deryn and how their friendship grew. I couldn't stop crying. It was utterly surreal to hear a famous comedian talking about Deryn so fondly in front of 6,000 people.

There were gasps and cries from the audience as Russ delivered the one-liners about Deryn making his dad promise to wear a Grim Reaper outfit at his funeral and the conversation about the penis costume. The crowd was roaring with laughter and I saw a few around me suddenly realise they were laughing at the story of a dying teenager. Then Russ introduced Deryn and he waddled on stage dressed as a bright pink penis with an enormous grin on his face.

The crowd lit up. Every single person gave Deryn a standing ovation. As I turned to look at the crowd behind me, I felt an almighty wave of love sweep over me.

Simon promptly burst into tears. Everyone around us was crying and clapping. Russ and Deryn left the stage waving to the fans. On the way back to the hotel, Russ's car was stopped by fans who wanted autographs and he hustled Deryn out of the car and handed him a pen.

They signed umpteen tickets and had their photographs taken, with Deryn loving every second and glorying in his newfound fame. Russ had given Deryn the best gift he could

CHAPTER 41

hope for – a reason to live.

With a week until Russ's next performance, Deryn asked if he could go back to his old school in Norfolk and say a proper goodbye to his friends now that we would be living hundreds of miles away. He hadn't set foot in school for well over a year and all his friends had come to terms with the fact that they would never see him again.

The reunion was wonderful. Deryn's head teacher was beside himself. He thought the world of Deryn and seeing him walk into school on a Friday afternoon finished him off. He broke down in tears of joy while Deryn acted like he'd never been away.

He sat in the dinner hall with his friends and ate some chips. Any fears I had that Deryn might no longer be able to socialise with people of his own age melted away in that moment. After a few pictures and an interview with the local newspapers, he said his goodbyes, astonished that he couldn't go anywhere anymore without being followed by paparazzi.

It was soon time to leave Watton. My mum took us out for lunch and spent most of the meal crying. I felt so guilty about leaving her but I knew that we had to make a fresh start. It was going to be strange walking into a shop where no-one knew my name or my business.

Deryn's performance in Newcastle caused a similar reaction to the one in Cardiff. Once again, Deryn was mobbed by fans wanting to meet him and be photographed with him, much to Russ's delight. Deryn lapped it up.

Unfortunately, his new found fame wasn't enough to get him eating properly on a regular basis. He would tuck away copious amounts when he was with Russ but once home, he was off food again. It was like living with two different people, the boy who was all smiles and happiness when out on stage in front of thousands versus the depressed anorexic. Deryn said he could only be himself at home and it saddened me that the miserable Deryn was the one he felt was the true him.

All we could do was try and give him a sense of wanting to live.

The exciting life that Russ showed him on the road gave him a huge thrill and something to look forward to. Travelling to various venues across the UK and staying in fabulous hotels that we could only dream about was thrilling for all of us. It was a celebrity lifestyle and although it couldn't last, we made the most of every minute.

The London shows at Wembley Arena and the O2 were incredible. By day we hung out with Russ, his friends and his crew while our evenings were spent backstage and in the audience watching the show.

At breakfast each morning, other hotel residents couldn't help staring at us. My pink hair and piercings always drew attention while Deryn was incredibly thin and pale and sporting a purple mohawk. I could understand why people were wondering what on earth we were doing there.

The staff somehow heard about Deryn and after arriving back at the hotel one evening, we were greeted with boxes of cupcakes, flowers and fruit. The table was covered in cards, all written by various members of staff, wishing Deryn all the best. It was mind-blowing.

Deryn's weight continued to plummet and being more active only exacerbated the problem. He was rapidly descending towards the 30kg mark and I was very concerned. There was still no sign of psychological help, as the person assigned to help him was off sick.

But at least his next blood tests confirmed that our hopes of recovery were not misplaced. A week earlier they went like this:

Platelets - 36

White blood cells- 2.08

Haemoglobin - 100

Neutrophils - 1.5

Now, they read:

Platelets - 53

White blood cells - 3.64

Haemoglobin - 119

Neutrophils - 2.27

I couldn't believe it! They hadn't looked this good for two years. They were almost normal. The nurses laughed as I high-fived a grinning Deryn in the corridor.

Linda Robson asked us to go and watch her filming the ITV show Loose Women which meant another wonderful day trip to London, with lunch at Harrods.

Given the wonderful experiences we were enjoying, I shouldn't have been surprised to read a few cutting comments at the bottom of a newspaper feature about Deryn. The article mentioned that he was struggling to deal with living after accepting his fate.

A few people commented to say that Deryn was selfish and should be grateful for a second chance. One said that Deryn didn't know how lucky or how spoilt he was. To the outside world, I understood how it might have looked like that.

Compared to most children his age, Deryn's life was fantastic; that was undeniable. As much as he loved the days out and the wonderful experiences, they didn't come close to making up for what he had been through and his team couldn't guarantee that Deryn's health wouldn't rapidly deteriorate at any moment.

The outside world didn't see Deryn at his worst. Those people had no idea how hard it was for Deryn to wrap his head around his new reality.

I vowed never to read the newspaper comments section again.

Chapter 42

With each stage appearance, Deryn's confidence grew. It was lovely to see our chirpy, cheeky son coming back to us. The glint in his eye had returned and he was developing some lust for life, even raising the subject of returning to school the following September.

The line removal signified the end of invasive treatment but the increasing time between appointments – three weeks – was the real game changer.

The first day I watched him swimming in a pool, totally submerged with no lines or bandages, was a joyful sight. His blood levels were almost normal and it was only his skeletal frame which still worried and upset me.

Having experienced how powerful the cannabis tincture had been, I was keen to get in touch with other people like us, who we could talk to openly and share our stories with. I didn't have to search for long before I found the Bristol Cannabis Club. I joined their Facebook page and started to learn about the community.

As much as I wanted to connect with like-minded people, I was still petrified that the authorities would discover our secret and take our children away from us. After being a silent member of the group for some time, I saw a post about a march taking place in Cardiff. I really wanted to go and meet others who wouldn't judge us for turning to cannabis when all else had failed.

The morning of the march arrived and we grabbed our bags

and headed off with the boys. We had trouble finding the meeting point but eventually, we stumbled across a lovely lady with a cannabis leaf painted on her face and she directed us towards a growing crowd of demonstrators, who ranged in age from young children through to pensioners. It was tremendous to see such a varied group as I'm ashamed to admit that we had preconceived ideas that they would be just a bunch of stoners who wanted to legalise cannabis so that they could sit around and get high.

We discovered that the woman with the cannabis leaf on her face was Jo Moss, Deputy Director of NORML UK – a non-partisan, non-profit organisation researching the benefits of cannabis for all purposes. She gave us lots of information and invited us to their annual general meeting to meet other like-minded souls.

On the march that day we met some wonderful friendly, caring people and when I was approached by Pippa Bartolotti, the Green Party leader for Wales, I found myself telling her our story. She promised to give me her full support when the time was right for me to talk more openly. My guard came down because I trusted her and passionately agreed with her campaign to legalise cannabis and publicise its healing properties.

All this time one name kept cropping up again and again, a name I first noticed during my initial research into cannabis. I was advised to talk to Jeff Ditchfield about our story. Jeff is a Liverpool-born cannabis expert who founded Bud Buddies in 2002, supplying cannabis to ill and disabled people free of charge and who now lived in Spain. I was told he was the right person to help us get Deryn back on track.

Simon and I spent hours watching documentaries and reading articles shared by our new friends. It was exciting to discover how widespread and supportive the cannabis community was.

CHAPTER 42

Many were chronically ill and had found that the class B drug was the only thing that helped them when their doctors had run out of options. Some had even been discreetly advised by their medics off the record to look into cannabis as a way of alleviating their suffering.

❖

By now, Easter was rapidly approaching and I bought the boys a chocolate egg each. Waiting to pay, I flashed back to a few months earlier and the tears I shed buying Advent calendars at Christmas. I couldn't quite believe that I was now buying two Easter eggs.

Deryn managed to eat his in one sitting, all 900 calories of it. Far from being annoyed, I thought it a good start to getting the calories he needed. He was growing taller which only further accentuated his protruding bones.

He loved swimming and it was one of the few exercises he could manage due to his atrophied muscles. We started going swimming together regularly and although he was painfully self-conscious of his frail body, he managed to swim a few lengths, which made him hungry, a double whammy.

With the gig at the Royal Albert Hall looming, we headed to London with some friends to watch Russ and his new stage partner in action once again, although the most remarkable moment of the night was witnessing Deryn walk up 20 steps without needing to hold onto a handrail. It was the first time he'd managed such a task in almost a year and he was so proud of himself.

My next challenge was making our new house into a home. We couldn't seem to settle, we all felt on edge, as if we were waiting for the next bad thing to happen. Life hadn't been this 'normal' for a very long time and it was unnerving.

I started to suffer from flashbacks and anxiety attacks. Certain noises set me off and on one occasion, when I pulled over to let an ambulance with blue flashing lights go past, I burst into tears and had to sit at the side of the road for some time composing myself.

We had a welcome distraction when Jamie the sculptor called to say Deryn's bust was ready to collect. We drove down to Brighton and found Jamie's studio on a backstreet.

Jamie proudly unveiled the sculpture but Deryn immediately blurted out that he found it creepy. I was embarrassed but Jamie wasn't offended and agreed that he too would find a cast of his own face creepy.

We enjoyed a lovely day in Brighton, eating ice creams as we strolled along the beach. Deryn managed without his chair for most of the day and it was wonderful to feel the bracing sea breeze on our faces.

Around this time, the Ellen MacArthur Cancer Trust got in touch. They had been very supportive over the years, sending regular messages asking how Deryn was. They wanted to know if Deryn would like to go sailing with them again.

As much as he wanted to, he didn't feel he could manage it. Not yet. He was far too frail so, with a heavy heart, I declined the invitation. The trust soon came back to us and asked if the whole family would like to spend a weekend sailing in the Isle of Wight on our very own yacht complete with two skippers. Even Ozzy was included!

We jumped at the chance. Deryn was beside himself with excitement. Sailing had brought my son back to me the first time and I had high hopes that the upcoming trip would do him the world of good once again.

I started making my own sun cream for the trip, which my dad was also going to join us on. He had spent months in Bristol looking after Ozzy and not once had he asked for thanks. It was

CHAPTER 42

nice to be able to reward him for his help.

At the trust headquarters, we met our skippers, Charles and Ellie, and were shown around the 40-foot yacht which would be our home for the next few nights. We sailed around the island and also enjoyed a speedboat ride to the mainland, stopping off at a museum for lunch. On our last day, as we dropped anchor in the middle of nowhere, we saw a figure rowing towards us in the distance.

As the small canoe got nearer, we realised that it was Dame Ellen herself. Along with her lovely collie Norman, she had rowed over just to have lunch with us. It was magical and Deryn was thrilled to see her again.

Deryn thoroughly enjoyed steering the yacht and Dylan was also in his element, throwing himself around the boat like a professional. As I sat watching Deryn steer, I couldn't help noticing once again just how thin he was. Now that the days were getting warmer, seeing Deryn in a T shirt highlighted his emaciated frame.

I tried not to focus on how ill he looked, instead I focused on what was in front of my eyes at that moment. Deryn was alive and eating as much as he could face. He was continuing to defy the odds, treatment was over and we were making memories that would last us a lifetime.

Chapter 43

Deryn's next examination with Dr Glam flagged up no major problems. He was trying his hardest to eat and the team took that as an indication that he no longer needed the help of the mental health team so he was discharged without receiving any assistance.

Dr Glam had greeted him with a warm smile and a polite enquiry as to how he was.

'Alive!' he barked back flippantly.

There was no denying his emotional maturity was seriously stunted. He sulked a lot when questioned by certain doctors while others got a wonderfully warm response from him. Deryn couldn't hide who he disliked.

Dr Glam had at least been honest with me, admitting at one point: 'In medicine, we don't know everything.'

We were planning a holiday in Spain, where we hoped to meet cannabis expert Jeff Ditchfield, and I had to hope that no-one would overrule our plans due to Deryn's emaciated state. Dr Glam thought a change of scene would do him the world of good. She had just two pieces of advice: drink bottled water and avoid salads.

Two weeks before our trip, late one evening, Deryn started shouting from the bathroom.

'Muuuuummm, my wee is really dark!'

He'd finished by the time I got to the bathroom and the toilet bowl was full of dark red water. He was peeing blood.

I felt sick.

We took him into hospital for tests and samples of blood, cultures and urine were examined. But other than the worrying amount of blood Deryn was passing and his low body weight, the doctor pronounced that Deryn was clinically very well and transferred him to the children's oncology ward for further assessment.

The following day, he was discharged with antibiotics as the bleeding appeared to have stopped. His urine was infected with E. coli, which required more pills and an ultrasound showing a huge blood clot in his bladder, hence the blood in his urine. On the plus side, his kidneys were in tip top condition.

What a relief. My darkest fears of it all going wrong again were put to rest.

After almost eight weeks with no weight gain at all, despite all my efforts to fatten him up with milkshakes and regular meals every few hours, his team wanted to discuss where we would go next. At his lowest point, Deryn weighed just 26kg. The latest weigh-in revealed he was 32.6 kg, which was still considered dangerously low, putting him at risk of infection and organ failure.

The hospital seemed to be classing him as someone with 'an anorexic mindset.' The subject of hospitalisation and force-feeding came up again, much to our horror, along with two other options, an NG feeding tube and a PEG – a tube that goes straight into the stomach via the abdominal wall.

Not surprisingly, Deryn wanted neither but it was unlikely he would be able to consume the 5 - 6,000 calories a day he needed to put on weight naturally.

I felt incredibly sad for him. We could all see that he was trying but his efforts just weren't enough. The dieticians had stopped giving us advice. They told me that I knew everything they knew. They also realised that I wasn't going to feed Deryn a high-fat,

CHAPTER 43

high-sugar diet of fast food just to help him gain weight in the short term. In my eyes, the long-term damage those foods could cause wasn't worth the risk.

Dr Glam had advised Simon to 'fatten him up on Mars Bars' to which Simon patiently explained that Mars Bars were made from glucose, excessive amounts of which were very unhealthy. We promised to find another way to encourage Deryn to eat. There had to be a safer and healthier way to get more calories into his body – it just needed to happen immediately.

The following 10 days were crucial as the team would be making a decision on their next course of action.

A physiotherapist was assigned to Deryn and took him for a hydrotherapy session at the hospital pool. He was a little dubious as to what to expect when he stripped down to his swimming shorts but the plan was that Deryn would slowly start to build his muscles back up.

Deryn's arms were like noodles and his knees far bigger than his thighs. Lucy, his therapist, confirmed that virtually all of his muscles had wasted away. It was going to take a lot of hard work to get them back. Deryn and Lucy bobbed around in the pool together and she tried to make it fun for him. He had a great time getting stuck in and giving it everything he had.

The German TV company RTL had been in touch to ask if they could interview Deryn. We jumped at the chance, hoping that our German donor might see it, although he would never know what a pivotal role he had played in Deryn's story as he was anonymous and wouldn't have been given Deryn's details.

We spent the days leading up to our departure for Spain making more sun cream and mosquito repellent (to avoid using chemicals on Deryn's skin) and shopping for holiday clothes as the boys had none that fitted. Deryn could easily have worn Dylan's clothes as, although he was five years younger, Dylan

379

now weighed more than him and was almost as tall.

Deryn had another session in the pool and the following day he woke up in agony – the hydrotherapy had clearly worked a lot of muscles his body had forgotten about and he was in immense pain. It did, however, mean that the exercises were working.

He was still passing blood clots and he was due back at hospital for repeat tests. Another course of antibiotics was prescribed, along with patience. But the biggest blow was the news that he had lost a further kilo in weight. He was a tad over 30 kg. It was enough to deflate him and make him feel like all his efforts at getting well again were wasted.

I was convinced Dr Glam would put her foot down and stop us going on holiday the following day. There was no way she was going to allow Deryn another two weeks' grace if he was losing weight and slipping back into depression.

I was so relieved when she confirmed that Deryn would be allowed to go away as planned. But the reprieve came with an ultimatum. If Deryn had not improved drastically by the time we returned from Spain, they would have no choice but to section him, sedate him and force feed him as if he were anorexic.

At midnight on June 11th, we did something we had only been able to dream about for so long. We packed up our car and left for sunny Spain.

❖

Our first road trip was finally underway, all 1,400 miles of it. We broke the journey up with many pit stops for wee breaks and food and as the service stations didn't have a lot to offer on the vegetarian front, we were fuelled for a couple of days by fruit, crisps and nuts.

We decided to stop for the night at a beautiful hotel in the Pyrenees. As we headed into the restaurant, I noticed a magazine with a picture of a cannabis leaf imprinted on a pill on the front cover. From what I could understand in Spanish, the article was all about the medicinal benefits of cannabis.

It seemed bizarre that just a few hours by car and we were in a country where cannabis wasn't demonised. Spain has a very different approach to the UK and it came down to mere geography as to whether someone suffered or not.

Simon and I were heavily involved with the Bristol Cannabis Club and had learned an awful lot about the drug's healing benefits through meeting people who had successfully reversed their ailments by consuming cannabis. Multiple sclerosis patients, Crohn's sufferers and people with chronic obstructive pulmonary disease had all told me their miraculous stories as well as cancer patients who were finding relief in the plant.

We finally arrived at the beautiful villa owned by some friends in the pretty coastal town of Moraira, south of Valencia, a two-hour drive from where Jeff Ditchfield lived. Our friends had kindly offered us their house as a base so that we could enjoy some much-needed relaxation together in the sun. They had no idea that we were attempting to meet Jeff. There was a huge pool, a gym and an entertaining area. Staying here was going to do us all the world of good.

The next few days were spent idly relaxing by the pool doing absolutely nothing apart from watching the boys splashing around. We sat up until the early hours chatting and swimming in the moonlight after visiting local restaurants. It was heaven.

Unfortunately, Deryn was still struggling to eat. Often, he would gag through trying to force feed himself and sometimes he vomited.

It came as a huge relief when Simon received an email from Jeff saying that he was happy to meet us. He had been in contact with Jeff for a while and had told him that we would love to meet him as we were very familiar with the stellar work he was doing with people like Deryn.

Jeff was revered and hugely respected by many and I hadn't met anyone with a bad word to say about him. He was working on a documentary called Project Storm, about a group of cancer sufferers who were using cannabis and documenting their experiences. It was already causing quite a stir and it wasn't even finished yet.

We drove to the rendezvous at an Irish pub in the middle of a predominantly British area and went to get a drink while we waited. A few minutes later, Jeff arrived in his trademark black cloth cap. I recognized him instantly from his pictures and felt quite jittery.

We introduced ourselves and Jeff gave absolutely nothing away with his facial expressions. The meeting felt like it was going to be hard work. He got straight to the point.

'What do you want?' he asked brusquely.

We told him we just wanted to shake his hand and show our gratitude for everything he'd done for children like Deryn. He softened immediately and gave each of us a warm embrace.

We sat for hours in the warm sunshine talking about what Deryn had been through. Jeff was clearly moved by Deryn's story. We left nothing out, filling him in on the ongoing pain in Deryn's joints and fingers as well as his starvation attempts and refusal to continue treatment.

It soon became evident why Jeff initially appeared cold. He was approached by hundreds of people every month all asking for help and, although he would never turn anyone away, over the last 20 years it had become tiring trying to prioritise people and his time. He told us that we had blown him away by driving for two hours just to shake his hand.

He invited us back to his villa and while Deryn picked lemons from his garden and Dylan swung happily in a hammock, Jeff showed us a volcano vaporiser. A large digital machine that fully used everything cannabis plants had to offer, this wondrous piece of machinery produced a large bag of cannabis vapour.

'Deryn, I need to ask you a question,' Jeff began gently. 'Why did you first start refusing to eat?'

Deryn didn't hold back.

'If I didn't eat, I knew I would die and then finally the doctors wouldn't be able to hurt me anymore.'

'And how about now? Do you still want to die?' Jeff continued.

'Yes, sometimes,' he replied hesitantly as a tear rolled down his cheek.

Jeff turned to me.

'If you'll let me mum, I'm confident I can help Deryn with his problems.'

Jeff asked Deryn to describe exactly how he was feeling, rating any pains on a scale of 1 to 10. Deryn's ankles scored a 10 while his knees and back came a close second at 8.

Jeff handed Deryn the large bag of THC vapour – Tetrahydrocannabinol, the main active component of cannabis. I had absolutely no reservations about what he was about to inhale. I had recoiled at the thought of radiotherapy and chemotherapy but I was looking forward to seeing what more this plant had to offer my son.

Deryn inhaled a lung full of vapour before breathing it out slowly and relaxing back into his chair. Jeff asked Deryn to stay aware of how he was feeling and describe anything that happened. I was highly impressed by the way Jeff dealt with Deryn. It was a far better way to be introduced to the drug than the way most youngsters first experience cannabis.

My own experience as a teenager was a good example. I had no idea what I was buying or what it would do to me. It was at a party where not one person was sober. It frightened me to think about what could have happened to me.

That was not going to happen to Deryn. He already knew way more about cannabis than I did at his age.

As we chatted, Jeff asked if we would be willing to be interviewed for his sequel to Project Storm. We had to think very seriously about the implications of taking part. I couldn't be identified and neither could Deryn. I ran a high a risk of losing my children if the truth ever came out. Jeff was patient and encouraged us to discuss it after giving us his word that no-one would know who we were until we wanted them to, if that day ever came.

Deryn reported that he was still feeling okay. The amount of opiates he had previously consumed meant that he could have developed a high tolerance for cannabis. Deryn finished off the rest of the bag while Simon and I decided that I should be interviewed for Jeff's documentary. It was liberating to talk openly about our journey without hiding any details.

Deryn now looked very mellow and was grinning from ear to ear as he asked Jeff for something to eat. Jeff and I made eye contact discreetly and smiled at each other. No words were needed. As Deryn's food was being prepared, Jeff turned the temperature up on the volcano.

THC vaporises at a lower temperature. The next component was CBD Cannabidiol, one of at least 113 other components and most commonly used for pain relief. After a bag of CBD, Jeff asked again how he was feeling.

The real Deryn was starting to emerge from behind his snapback hat, which had the words 'Scarred for Life' emblazoned across it. He was cracking jokes and reverting back to the cheeky character that we hadn't seen in such a long time.

'How are your ankles feeling now Deryn, can you rate them out of 10 again?' Jeff enquired.

'What ankles?' Deryn quipped before bellowing with laughter. Jeff smiled.

Deryn was high but he was fully aware of his surroundings and completely in charge of his faculties, in stark contrast to how I had seen him on prescribed opiates. I would take this kind of high over morphine any day; out of pain without being out of his mind.

His food arrived and Deryn eagerly polished off the entire plate in minutes. A wonderful sight. Jeff handed Deryn a small syringe full of cannabis oil. It looked identical to the substance that I had given away months earlier. He asked us to give Deryn a small amount each day to see if it would help.

We were incredibly grateful. After talking to Jeff, it was clear that there was not enough oil to help everyone who came to him and Jeff was having to turn adults away so that he could help more children.

For the first time, I realised I no longer felt terrified of cancer. I didn't fear it because I believed that the oil could get Deryn back on track. And now, along with a new healthy diet, he would be unstoppable.

After lunch Jeff helped Deryn plant his very own cannabis cutting. Once the plant was fully grown, Jeff told us he would make oil out of it for Deryn.

'We need to label this plant H, Deryn,' Jeff said.

'Like H from the pop group Steps?' I quipped.

'I was actually thinking of Harry Pot-ter,' Jeff chuckled mischievously.

Jeff wrote the letter 'H' on a marker and pushed it into the ground next to the small plant.

❖

Early the next morning, I squeezed a tiny amount of oil from the syringe onto a cracker. Jeff had advised us to start with a blob the size of half a grain of rice.

Deryn eagerly chomped on the cracker. The oil tasted quite bitter and he followed it with a glass of fruit juice.

I was incredibly nervous. I knew that if he had too much, he would simply sleep it off. I'd seen him high a thousand times on drugs that were far more dangerous than cannabis. I wasn't scared of that, I was scared of getting caught.

Within 30 minutes, Deryn was sitting by the pool eating a huge bowl of pistachios while we made his breakfast.

'Can I have loads of food please, mum,' Deryn shouted from the pool. 'I'm starving!'

Simon and I quietly wept with joy. Simon had also suffered so much over the last few months and had used his prowess as a baker to try and tempt Deryn with all sorts of wonderful goodies. Sometimes he had literally begged him to eat.

By the time breakfast was ready, Deryn looked quite stoned. His eyes were bloodshot and he was cracking jokes and larking about in the pool with his brother.

That day, Deryn ate for 10 hours straight, one meal after another, with bowls of nuts in between. Nothing could satisfy his hunger. In the evening, as the oil was wearing off, we drove down to one of our favourite local restaurants, where the staff joked about how much Deryn managed to put away.

Having lived with a teenage boy who weighed 30kg for so long, we had lost perspective on how Deryn looked to others. We started to understand why so many people stared at him. Deryn looked like he was dying.

Every morning, he ingested a tiny blob of oil and the day would pan out the same way. He would eat copious amounts of food and spend his time swimming and playing with Dylan. Our evenings were whiled away in town, watching the various parades and colourful fiestas. Deryn was a different person. Lively, funny, caring but most important of all, pain free and eating.

On our way back to the villa, Deryn had stopped at a service station for a pee. He'd come hobbling out as quickly as he could, telling us to drive away quickly.

'I used the urinal and a blood clot came out,' he explained. 'It looks like I've murdered someone in there!'

Just two days after starting on the oil, the blood stopped. It could have been the antibiotics, of course, but we couldn't help feeling that the oil was playing its part in a variety of ways.

Most astonishing of all was that with each dose of oil, Deryn started experiencing strong electric shocks travelling down each of his damaged fingers. Within a week, he was experiencing some sensation in the tips. Could the oil also repair damaged nerves?

The rest of our holiday was magical. Deryn was himself again, in fact, he was better than his old self. The oil seemed to have brought out some empathy in him and his emotional outbursts ceased as he learned to deal with things more rationally. He was a delight to be around.

On the final day of our trip, Deryn had the last tiny blob of oil and we started the two-day drive back to England.

We left Spain with a very different boy to the one we arrived with. A boy who wanted to live again. I had witnessed another miracle. Cannabis had saved my son's life. Again.

Chapter 44

As soon as we arrived back home in Bristol, Deryn immediately rushed to jump on the bathroom scales. We had no idea how much weight he had gained in Spain and Deryn wasn't willing to wait a moment longer to find out.

As we unpacked, he shouted downstairs: 'I've put on THREE kilos!'

I ran upstairs and stared at the scales in disbelief. For such a long time, Deryn had failed to gain any weight at all and in just 10 days, he'd put on almost half a stone.

My only concern was that the holiday had been the main source of Deryn's new lust for life. Being in Spain with no worries and beautiful weather was enough to cheer us all up but would the return to England cause a reversal in his improved mental health?

The obvious difference the cannabis oil had made to Deryn's appetite and general wellbeing was undeniable, however, we didn't have any in the UK and the chances of us getting further supplies were incredibly slim. Or so we thought.

Only two days after returning home, a package was left on our doorstep. Inside were three large syringes containing 25g of organic cannabis oil. We had no idea where it had come from but we knew straight away who was behind such a wonderful delivery.

Jeff Ditchfield founded Bud Buddies UK, a non-profit medicinal cannabis organisation with a mission to assist, educate and empower people. With almost 13,000 members, it is a huge support and resource for many. Someone in his network had been kind enough to donate this oil anonymously to Deryn having never even met us. As I carefully stored the precious syringes somewhere safe I cried tears of joy.

Each day, we followed the same protocol we had followed in Spain. I'd bought some micro scales to make dosing far easier. I also ordered some empty capsules online to make suppositories with the oil as they drastically reduced the high associated with cannabis use. The medical benefits are still present but it allows cancer patients to continue leading a normal life without getting too high.

However, it was the high that was aiding Deryn's appetite so until his weight reached an acceptable level, we would be sticking with the oral method. Throughout our journey with cannabis oil, we were never left in the dark. Jeff was always on the end of an email and our new friends within the Bristol Cannabis Club and NORML UK were on hand day and night.

On July 10th 2014, Deryn and I sat in the waiting room ready to see Dr Glam and Dr Ponni. We were both nervous about what they would say. I was concerned that they might detect the cannabis oil in Deryn's blood. The tincture had never shown up and I hoped that it was something that wouldn't be found unless they were looking for it. They had no reason to suspect anything so no reason to look.

A nurse arrived to carry out the usual observations and take a sample of blood. I felt sick with worry. What if they found out? They would take the oil away from Deryn and his recovery would be thwarted. What would happen to us?

Deryn hopped on the scales as the nurse stood alongside with her clipboard, ready to write down the results. The screen flashed up with 35.2kg. Deryn had added just over another kilo.

Dr Glam called us in and commented on how well Deryn

looked. I had to agree. He was no longer pale and sickly, he had colour in his cheeks and a glint in his eye.

'Well, it's clear that you've put on some weight, Deryn,' Ponni said with a smile.

'Yeah, four kilos actually,' Deryn replied with a dazzling grin.

He told them that he felt amazing, the best he'd felt in a long time. While he was examined behind the curtain by Dr Ponni, Dr Glam glanced at me, pointing to her head.

'He's a million times better in his mind now, isn't he?' she whispered.

I agreed. Deryn was so much fun to be around. Cracking jokes, singing, dancing and just being jovial. No more depression, no more eating issues, no more sickness. It was beyond belief.

His knees and ankles were still problematic, however, the oil was dealing with the pain in a way we had never witnessed with opiates.

Dr Glam was concerned about Deryn's lack of puberty. His treatment had made the pituitary gland sluggish while radiotherapy to his head and excessive chemotherapy had stunted Deryn's growth, delaying the onset of puberty. The team planned to test his hormones and testosterone levels so that they could treat him accordingly.

Deryn's bloods came back in tip top shape and Dr Glam announced that she didn't want to see Deryn again for four weeks. Very soon, Deryn would be on three monthly check ups.

Life was becoming more about living and less about hospitals. It felt like the last four years were finally behind us.

As we left the room, Dr Glam gave me a warm hug.

'I truly cannot believe that Deryn has put on four kilos and he no longer wants to die,' she said happily. 'That holiday clearly did him the world of good.'

'Yes' I agreed with a smile. 'It was definitely the holiday!'

Epilogue

I'M PROUD TO TELL YOU THAT DERYN HAS GONE FROM STRENGTH TO strength since our holiday in Spain in 2014.

In September that year, I was invited to talk at Number 11 Downing Street by Callum Fairhurst, who had founded cancer charity The Liam Fairhurst Foundation in his 12-year-old brother's memory. Callum's charity had assisted Deryn a number of times and I was more than happy to tell a room full of people all about their good work.

The experience of public speaking in such a grandiose venue didn't frighten me. I enjoyed every nerve-wracking minute. The family was there too and the reception Deryn received was overwhelming.

I spoke at length about Deryn's journey – although reluctantly leaving out the most important details about how cannabis had aided his pain relief and recovery. Omitting those crucial points wasn't easy for me. Every time I told his story, I wanted to share the full, unabridged facts with everyone because I believed that they could help others in a similar situation.

But at that time, I simply couldn't take the risk.

I hope that all the wonderful people who have followed our story don't feel betrayed and understand why I had to hide the facts for so long. I still believe it was a miracle, regardless of how it came about. I also believe in the power of prayer and positive thinking.

Deryn's unique story has led to me being contacted every week by parents who are desperate for a miracle similar to the one we were granted. I have trusted many of them with the truth and pointed people towards the same path we took.

I became heavily involved with Jeff and he would refer parents to me anonymously so that I could advise them and share my knowledge and our experience.

Meanwhile, my panic attacks reappeared with a vengeance. I was crying for no reason, I stopped going out and I refused to socialise. I became a virtual hermit, forcing Simon to take Deryn to his appointments as I couldn't bear going near a hospital. I was diagnosed with post-traumatic stress disorder, depression and severe anxiety. In short, I was on the brink of a nervous breakdown.

My GP offered me some pills but I refused. I knew exactly what would help…cannabis. My anxiety disappeared and I've only had a handful of panic attacks since.

Setting up Deryn's charity, DoEveRYthiNg, was a labour of love but it continues to raise money to fund a centre for teenagers with cancer.

Deryn was prescribed growth hormones and each evening he would inject himself. His bones were left very weak from the treatment and he has mobility issues to the point where he still struggles to walk normally. Happily, his hand and fingers continue to improve.

One of his proudest moments was being awarded a Special Recognition Award by the Eastern Daily Press newspaper, which had followed his story from the early days.

Some things haven't changed and Deryn has never wanted to stop crossing things off his bucket list.

He went back to high school in Norfolk where he thrived among his friends and peer group and following just nine months of schooling in the space of four years, Deryn left school in June 2016 with seven GCSEs.

EPILOGUE

His weight is no longer a problem and he has decided to pursue a career as a vegan chef. That irony is not lost on us, but maybe years of eating bland hospital food gave him a passion for more flavoursome and exotic dishes. He's incredibly good at creating them too!

He and Dylan continue to be close and Dylan is hoping to go to stage school to pursue his acting dreams.

As each day passes, the prospect of cancer returning decreases. I'll probably never be totally free of that fear, and if he so much as coughs, my hair stands up on end.

We may have had no choice in the blows we received but we had a choice in how we dealt with them. We made the best of every situation and had faith that everything would work out exactly as it should.

I am reminded of my miracle boy every time I look at Deryn and I know deep in my heart that whatever the future may throw at us, we can cope.

We always do.

Acknowledgements

ABOVE ALL, I HAVE TO THANK MY SON DERYN, FOR WITHOUT HIM none of this would have been possible. He took me on a journey that I never wanted to go on, but am so very grateful that I did. Deryn has changed us all for the better and for that I am truly thankful.

My youngest son Dylan, for being the strong, sensitive, most hilarious, caring little guy. He never grumbled or complained. Dylan often healed my heart with one of his divine hugs.

I have to thank my wonderful soul mate, my husband and rock, Simon. We have been through times that would have ripped many couples apart, not only with Deryn but throughout our personal lives, too. My life wouldn't be what it is today without the love, patience and support of the most wonderful husband.

My mum and dad, Julia and Ian Wilson. They always did what they could, albeit I didn't always realise that. No questions asked and they never asked for anything in return. They are the epitome of selflessness.

Karen's wonderful mother-in-law Jean Kershaw, for had it not been for her caring nature and my mum's inability to keep quiet about my life, this book probably wouldn't have been written.

Our immediate family, who have supported us from afar but who stepped forward whenever asked. My brother Ian Dylong, Simon's mum RoseMarie and step-dad Steven Lovejoy, Simon's dad Brian Blackwell, his sister Gemma Blackwell, her partner Ben Roberts and our lovely little nieces Isla and Isabelle.

Our dear friends, Wendy Binmore, Julie Hardiman, Patrick Welsh, Alex Hart and Jake Eames – your help and support over the years has never gone unnoticed. Thank you all so much for stepping forward, helping us and making our lives a little easier.

Erika Burnett and Jodie Rowlandson for the unwavering support during our time at Addenbrooke's and beyond.

To the staff at Addenbrooke's Hospital, Bristol Children's Hospital and Charlton Farm Hospice, we owe you more than we can ever put down in words.

Our amazing team at Mirror Books, specifically Paula, Jo and Julie for their support and enthusiasm in bringing this book to life, and our agent Valeria Huerta.

The companies that answered Deryn's wishes and the charities which supported us through thick and thin and gave our family some of the most amazing experiences.

The celebrities who took time out of their busy schedules to come and brighten up Deryn's life, many of whom have become firm friends.

Mr Allot and the staff at Wayland Academy for the phenomenal support you have given both of my boys, thank you for making their school lives enjoyable.

To everyone who has stepped into our lives. Some have drifted away over the years but everyone we met has shaped our lives in some way or other and I want to thank you for the part you have played.

A special thank you has to go out to our loyal supporters on social media. Our Facebook and Twitter followers have at times given this painful journey meaning. Perfect strangers online often eased my pain during the most dire of moments and I took great comfort from people I will probably never meet. You are all wonderful.

I couldn't finish this book without thanking the wonderful

ACKNOWLEDGEMENTS

unsung heroes of the cannabis community. A selfless group of strangers who have gone above and beyond, simply because they want to see the world become a better place for people who are suffering needlessly.

And last, but most definitely not least, the wonderful people whose real names have graced the pages of this book. Without you, our lives would have been completely different. Each one of you will forever be etched into our hearts for the guidance, support and love you have shown us all.

Thank you x

I also want to thank Karen, my co-author. Your endless support and love has guided me and allowed me to fulfil a lifelong dream. You are an amazingly inspirational woman who has shown me that I am good enough, I am capable and I am worthy.

Also by Mirror Books

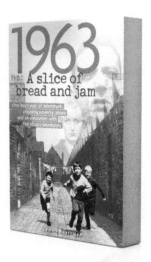

1963 - A Slice of Bread and Jam
Tommy Rhattigan

Tommy lives at the heart of a large Irish family in derelict Hulme in Manchester, ruled by an abusive, alcoholic father and a negligent mother. Alongside his siblings he begs (or steals) a few pennies to bring home to avoid a beating, while looking for a little adventure of his own along the way.

His foul-mouthed and chaotic family may be deeply flawed, but amongst the violence, grinding poverty and distinct lack of hygiene and morality lies a strong sense of loyalty and, above all, survival.

During this single year − before his family implodes and his world changes for ever − Tommy almost falls foul of the welfare officers, nuns, police − and Myra Hindley and Ian Brady. An adventurous, fun, dark and moving true story of the only life young Tommy knew.

Also by Mirror Books

Eating the Elephant
Alice Wells

A shocking but inspiring true story that tackles the dark, modern crisis of internet pornography in a frank and groundbreaking way.

Alice, a dedicated doctor and mother of two children, bravely tells the story of her marriage to a man hiding a terrible secret – one into which he has drawn their 4-year-old daughter, Grace. As the shocking truth about their family life unfolds at a heartstopping pace, Alice struggles to learn how to survive the impact and piece together her shattered world.

The devastation of what she is forced to face when her life is hit by catastrophic pain, and the horror of wondering if she overlooked the signs, is laid bare in a moving and honest way that will stay with you for a long time to come.

How do you eat an elephant?
One piece at a time

Mirror Books

Also by Mirror Books

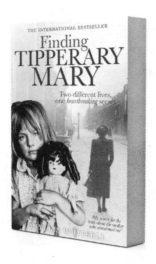

THE INTERNATIONAL BESTSELLER
Finding Tipperary Mary
Phyllis Whitsell

The astonishing real story of a daughter's search for her own past
and the desperate mother who gave her up for adoption.

Phyllis Whitsell began looking for her birth mother as a young
woman and although it was many years before she finally met her, their
lives had crossed on the journey without their knowledge.
When they both eventually sat together in the same room,
the circumstances were extraordinary, moving and
ultimately life-changing.

This is a daughter's personal account of the remarkable
relationship that grew from abandonment into love,
understanding and selfless care.

Mirror Books

Also by Mirror Books

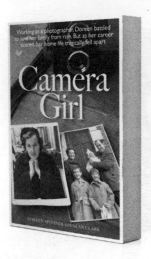

Camera Girl
Doreen Spooner with Alan Clark

The true story of a woman coping with a tragic end to the love of her life, alongside a daily fight to establish herself and support her children.

A moving and inspiring memoir of Doreen Spooner – a woman ahead of her time. Struggling to hold her head high through the disintegration of the family she loves through alcoholism, she began a career as Fleet Street's first female photographer.

While the passionate affair and family life she'd always dreamed of fell apart, Doreen walked into the frantic world of a national newspaper. Determined to save her family from crippling debt, her work captured the Swinging Sixties through political scandals, glamorous stars and cultural icons, while her homelife spiralled further out of control.

The two sides of this book take you through a touching and emotional love story, coupled with a hugely enjoyable portrait of post-war Britain.

Mirror Books

Also by Mirror Books

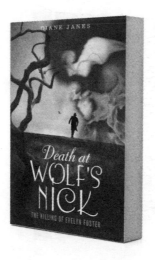

Death at Wolf's Nick
Diane Janes

In January 1931, on a lonely stretch of Northumberland moorland known as Wolf's Nick, flames rose up into the night sky. Evelyn Foster, a young taxi driver, lay near her burning car, engulfed in flames, praying for a passing vehicle.

With her last breath, she described her attacker: a mysterious man with a bowler hat who had asked her to drive him to the next village, then attacked her and left her to die. Local police attempted to track down Evelyn's killer – while others questioned the circumstances, Evelyn's character and if there was even a man at all…

Professional crime writer and lecturer Diane Janes gained unprecedented access to Evelyn's case files. Through her evocative description, gift for storytelling and detailed factual narrative, Diane takes the reader back to the scene of the crime, painting a vivid description of village life in the 1930s.

Central to this tragic tale, is a daughter, sister and friend who lost her life in an horrific way – and the name of her murderer, revealed for the first time…

Mirror Books